The Book of Christian Men

*God Created Man First: The Laws of Men,
Awakening Faith, Family, and Legacy*

The Lord has made everything beautiful in its time. He has also set eternity in the human heart; yet no one can fathom what God has done from beginning to end. Man is the first form of Godlikeness within the realm. (Ecclesiastes 3:11)

Gabriel Marcelin

Copyright © 2025 by **Gabriel Marcelin**

The Book of Christian Men.

All rights reserved.

This book is protected under the copyright laws of **Canada, the United States of America**, and all applicable international treaties. No part of this publication may be copied, stored, or transmitted in any form, electronic or mechanical, without prior written permission from the author, except for brief quotations used in reviews or articles.

Permission will be granted upon request. Unless otherwise identified, Scripture quotations are taken from the King James Version. Copyright ©1982, 1984, by Thomas Nelson, Inc.

Used by permission. All rights reserved.

Scripture quotations marked NIV are taken from the **HOLY**

BIBLE, NEW INTERNATIONAL VERSION, © 1973, 1978,

1984 International Bible Society, used by permission of

Zondervan. (fix the space)

The book of Christian Men is a work of nonfiction. Any references to historical events, real people, or the Bible are accurate to the best of the author's knowledge. Scripture

References: Unless otherwise noted, Scripture quotations are taken from the Holy Bible, New International Version® (NIV®). Copyright © 1973, 1978, 1984, 2011 by Biblica, Inc. Used by permission. All rights reserved worldwide.

All ideas, stories, and teachings in this book are original and authored by Gabriel. A big thank you to <u>the **editors**</u> who supported the refinement process, ensuring clarity and quality without altering the heart of God's Kingdom.

ISBN (Paperback): 978-1-0696240-7-9
ISBN (Hardcover): 978-1-0696240-8-6
ISBN (Ebook): 978-1-0696240-6-2

Dedication

In the memories of countless Christian men who tried or died trying to build their homes on God's laws, but were failed or killed, thrown out of their own homes, or imprisoned under different circumstances for women and children: "The Book of Men is for you. Be still, and know that I am *God*. "Be on your guard; stand firm in the faith; be courageous; be strong. Do everything in love." (1 Corinthians 16:13-14)

To all **fathers** and **stepdads** who have never given up, **brothers** rebuilding after betrayal, young single **men** seeking marriage, and children committed to walking in wisdom and grace: **to all men who have loved deeply, fought quietly**, and found themselves alone in the wilderness of broken promises.

To my uncle **Jean Pochette**, my cousin **Croilnor**, and my best friends **Denis** and **Jude**, good men who have sought to build their homes under the sacred covenant and the laws of heaven.

Above all, **to all Christian men, devoted husbands and stewards of their homes**. Remember that the one true God, **who first created man and breathed life and knowledge into his soul**, still calls us to rise again. **The Book of Christian Men** beautifully reminds us of the true principles of **Men's Laws and the Source of masculinity**. Let's read to discover your divine purpose and awaken the hearts of all husbands.

Introduction

The Book of Christian Men

Welcome to **The Book of Christian Men**, a spiritual teaching and declaration of truth for men worldwide. Whether you are divorced, single, married, or preparing for marriage, this book speaks directly to the man who has been wounded in silence, betrayed, or overlooked, and still dares to hope that God is not finished with him yet.

This is a book about husbands and potential bachelors. It is written for women who genuinely want to understand men, serving as a blueprint for rebuilding without seeking revenge and as a guide for strong Christian men.

This book has its roots in resilience, is shaped by years of silence, and is grounded in Scripture. It speaks kindly to the man who has prayed for peace during storms, to the one carrying the quiet burden of disappointment, and to the man searching for meaning after losing everything he once built.

The Book of Christian Men exists for one purpose:

To awaken the men of God, from divorce and loss to healing and rebuilding with greater wisdom.

We live in an era where masculinity is misunderstood and leadership is belittled. Fathers are left behind, husbands are disrespected, and the role of a man has become a punchline. The Book of Christian Men restores the sacred calling of being a man of faith, purpose, and spiritual dignity and authority. Inside, you'll find:

- The wisdom **of David** and **Solomon**
- The boldness of **Elijah** and **Jesus**
- The lessons of **Paul** and **Gabriel**
- The unshakable manhood of **divorced men** and **their untold truth.**

You'll also encounter warnings, **the laws of husbands**, and references to man as the first student at **the University of God**. These principles aim to strengthen a man's soul and protect his legacy from **selfish theft**, whether from **government, courtrooms,** or **culture.**

This book is not only for divorced men but also for:

- The **bachelor** preparing for marriage
- The **young single man** seeking God's will
- The **husband striving** to lead faithfully
- The **man** who has been burned, broken, or betrayed but refuses to remain a victim

Through **real-life stories**, **biblical truth**, and practical wisdom, **The Book of Christian Men** will teach you how to:

- Lead without **fear**
- Love with **wisdom**
- Recover from **betrayal**
- Build again with **purpose**

Walk confidently in the **identity God** has given you and in the **protection of your wealth.**

You were not created to be a passive bystander. You were made to **rebuild, redeem**, and reclaim your role as a **husband, father, brother, leader**, and **warrior in the Kingdom of God.**

These are not opinions. **They are laws, signed by the Throne of Heaven**, echoed in Scripture, and proven in the hearts of men who refuse to quit.

Jesus reaffirmed that God's original plan for marriage is a lifelong, covenantal union. Therefore, you must approach it with clarity, spiritual insight, and understanding, whether you have **struggled, married, remarried, succeeded,** or **have not yet begun**. This is your opportunity to become **the man you were always meant to be.**

For Adam was formed first... (1 Timothy 2:13)

You are not **forgotten.** You are not **finished.**

You are not **disqualified.**

You are being called back to the truth: to intentionally build with explicit knowledge, to strengthen your mind, and to **become a high-value Christian man rooted in biblical manhood.**

This is more than just a book. It is for **strong Christian men**; it is your **mirror to wake up** and **earn the respect you deserve.**

*If you are **tired of silence**, **ready to heal**, and **brave enough to lead and claim your role as a husband**, this book is for you.*

Welcome to The Book of Christian Men.

Let the awakening begin.

TABLE OF CONTENTS

Chapter One 1

Chapter Two 12

Chapter Three 25

Chapter Four 37

Chapter Five 50

Chapter Six 64

Chapter Seven 84

Chapter Eight 96

Chapter Nine 106

Chapter Ten 117

Chapter Eleven 127

Chapter Twelve 137

Chapter Thirteen 150

Chapter Fourteen 163

Chapter Fifteen 176

Chapter Sixteen 190

Chapter Seventeen 205

HEAVENLY CITIZEN

CHAPTER ONE

Mr. Right and Mrs. Right got married.
*"Therefore, what God has joined together, l
et no one separate." Mark 10:9*

"There is a time for everything, and a season for every activity under the heavens, a time to heal, a time to tear down, and a time to build." (Ecclesiastes 3:1, 3) When a man is ready to assume the role of husband, he develops a deep sense of self-awareness, spiritual insight, and emotional maturity.

It's never just a simple choice based on fleeting feelings or societal expectations. Instead, it's a sacred covenant, a bond established by God. Marriage is more than a social institution, a religious commitment, or a legal agreement with the government; it's a sacred union created by the Creator, rooted in love, responsibility, and mutual growth.

To truly grasp the importance of commitment.

One must view it through the lenses of authenticity and responsibility. A man who is genuine at his core is better prepared to understand the sacred duty of leading and caring for a family. Reflecting on the very beginning offers profound insight into God's original design. *In the Garden of Eden, God demonstrated divine purpose by creating the first man, formed from dust and brought to life by God's breath (Genesis 2:7).*

Man's intelligence was not just natural; it was divinely given. Taught directly by the Creator, man gained wisdom not through trial and error or human instruction, but through direct, personal communion with God Himself.

There was no sin to distort his thinking, no guilt to cloud his judgment. His mind, pure and enlightened, could understand the mysteries of creation as God revealed them to him. Time had no power over him, for death had not yet entered the human story. Man was created to live forever, designed by God to walk in constant, unbroken fellowship with Him.

This man didn't need sermons, rituals, or intermediaries to understand his purpose. His very existence was an act of worship. He lived in the presence of the Almighty, with every breath aligned with divine will. There was no need for effort, only perfect peace within God's plan. His life was based not on survival but on stewardship. He was driven not by ambition but by divine calling. The very breath that gave him life sustained him as he walked in wisdom, clarity, and joy.

This origin story explains why the Lord created humans first: not to wander, but to live intentionally with a divine purpose.

His role was not driven by personal ambition, but assigned by God Himself. Man was made to lead with integrity, endowed with greater vision than other beings that were created, named with authority, guarded with strength, and loved faithfully, all while staying rooted in his Creator. In the design of that first man, we see the lasting call for all men: to live genuinely, embrace responsibility, and walk humbly in fellowship with the One who made them.

Christian men are intelligent enough to know not to depart from the Lord's teaching, no matter the darkness. *"I am the vine; ye are the branches: He that abideth in me, and I in him, the same bringeth forth much fruit: for without me ye can do nothing."(John 15:5)*

In this ideal state, man did not experience sickness, pain, anxiety, or fear. No disease could affect his body; no emotional wounds could scar his heart. There were no hospitals, no wars, no jails or police, because there were no rebellious women around. The very presence of God was his covering and his healing. His world was not driven by survival, but by stewardship directly from the throne of heaven.

The environment reflected God's laws, being balanced, fruitful, and overflowing with life. There was no struggle, only a clear direction. The breath of God that gave him life continued to empower him as he fulfilled his calling with peace and joy. *God entrusted the first human (a man) with a sacred responsibility, beginning with the development of his intellect as a complete and mature creation (Genesis 2:15).*

This was more than just tending plants; it involved overseeing paradise itself. *Man was also given the privilege to name every living creature (Genesis 2:19-20).* So, he called all the livestock, the birds in the sky, and the wild animals.

This task required far more than simple observation; it demanded a remarkable blend of memory, creativity, and deep intelligence. It called for discernment sharpened by wisdom, insight rooted in understanding, and the ability to perceive the nature, purpose, and function of each living creature. Knowledge of the different sea temperatures was also essential.

Such a responsibility was not merely intellectual; it was spiritual in nature. It required the capacity to name according to essence, not appearance, to recognize patterns, distinguish traits, and assign identity with authority and purpose. Only a mind truly aligned with the wisdom of the Creator could execute such a task with precision and intention.

Every name perfectly aligns with its meaning, territory, and environment.

Throughout the Bible, choosing a name is more than just labeling; it reflects authority and spiritual understanding. Man recognized the distinctive nature and purpose of each creature and named it accordingly, based on its God-given role. This task required not only mental acuity, but also a soul in harmony with the Creator's plans.

The Laws Within the Blueprint of Righteous Manhood:

Mentally sharp, spiritually in tune, physically whole, and relationally connected to God. He was neither passive nor unclear about his identity or purpose. He was a steward of creation, a ruler under God, and a worshiper in perfect communion with Him. His strength did not come from dominance, but from obedience and aligning himself with divine order. Adam's life, before the fall, reveals the dignity and nobility of man as God intended, capable of leading, creating, cultivating, and loving in righteousness and truth.

He was the crown of creation, made in the image of God, walking in the light of perfect intimacy. The Lord revealed to man the divine order of creation and its relationships. ***"Then the Lord God made a woman from the rib He had taken out of the man, and He brought her to the man."***

This moment is filled with sacred symbolism. The woman was not made from man's head to dominate him, nor from his feet to be beneath him, but from his side, close to his heart, to walk with him in unity, love, and mutual respect.

This divine moment reflects the eternal truth of many love stories. When the heart is prepared, the right person will come not by chance but through divine appointment. When a man chooses to take this step, the first authority he must speak to is his parents. ***This is a sacred conversation, a*** *declaration that he is ready to leave his father and mother and be united with his wife (Genesis 2:24).*

A Christian man doesn't marry in isolation. His parents, especially if they are Christians, work with God to shape him into a man of honor. Parents should be involved in the selection process, not to control, but to exercise discernment. They will naturally want to know who this woman is. Is she good enough, faithful enough, strong enough, and respectful enough to be a wife? Does she respect her parents? Does she walk with humility and integrity?

Did she grow up witnessing her mother be an exemplary wife to her father? These questions are not meant to discourage love, but to protect the sanctity of the lifelong covenant that is about to be formed.

Recalling God's act, as a father, before marriage, Adam had to wait for Eve to be presented to him by her father, the Lord Himself. Adam needed to work, understand how everything functions to protect and care for his wife, and be prepared to be the husband God wanted him to be before the Lord initiated the first wedding on the planet. All the angels were present; this covenant law is a serious contract before the Lord, registered in the parliament of the throne of heaven.

This gesture symbolizes trust and respect. The father entrusts his daughter to a man who, like Adam, will recognize her worth and welcome her with joy. Just as Adam exclaimed, "***This is now bone of my bones and flesh of my flesh" (Genesis 2:23),*** A godly husband recognizes the deep spiritual and emotional bond that now unites him to his wife.

This unity, the union of man and woman in marriage, is not only physical; it is deeply spiritual. It reflects the connection between Christ and the Church. Just as Adam's side was opened to create Eve, Jesus' side was pierced to give birth to the Church.

(John 19:34). When a soldier pierced his side with a spear, blood and water immediately flowed out. Eve's creation foreshadows Christ's sacrifice. When a man chooses marriage, he decides to sacrifice his life, not to lose it, but to invest it selflessly in his wife and future family.

When God gave Adam dominion over all creation, he didn't immediately give him a wife. Instead, God assigned him a task, a sacred mission that required vision, discipline, and responsibility. ***Adam was placed alone in the Garden of Eden with a clear mission to cultivate and care for it (Genesis 2:15).*** This reveals an essential truth: before blessing a man with a wife, God first blesses him with a purpose.

Work comes before a relationship. God's purpose shows that a man's identity does not rely solely on romance or partnership, but on his vocation and responsibility. Adam had to discover who he was and why he was created before he could understand how to love and lead someone else.

The waiting period for a man holds deep significance.

This is not a time for passivity but for purposeful preparation. Before a man chooses a woman to marry, he must first align his mind, spirit, and priorities with divine principles. Solitude in maturity becomes sacred, a time set aside for growth, self-control, and spiritual development. During this season, a man is called to explore, organize, and establish a structure for what God has entrusted to him. This is not a delay but a divine process of learning to protect his wealth.

Naming Creation: A School of Discernment and Authority

Naming everything on earth and in the sky, as recorded in Genesis, was more than just a task; it was an exercise in authority, creativity, and discernment. Each name carried significance, reflecting humanity's ability to perceive purpose, assign identity, and establish order within creation. This was God's way of training man to govern nature, eventually his household. It served as an early apprenticeship in dominion, an introduction to the responsibilities of stewardship, vision, and leadership with God as an exemplary father.

Through these university courses, men were not simply preparing for marriage; they were being equipped for leadership. God was shaping their minds, refining judgment, and testing character. Leadership begins long before marriage; it begins in solitude, where a man learns to think critically, act responsibly, and lead with wisdom. In the beginning, God did not just give man a wife; He first gave him purpose, responsibility, and the wisdom to walk in both knowledge and understanding.

At this point, the man was alone at the helm of his enterprise, which had only one employee: himself. Yet the scope of his mission was enormous. He was responsible for managing the first cultivated spaces on Earth and documenting all the creatures on the planet, by name and with their meanings. He was swamped and supervised by God himself; he was immersed in a project given to him by God that challenged his mind and tested his intelligence.

There was an urgency in him to "**complete**" the job, even though he was all alone. He didn't know a woman. God first created a man, a man who would one day love, protect, and provide for a woman, but only after he had proven his faithfulness in the business or the field.

The Lord had expected his competence and evaluated his work performance, then promoted him to take on the role of husband. Adam's story shows us today that a man's purpose comes before partnership; our goal takes priority before we decide to get married. A man's worth isn't based on his relationship status but on his alignment with God's calling. Before seeking a wife, a man must first find his divine mission and purpose. Work builds character, responsibility, and maturity, and obedience shows our willingness to go further.

Man worked alone in the vast realm of creation with clarity, determination, and serenity. His mind was free from concerns about governments, courts, or conflicts. There was no confusion or drama, only divine order. His mind, created by God and filled with wisdom, could bear the weight of life without anxiety or distraction. However, everything changed when he chose to listen to his wife rather than God's commandment. From that choice, time began to deteriorate, mortality appeared, and consequences replaced peace.

The Book of Men: A Manual for the Christian Man

The Book of Men serves as a manual for biblical manhood in a fallen world, not as a reaction to bitterness. Its laws and principles are designed to safeguard a man's heart, sustain his purpose, and shield him from traps set by women, which can threaten his family, integrity, and potentially lead to the loss of half (50%) of his wealth. In a world where relationships can be manipulated, men need more than love and grace; they also need discernment and structure to prevent unauthorized access to their life's legacy. Through other Christian men who have acquired this knowledge, we can teach and protect our offspring.

When God saw that man had taken his role seriously, competently, and faithfully, He responded not by giving more tasks but by offering a reward. Only after man demonstrated his dedication to stewardship and obedience did God provide him with a companion. This establishes a pattern: responsibility first, then relationship; preparation first, then partnership. The modern Christian man must restore this order if he wants to lead effectively and finish strong.

Adam was only allowed to marry not to complete him, but to support him in the mission already given to him. Before starting a family, a man must learn to cultivate the garden that God has placed in his heart. Your goal is to understand certain legal matters to protect your assets. There's nothing wrong with men being good at math and calculating everything before committing to a woman in your program.

If she remains in the marriage, we have a responsibility to provide her with all the necessary means; however, if she chooses to destroy everything, she will have to leave and build her wealth. That is why she should obey and stay, to serve the Lord's purpose in marriage: for better or for worse, in sickness and in health, to love and cherish each other until death do us part.

Similarly, a religious man does not marry to discover his destiny; he is meant to marry for a specific purpose. He already knows that being married involves taking on the role of provider and heading a family. He embraces the joys of a woman's companionship, even if he was pleased alone: **"Do not be afraid; you are worth more than many sparrows." Matthew 10:31.**

The Challenges of Marital Commitment

Challenges in marriage commitment often stem from an unequal support system for the bride and groom. Typically, the bride has a larger network of people actively involved in her marriage and household affairs, whereas the groom tends to have less support. A man entering into marriage must be prepared to assume significant responsibilities, such as managing household duties, helping to raise children, respecting and supporting his in-laws, working to create a peaceful and stable home, and maintaining love through both good and bad times.

When it comes to the wedding day and the reality that follows, the groom is often supported mainly by his parents, a few loyal friends, and sometimes his close siblings. In contrast, the bride is typically supported by her parents and extended family, her circle of independent friends, and, more broadly, by lawyers and courts that uphold government rules, which can play a significant role in areas such as family law, child custody, and matrimonial rights, especially pushed a man to ask tangible questions: Is it a good deal?

Divorce settlements, where assets accumulated over years of labor may be divided, often result in unequal distributions of the husband's wealth. Child custody battles, where fathers may struggle to maintain consistent access to their children, could even lead to imprisonment. Alimony and spousal support involve a man possibly being legally required to provide ongoing financial support, sometimes for years after the divorce. In such cases, she might choose a partner she considers a 'loser' and demand that you contribute to their living expenses.

False allegations can lead to a husband's arrest and detention, initially, until proven innocent, which can damage a man's reputation and influence legal outcomes even before evidence is presented. Restraining orders, which can be issued preemptively, restrict a man's freedom or access to his home and children. Property division, where jointly owned homes or businesses may be awarded to one party, often the wife, regardless of who originally financed them.

Prenuptial agreement disputes, where previous contracts might be challenged or overridden in court. Legal bias, whether perceived or real, that favors one gender in custody battles or financial decisions.

This difference highlights a subtle truth: a man must be prepared to demonstrate his intelligence before committing to a woman, take on his responsibilities, and lead with love and wisdom. Even when you are in love, you should legally protect your assets from her and her influential friends, even when men feel outnumbered or misunderstood.

Marriage is not just a celebration of love; it is a lasting alliance that requires maturity, a ritual in which all men are expected to ensure that their wives stay committed until death, not a contract meant to dismantle everything we have worked for, so, when you consider all these groups and the scope of legal government entities: the marriage breakers, the family court and child cartel, the divorce industry, the home wreckers in suits and ties, and the government machine growing its power against the Lord's ordinance for marriage. "The Lord witnesses the covenant between you and your wife of your youth. ...

Therefore, stay vigilant and remain faithful to your youthful wife. *'I hate divorce,' declares the Lord God of Israel." Malachi 2:14-16.*

It is concerning that few branches of government, courts, or legal systems prioritize preserving a man's hard-earned wealth following a wife's breach of marriage vows. Instead, family courts and matrimonial laws are generally structured to protect women, who are often seen as the most financially vulnerable party, from men.

The spirit of a Christian wedding.

The Scriptures are clear: 'The Lord has been a witness between you and the wife of your youth. Guard your spirit, and let none of you be unfaithful to the wife of your youth. *For I hate divorce,' says the Lord, the God of Israel. He seeks godly offspring."* (Malachi 2:14–16)

The legal system heavily favors fair division of property, spousal support, and child support, often regardless of who earned or saved the money. In practice, if a person wants to protect their wealth, they must actively utilize legal tools before marriage, such as prenuptial or postnuptial agreements, precise financial planning, and solid legal advice. Without these precautions, once vows are exchanged, a man's economic security largely depends on the courts, which focus on what they perceive as fairness and the family's overall well-being rather than the man's interests in what he has accumulated.

A man's role is to listen, learn, grow, and create a space where his wife and children feel safe, valued, and supported. He does not see her as an adversary, but as a partner, a helper who complements him perfectly. And he understands that in helping her, she will also need his strength, his gentleness, his presence, and his power. But if she chooses to leave, nothing stops her from starting over and building her wealth.

Under these conditions, until death do us part, you may leave if you want to, but not with our lives; you go only with what you've earned. See you, bye! ***Numbers 23:19: "God is not a man, that he should lie; neither the son of man, that he should repent:***

hath, he said, and shall he not do it? Or hath he spoken, and shall he not make it good?"

HEAVENLY CITIZEN

CHAPTER TWO

**Purpose Before Partnership:
The Genesis Blueprint for Manhood.**
*How God Trains Men in Responsibility, Leadership, and
Stewardship Before Granting Them a Wife.*

Marriage: A Divine Sacred Covenant

Marriage is not a decision to be taken lightly. It is a lifelong covenant, and for a Christian man, it is a divine mission. Men and women must approach it with respect. Their parents, for their part, become wise advisors, discerning voices, and protectors of the families.

When a man and a woman stand before God, their family, and the Church, they are not only making a promise to each other; they are making a promise to God. They say, "I will love you, honor you, and cherish you." But more than that, they say, "I will respect this sacred covenant, not only in words but also in deeds and actions, in good times and in bad." However, if the marriage endures a difficult period, she can choose to leave today.

Even after swearing to stay together until death, she can still decide to pursue her path to wealth. In this case, the man must be wise and take steps to protect the family's assets, as they belong to the family as a whole, not to the fugitives who abandoned their vows without probable cause or abuse.

The marriage of Mr. and Mrs. Everyman is not a fairy tale. It's a sacred story that begins when two people, entirely devoted to God, come together in accordance with His plan. Their union isn't perfect, but it is meant to be. Their love is not free of difficulties, but it is built on grace. ***Mark 10:9 states, "What God has joined together, let no one separate."***

When you choose each other, when your parents give their blessing to this union, and the Church bears witness to it, God seals it. The union is sealed in heaven. That is why, as believers, we must seek God's will in our relationships. Because when it's God's hand that brings two people together, no man, no situation, no struggle can separate them.

The world may have its opinions about marriage, but The Book of Men states that: Marriage is a ministry. It's a learning experience. It is the crucible in which two souls are bound into the image of Christ through love, forgiveness, sacrifice, and joy until death."

So, when Mr. and Mrs. Right got married, it wasn't just the start of a new chapter. It was the beginning of a sacred calling, two lives bound together by a selfless goal. A legacy forged not just by vows, but by daily choices, prayers whispered in the dark, dreams built together, and a faith carried through seasons of change. Young and old, healthy and sick.

They said **"YES"** not only to each other, but also to God himself, who created them, found them, and united them.

This is the true miracle of marriage.

Rebuilding After the Covenant Breaks

According to Scripture, God's design for marriage was never meant to be divorceable, negotiable, or driven by passing emotions, modern trends, or cultural expectations. In God's view, marriage is not a casual agreement, a romantic experience, or something to be annulled when feelings fade. It is a spiritual covenant, a sacred bond made in His presence. This means that the opinions of friends, family, or your social media contacts have no authority over your marriage once the vows are exchanged. Whether you are experiencing joy or hardship, the sacred weight of the covenant remains fixed. ***King Solomon in Ecclesiastes 5:4-5 says: "When you make a vow to God, do not delay in fulfilling it, for it is better not to vow than to vow and not fulfil it."***

Marriage rests upon unwavering fidelity: it is a choice of eternal love. It is therefore not meant for children, but for adults who, in maturity, lay aside the things of childhood.

Parents first, then the angels of the Kingdom, along with family and friends, may serve as witnesses. Yet in the end, it is you alone who freely choose the person you will present before the throne of heaven, pledging to honor this sacred covenant for the rest of your life.

Today, many Christians are finally recognizing that love alone is not enough to sustain a marriage. Feelings come and go, but it's commitment that keeps the house standing. You don't stay married because you still feel in love. The butterflies you felt in your heart when you were dating were emotional reactions, brought on by a deep sense of attraction and chemistry. But these feelings have nothing to do with the conscious, deliberate decision to marry. Marriage is not motivated solely by emotions; it's a choice grounded in commitment, responsibility, and a genuine alliance. ***Romans 7:2: We stay married because we've made a choice, for better or for worse, for richer or poorer, in sickness or in health.***

The rising divorce rate has made many men more cautious about entering the sacred bond of marriage. Men are increasingly aware that choosing the wrong partner can result in significant personal costs, both emotional and financial.

According to the Bible, when a man chooses his wife poorly, he risks experiencing deep grief, ongoing quarrels, and spiritual obstacles in his life and at home. King Solomon warns all men in Proverbs that "*a quarrelsome wife is like the constant dripping of a leaky roof" (Proverbs 19:13),*

Demonstrating how an unwise marital choice can lead to endless conflict and drain a man's peace and strength. The story of Samson (Judges 16) illustrates how loving the wrong woman can lead to betrayal, a significant loss of purpose, and even destruction.

Similarly, Solomon's many foreign wives turned his heart away from God, resulting in the downfall of his kingdom (1 Kings 11:1-11). That's why the Bible encourages men to seek a wife of noble character who fears the Lord so that they can have a life with both married parents. *"She is worth far more than rubies" (Proverbs 31:10), thus* safeguarding their lives, heritage, and faith.

Until a man decides to put a ring on a woman's finger and make a commitment, all potential women will remain in line to enter the man's program. Today, more single men and bachelors are carefully considering the types of women to avoid, especially those who approach marriage with a conditional mindset, saying,

"Only for the best, never for the worst."

If you're a woman who genuinely desires a husband, a key first step is to break free from the mindset shaped by extreme modern feminism; the kind that encourages independence at the expense of partnership, and power at the cost of purpose. Be honest with yourself: are you ready to reverse traditional roles and biblical laws? Would you buy a ring, choose a man, and propose marriage to him? Even if you're a 'ten," beautiful, educated, and successful in your career or business, does that mean you're willing to pursue and *initiate marriage*?

Now consider this: the man you desire, how many other women, perhaps younger, equally accomplished, or even more attractive, are also seeking him? Do they recognize his value?

More importantly, do you? This is where wisdom comes in. Many women delay understanding relationship dynamics until it's too late. Time is not a neutral force; it affects men and women differently. A man can build, grow, and marry at nearly any age. But for a woman, fertility and childbearing capacity tend to decline between 25 and 35, with menopause approaching around 40 years old.

And while many women focus their hopes on the elusive "top 1%" of wealthy men, powerful, or high-status, they often overlook the honorable, faithful, and steady men all around them: at the gas station, on the train, delivering packages, serving tables, managing businesses, and working diligently in their trades. These men may not flaunt luxury, but they possess character, loyalty, and commitment; the proper foundations for a lasting home with great family value.

So, ask yourself: are you willing to cling to unrealistic standards, waiting for the perfect image, while missing genuine, godly husbands right in front of you? Waiting isn't always wise. Sometimes, it's a costly delay. Stop taking relationship advice from those who are divorced or have remained single for years while standing in the same line as you. Often, their perspective is shaped more by pain or pride than by wisdom or truth. Meanwhile, men are increasingly educating each other on how to avoid women who carry certain mindsets, mindsets that may not be spoken but are quickly revealed in actions and expectations.

Here's the pattern they've learned to recognize:
"Only for the best, never for the worst."
"Only for wealth, not for poverty."
"Only in health, not in sickness."
"Love only when it feels good, and cherish only when it's convenient."
"Stay until love fades, or walk away when life gets hard."

This kind of conditional love isn't true covenant love; it's more like consumer-driven love. Men are increasingly aware of the dangers of committing to a life with women who see marriage as a temporary feeling rather than a lifelong commitment. If your loyalty only remains during good times and prosperity, then it's not genuine love; it's motivated by self-interest. A wise man will recognize this clearly before he makes his vows.

This does not accurately reflect the true spirit of marriage, as described in the Bible. The genuine covenant of love, as established by God, is not based on circumstances but on strong commitment, daily sacrifice, and mutual loyalty.

You chose to honor the vow, keep the promise, and work through the trials of a lifetime with someone you love. If one morning you "don't feel love" anymore, that's not a reason to put on your sneakers and run away from home; it's a signal to look deeper within yourself. Often, the dissatisfaction people feel in marriage isn't about their spouse at all; it reflects internal emptiness or unrealistic expectations that may not even exist in other couples.

This issue is not unique to online relationships. Ninety percent of honeymoon displays online are only for show; it's only when you meet these individuals separately, in a therapy session, that you understand it's only you who can make yourself happy, and self-love is unconditional. Your spouse is just an addition to your sense of completion. Your spouse contributes to your happiness, but isn't the sole source; the Lord is. "Lord, you alone are my portion and my cup; you make my lot secure. The boundary lines have fallen for me in pleasant places; surely, *I have a delightful inheritance." Psalm 16:5-6.*

Expecting one person to be your emotional counsellor, financial provider, spiritual leader, cheerleader, romantic husband, and best friend all at once is not only unrealistic but also unfair to that person.

Let's be honest: no man, no matter how devoted or skilled, can check off every item on the list that modern women sometimes carry. Here's a sample list many women today expect from a man:

A. A man who expresses feelings honestly
B. Listens without judgment
C. Communicates with empathy and patience
D. Is emotionally and mentally mature
E. Handles stress and life with resilience
F. Earns a high income or is financially stable
G. Is loyal, faithful, and respectful of boundaries

H. Respects her voice, values her dreams, and isn't controlling
I. Leads spiritually without dominance (Ephesians 5:25)
J. Supports her ambitions while emotionally serving her
K. Is fun, humorous, and physically and romantically attractive
L. Is fully transparent about finances and plans, and the list continues.

However, the Bible never demanded perfection from husbands or wives; it called for the submission of wives in Ephesians 5:21: "Wives, submit yourselves to your husbands as you do to the Lord." For the husband is the head of the wife, just as Christ is the head of the church. Yes, wives are told to "submit" to their husbands, but not in a demeaning or oppressive way. Meanwhile, husbands are instructed to love their wives as Christ loved the church, with humility, sacrifice, and care.

If you want to wear your Misses fake to enter marriage:

Fake hair, false eyelashes, fake long nails, fake makeup, fake contact lenses, spray tans, fake bras, fake body shapers, Botox, body implants, fake tattooed eyebrows, and fake height-boosting.

You don't listen to anyone when you want to change your name to Miss Fake.

Unfortunately, in many parts of today's Western culture, biblical laws have been dismissed or reversed. Wives are no longer encouraged to honor, support, or respect their husbands unless they check every box, and if he doesn't, many feel justified to leave, file for divorce, and take half of their lives with them.

Marriage is not a game. It's not about constantly evaluating whether your partner "deserves" love; it's about giving it. If you want a marriage that lasts, build it on grace, truth, and covenant, not on conditions and criticism. Because no human can meet all your needs, only God can.

Take a close look at that long list of qualities you expect from a man. Even after getting married, you might find yourself checking off your crazy boxes, wondering if you made the right choice or if it was a mistake, or if someone else might have been a better option. Let's be realistic for a moment: instead of constantly judging him, create a list of expectations; then go through it one by one and ask yourself how many of these traits you bring to the relationship with him.

Now, on the other hand, if you travelled around the world and asked men what they want in a wife, most wouldn't give you a long list. Most men (99%) would prioritize three basic needs: Respect, Peace, and Intimacy.

Men desire to be respected not only for what they do but also for who they are. The Book of Men affirms this in Ephesians 5:33, where Paul wrote, "The wife must respect her husband." Respect is not earned through perfection; it is given as a sign of honor, trust, and reverence in a covenant relationship. Sarah demonstrated how every wife should show respect to their husbands, saying:

"After I am worn out and my lord is old, will I now have this pleasure? «Genesis 18:12 Men desire a peaceful and emotionally safe home, a true refuge rather than a battleground. King Solomon wisely said, *"Better to live in a desert than with a quarrelsome and bitter woman" (Proverbs 21:19).*

Sadly, in today's world, many responsible men are calling for all women to take a simple course in the men's program called "the shut-up program." A man's spirit thrives in an environment of quiet respect and steady support, but it can be shattered by relentless conflict, harsh criticism, or a woman who believes she knows better and can do better than her husband. *"A wife of noble character is her husband's crown, but a disgraceful wife is like decay in his bones." (Proverbs 12:4)*

The Contemporary Crisis of Marriage

In recent decades, an increasing amount of sociological and psychological research has highlighted a concerning trend in the dynamics of long-term marriages. After years, sometimes decades, of building a life together, raising children, and facing the challenges of married life, many women choose to divorce, often in midlife or later. According to a 2015 study by the American Sociological Association, nearly 70% of divorces are initiated by women, with the rate being even higher among college-educated women with promising careers and good salaries.

They feel more wanted than their husbands; they need something new. In the 21st century, you'll find numerous new things that your brain won't be able to process.

Men tend to close their hearts quickly when a woman decides to leave. By the time you look back, they may have already moved on, possibly remarried, and be living as if you no longer matter. This isn't out of spite, but a matter of resolve. Men are created to adapt swiftly to new situations and seek results, not pity. After investing years in building a life together, being left behind can fundamentally change a man. If you find the courage to go after all that, don't expect the door to stay open. Many men will firmly shut it, not out of hatred, but out of respect for themselves. Some even move on with younger, more vibrant partners or choose a new life with two, having learned not to risk their peace again.

One common reason given is the pursuit of a "**better life**", often seen as emotional fulfillment, a new partner, or personal reinvention. In many cases, this pursuit causes women to break apart the very household they once promised to protect, seeking alimony, child support, and a fair division of assets accumulated mostly through the husband's financial effort. Although this legal right is protected by civil law, it can lead to emotional and economic hardship for the partner left behind, typically the woman, especially after a long marriage.

Psychological research and personal stories reveal that the happiness often associated with "starting over" with a new partner doesn't typically materialize for divorced women. As we age, changes occur, and qualities that once attracted attention may no longer stand out as they once did. What seemed like a lasting spark often turns out to be a fleeting flicker, leaving one in darkness.

The excitement of a new relationship tends to be brief and may not provide the long-term compatibility that many years of shared history previously offered. These new partnerships often lack a deep understanding of each other's core values, routines, and future goals, which can lead to disappointment or separation.

The Mirage of a "New Life"

A clear consequence of these choices is a higher risk of loneliness in old age. Many studies on aging show that divorced women tend to feel lonelier than those who are married or widowed, often living alone with pets as their main companions. While pets provide comfort, they can't match the depth of human connection built through shared experiences and commitment.

Sometimes, what starts as a desire for freedom or adventure ends in isolation and regret, a realization that many come to only too late.

If you are married and follow Christ, don't wait until love fades. Share the principles from *The Book of Men* with your spouse. Read, reflect, and pray over them together. Create space not only for correction, but for connection. Instead of walking away, choose to continue loving each other.

Travel together and plan a quick weekend escape. Changing your scenery can reignite your sense of wonder together. Attend events or small plays to create new memories and experiences, replacing routine with excitement. Write letters or heartfelt notes, not just text messages. Written words carry lasting weight and tenderness. Schedule weekly date nights and protect that time. It's not a luxury moment; it's a lifeline of love.

Marriage is not self-sustaining; it thrives on intentional care, shared prayer, and mutual investment. You don't abandon a garden because it stops blooming; you water it, protect it, and tend to it. Do the same with your covenant. Choose to set an example for your family and friends. Stay together as if you are both answering the call before the final judge, as a couple who fought the good fight and prevailed.

God created marriage to foster emotional and physical closeness. In Genesis 2:18, the Lord says, "It is not good for man to be alone." Men deeply desire a wife who is more than just a roommate, someone who shares not only their bed but also their life, their vision, and their faith. Intimacy is more than just a physical connection; it is the glue that bonds vulnerability, maintains affection, and unites common goals.

The court of public opinion does not judge this commitment. It is not subject to "**likes**," comments, or applause from others. It is a sacred, serious, intimate, and private bond between two people under God's watchful eyes. It deserves to be respected, kept private, and protected. The vows exchanged at the altar should not be broadcast for show or debate, but kept within the sacred space of the marriage.

Vows are a sacred and unique part of the wedding ceremony. While the celebration may include parents, siblings, and friends, the faithful covenant of marriage begins with a private decision, when two people choose each other for life, heart to heart, soul to soul. That choice is made before God, long before it is witnessed by guests or sealed with a ring.

After the music fades and the wedding clothes are put away, real life begins. Challenges will come, including pressures from work, financial concerns, parenting, and personal growth. But just as choosing to marry was a private moment, dealing with struggles should also stay personal and sacred.

Only two people got married, not their families or friends. To protect the bond and prevent the erosion of trust that can lead to divorce, it is wise and mature to keep marital issues private between the couple. Seek God first, not public opinion. Invite accountability only from trusted spiritual mentors, not social media, gossip, or extended family. Your marriage is your ministry; guard it with wisdom, discretion, and prayer. ***"So, they are no longer two, but one flesh. (Matthew 19:6` Therefore, what God has joined together, let no one separate" (Matthew 19:6)***

Means that in marriage, a husband and wife are no longer two individuals, but one unified entity, emotionally and spiritually. As a result, neither spouse should expose the other to outsiders or speak negatively about the other. What concerns one, concerns both, and their issues should be handled with discretion, love, and unity, protected from interference or division. This sacred bond is not meant to be shared with the world but to be honored and safeguarded as one.

Unfortunately, in today's culture, weddings are often showcased online to impress strangers, while the sacred vows themselves are treated as temporary suggestions. The Book of MEN warns Christian men against the foolishness that leads to this. "When you make a vow to God, do not delay in fulfilling it. He does not like fools; fulfil your vow. ***It is better not to make a vow than to make one and break it" (Ecclesiastes 5:4-5).***

A wedding is not a party; it is a promise to keep until death do us part. Only God has the authority to unite two people in marriage, and only He has the right to speak into that covenant. He said, "Let no one separate." This means no friend, family member, counsellor, or courtroom has the power to break what God Himself has sealed. When two people stand before God and bind themselves to each other in love and obedience, they are accountable first to the Lord, remaining so until death.

Not to culture, not to trends, and certainly not to personal convenience. Marriage is not a game, and those who enter it must do so with the weight of eternity in mind, **UNTIL DEATH**. The two who say "I do" must also say, "We will stand with each other no matter what," every day afterward, not because it is easy, but because it is holy.

When a man and woman enter into a covenant before God, they are no longer two, but one flesh. However, in a fallen world, not all marriages last.

The Book of Men writes in

1 Corinthians 7:15:
"But if the unbeliever leaves, let it be so. The brother or the sister is not bound in such circumstances; God has called us to live in peace."

This teaching acknowledges that sometimes one partner may choose to end the marriage, particularly when there is a conflict of faith, values, or commitment. In such cases, the believing spouse is no longer spiritually bound. You cannot begin to rebuild a new life while still tied to a covenant that has been spiritually, emotionally, or legally abandoned. Just as a condemned building must be torn down before reconstruction begins, a person must be released from their former vows to start anew.

Government laws, especially in the United States, often conflict with biblical teachings. In The Book of Men, it was the husband who had the authority to issue a certificate of divorce in cases of adultery or abandonment of marital duties (Deuteronomy 24:1-4, Matthew 19:9).

Today, however, the government grants equal or greater power to women to initiate divorce, regardless of biblical grounds. Many women, especially in cultures influenced by secular ideologies, leave their homes not out of fear or abuse but out of dissatisfaction or personal gain.

In too many cases, a woman will leave her husband if he is financially stable, taking advantage of state laws to claim half of his fortune, as well as long-term child support and alimony for herself. What was supposed to be a sacred union becomes a legal trap, where the man finds himself financially and emotionally devastated, while the state rewards the woman who walks away.

This abuse of government laws has undermined the sacred institution of marriage. In some cases, women may claim mental instability or emotional trauma to avoid working and to gain extended financial support from their husbands, regardless of whether they contributed equally to the marriage or fulfilled their roles. While Scripture encourages compassion for the brokenhearted, it never justifies manipulation.

Marriage is meant for mutual sacrifice, not for claiming privileges. Men who want to follow God's laws must be guided by wisdom and spiritual discernment. If a woman chooses to abandon her role as a wife and there is clear proof of neglect, betrayal, or rebellion against God's design, then a man has biblical grounds to free himself from these bonds. Only then, when the old foundation is removed, can he truly rebuild spiritually, emotionally, and perhaps someday with a new partner who will honor the covenant as God intended.

HEAVENLY CITIZEN

CHAPTER THREE

A divorced Christian Man.
"The Lord is close to the brokenhearted and saves those who are crushed in spirit." Psalm 34:18

I am a Christian who once believed with all my heart that my marriage would last until death do us part. I was convinced that if I followed God's path, my home would stay strong. I promised before God and in the presence of witnesses that I would love, honor, and cherish my wife, and for more than twenty (20) years, I kept that promise every day, not as a burden, but as my highest calling. I took on the roles of husband, father, provider, protector, and spiritual leader of my family with pride and a deep sense of responsibility.

Looking back now, I see just how earnestly I tried to live out the words of Joshua. ***"But as for me and my house, we will serve the Lord." Joshua 24:15***

I wanted nothing more than to build a home with God as the foundation and love as its unshakable walls. God blessed me with two sons, strong, smart children, who became the center of my life and the greatest gift from the heavenly Father to me, even when I stumbled. They were my entire world, my legacy, and my reason for enduring storms that many men would have abandoned long before I did. Imagine yourself in my place, standing weary and doubtful, wondering how to stay godly when your marriage feels distant from God. I write these words for you. Brother, understand this: even if your plans fall apart, your story isn't finished yet. As it says in scripture, ***"Many are the afflictions of the righteous, but the Lord delivers him out of them all." (Psalm 34:19).***

I have experienced this truth firsthand for a long time, and you will too if you continue to hold onto the Lord. From the moment I said 'I do, I made a covenant not just with my wife but with God, to provide, protect, and lead. For fifteen years, I bore the full weight of our household with unwavering dedication, regardless of the toll it took on me, physically, emotionally, or spiritually. I showed up. I paid every bill, maintained the mortgage, took care of the cars, and funded every family vacation, date night, and small joy my wife or children desired. I gave it all, not out of obligation, but out of responsibility and faithfulness to the promise I made before heaven.

In my culture, as in many others, a man is expected to support his entire family. I dedicated my strength and youth to building what I believed would be a stable home. I never asked how much my wife earned once she started working, nor did I question her bank deposits. To me, love meant trusting her. I might have been naïve; I could have gained more insight from the wisdom in The Book of Men, but I chose to remain steadfast, acting like a foolish and blind husband.

While I worked hard and made sacrifices, she quietly built her wealth, eventually able to afford things I could no longer provide. One day, she declared, "This is America, I don't need a man to support me. I can take care of myself. I am independent." In that moment, without speaking a word, she signed the end of our marriage. God, in His perfect wisdom, created man first and instilled in every man's heart what no one else needs to teach: at that moment, I knew deep inside that I was no longer her husband. The vow had died, not by my choice, but because of her pride.

I dedicated myself to early mornings and late nights, making countless sacrifices without complaint, because it is written: "Whatever you do, work heartily, as for the Lord and not for men. ***Colossians 3:23. The clock is set, and the Lord is watching every move.***

For twenty years, I provided for our household, covering all expenses. I was proud to be the provider, not for recognition, but to ensure my wife and sons felt safe, protected, and loved. I never imagined she would leave, especially after everything we shared. She was in her forties, five years older than I am, with a wealth of history behind us. I wasn't heartbroken by her departure; it was the realization that she had left us long before it became apparent.

Even while living under the same roof, she had already emotionally and spiritually distanced herself from the family. Still, she stayed, quietly enjoying the security and provisions of the household, as if she were still rooted in the home, when in fact, her heart had drifted elsewhere a long time ago. Be cautious of those who hide their deceit behind a mask of righteousness.

1 Corinthians 13:7–8:
"Love bears all things, believes all things, hopes all things, endures all things. Love never fails."

I was convinced that my love, my work, and my faithfulness would strengthen our marriage. I was mistaken about her heart, but never about my obedience to God. That obedience became my anchor during the storms that followed.

When she started her new job with a higher salary, I felt proud of her achievement. I believed it would reduce my burden and help her feel satisfied. I cheered her on, supported her education, and was always there to offer my help.

What started as a blessing gradually created a rift between us. I noticed her new salary boosted her confidence. Her social circle also shifted, as she began spending more time with women who claimed to be "*independent*" but secretly harbored resentment. I saw them leave their husbands one after another, applauding each other for their "freedom." They persuaded my wife that she didn't need me.

I could see Proverbs 14:1 unfolding in my home: "The wise woman builds her house, but the foolish pulls it down with her hands." Proverbs 14:1

I asked the Lord to rebuild what I could no longer hold together with my own hands. The Lord chooses to rebuild me instead of the marriage. The Holy Spirit began whispering directly to me, "I will build you up again; I will never forsake you."

Divorce can provide a feeling of freedom from responsibilities, but for older women with children, that independence often comes at a high cost. After years of managing a household and raising kids, many women find themselves reentering the dating scene after divorce with limited resources and opportunities. The financial strain is especially severe; studies show that women aged 40 and older see a 55% drop in their standard of living after divorce, compared to just 11% for men. This gap is caused by factors such as interrupted careers and wage disparities.

Emotionally, the journey can be just as challenging. The urge to reconnect with. She didn't realize she was tearing down her roof while claiming she was building herself up. She forgot that a family's strength comes not just from money, but from unity under God's hand. And while her heart drifted away, mine stayed, praying, working, and watching in quiet pain. I asked my God for guidance and to show me when it's time to let her go. I prayed often over my children, guided by the promise in Psalm ***127:1: "Unless the Lord builds the house, they labor in vain who build it."***

I asked the spouse, and rebuilding the bond once shared might lead to efforts that don't consistently achieve the desired result.

In my experience, I planned a long road trip from Boston to Delaware, hoping that the change in environment would rekindle our connection. Seven hours on the highway, two children sleeping in the back seat, my wife beside me, I thought maybe the distance from her friends would soften her heart toward our family again. She enjoyed the trips, the dinners, the hotels, but her heart had checked out long ago. Feminist independence had already taken root before anyone could notice the change.

We used to be close friends. I was trying to recreate the atmosphere that had disappeared. I thought that spending more time together would help bridge the gap that had grown between us. I didn't realize that the influences she had taken on had changed her beliefs and priorities. What I saw as a chance to reconnect was, in her eyes, a clash of ideologies.

This was the moment when The Book of Men's Laws began to speak directly to my situation, and I finally started to listen. The first lesson? Silence. *Shsshshshsss!* ***"I said, 'I will take heed to my ways, that I sin not with my tongue: I will keep my mouth shut with a bridle, while the wicked is before me.'"*** *Psalm 39:1, she was no longer my problem.*

So, I stopped speaking. I held my tongue, not out of fear, but out of wisdom and understanding. Then I remembered:

"For the Lord gives wisdom; from His mouth come knowledge and understanding." *Proverbs 2:6*

He had taught men how to think clearly and discern

Quickly, so I could start to see the end of a thing before it fully unfolded. That's when I began to prepare, not just outwardly, but internally. I gathered my dignity, guarded my heart, and walked alone with the Lord. At that point, the battle was no longer mine. The Holy Spirit whispered again with clarity: "It is time for you to leave."

At that moment, I realized I needed to fight for my family differently, not with anger, but with strategy. It's crucial to understand the complexities of life after divorce for older women. It's not just about emotional resilience, but also about handling the financial and social challenges that can linger long after the legal separation. I envisioned a fresh start in a new state. Delaware had a similar network of private schools for boys and affordable new homes. I thought to myself, "If she sees that I'm willing to leave everything behind again for her and the children, she will surely remember my love."

At first, she was impressed. She saw that I could provide for her and that I was still the man who gave her a sense of security. But her heart was already gone. I now understand what The Book of Men says in Proverbs 4:23: ***"Above all else, guard your heart, for everything you do flows from it."***

The Holy Spirit told me that this woman was going to cause you and the boys a lot of pain, and that if you didn't pay attention and make peace with the situation, you would end up being condemned by the government for tearing your home apart or going to prison.

I had guarded my heart, but she hadn't. A heart led by pride and unhealthy influences becomes a stranger; even in your bed, you no longer recognize the person next to you. If you're someone of prayer like me, the Lord will show you signs to teach you that your place is no longer in this house, that you will need to make other plans. This train is complete, and there is no place for the husband on board.

You must leave when the time is right. I tried anyway. I thought that if I changed our environment, I could distract her from the voices whispering to her that independence was synonymous with disrespect and divorce for a man. But a wise man learns from The Book of Men that "you cannot change the fruit without changing the root, and by then, the root was already too deep."

Holding on for the children?

No, it's out of the question. Don't put yourself through that. The challenges you'll face aren't documented in any book, except in The Book of Men. Trust me, it will teach you that when you decide to change the game, it's time for a fresh start. Only men understand the rules now. She is no longer your concern; her interests, decisions, and outcomes are not your burden. It's just you and God. Develop a new plan.

Protect your purpose. Rearrange your life so she cannot influence your peace or prosperity. Change the rules subtly, wisely, and without anger as you build something new. Be present for your children. Stay consistent, loyal, and quietly intense. You are no longer just reacting; you are reconstructing with God as your guide.

I had to accept the truth; I couldn't fix what she no longer valued. Her father, a man I deeply respected, sat down with me one evening and said softly, "If I were you, I would have left already." He apologized to me after seeing the mountain I had to climb to keep things together. I remember that night vividly.

I looked at my two sons sleeping in the next room and thought of Psalm 127:3: ***"Behold, children are a heritage from the Lord, the fruit of the womb is a reward."***

The Lord will protect them; He will provide for their needs and shield them from anything that might come in the future.

My sons were my reason for staying strong when my marriage fell apart. I refused to let them grow up in a broken home too soon. I prayed, "Lord, give me the strength to persevere, not for her, but for my boys who look up to me as their role model."

The Book of Men's Laws is to pray to God for everything and anything we cannot control. So, I entrusted their souls and lives to my Lord and Savior, Jesus, saying these words: "Don't worry about anything; instead, pray about everything. Tell God what you need, and thank Him for all He has done. Then you will experience God's peace, which surpasses all understanding. ***His peace will guard your hearts and minds as you live in Christ Jesus."*** *(Philippians 4:6-7)*

I enrolled my sons in taekwondo so we could learn together, fostering discipline, respect, and resilience as father and sons. On weekends, we swam at the YMCA in Hyde Park, Boston. I focused on developing their bodies and minds, praying daily for their morale. I vividly remember Isaiah praying for me when I was too tired to drive them home. I took the time to follow a simple procedure that the Lord gave to King Solomon in Proverbs 22:6:

"Train up a child in the way he should go, and when he is old, he will not depart from it."

Even as my marriage ended, I fought for my sons' souls. I wanted them to see that their father was still faithful, still present, and still a man of God, regardless of what their mother chose to become. I will never leave them. *"Never will I leave you; never will I forsake you." Hebrews 13:5*

The Book of Men's Laws once again confirms the truth in Proverbs *21:9: 'Better to live on a corner of the roof than share a house with a quarrelsome wife.'*

This is not just poetry; it reflects the reality of millions of men, past and present, who suffer silently within their own homes. We endure not out of weakness, but out of love, duty, and covenant. As men, we stand tall even when we're crumbling inside.

We often sacrifice our dreams, energy, and sometimes even our sense of self for our families. And yet, there may come a day when the burden exceeds our capacity, when our plates are empty, our hearts are weighed down, and our bodies start to falter under the silent burden. Instead of "until death do us part," it starts to feel as if death is sprinting toward us alone.

But God's Word never fails. In my darkest moment, Galatians 6:9 breathed life back into me: *"And let us not grow weary in doing good, for at the proper time we will reap a harvest, if we do not give up."*

I chose not to become bitter. I decided to stay faithful, not because of her, but because of Him, the God who sees, hears, and rewards. In response, He gave me the strength to endure. Many men suffer the devastating effects of marital distress quietly, until now. The Book of Men will speak on your behalf: a calm, peaceful heart is closely connected to physical health, whereas stress and envy can harm the body.

Emotional shutdown, chronic fatigue, and identity erosion are more than poetic phrases; they are scientifically documented reactions to long-term relational stress, especially in married men. Research from organizations like the American Psychological Association and Harvard Medical School has demonstrated that men in high-conflict marriages or emotionally neglectful relationships face a much higher risk of depression, anxiety, insomnia, and stress-related health issues, such as high blood pressure and heart disease.

Prolonged emotional suppression, frequently ingrained in men from an early age, may result in loneliness, substance abuse, and a profound sense of failure or shame. In the absence of sufficient support, numerous men internalize their distress, leading to what psychologists describe as "silent despair," a state wherein individuals are physically present yet emotionally numb and spiritually vacant. Even in the depths of emotional exile, God's Laws offer hope for these Christian Men. ***"The Lord is near to the brokenhearted and saves the crushed in spirit" (Psalm 34:18).***

When someone is betrayed, abandoned, or falsely accused, and the burden threatens to overwhelm them, they can still rise, not by their own strength, but by anchoring themselves in God.

The prophet teaches men not to be discouraged in Isaiah 41:10:

"Fear not, for I am with you; be not dismayed, for I am your God; I will strengthen you and help you; I will uphold you with my righteous right hand."

Even when alone, God is present. For those who trust in Him, there is restoration, honor, and a renewed identity, no longer defined by what was broken, but by the One who makes all things new.

The Betrayal Uncovered was not unexpected. One thing I've learned as a Christian man is this: the truth always comes out. A man of prayer often senses what's happening long before it is revealed. For years, I prayed, "Lord, let this cup pass from me, don't let it be true." But the Holy Spirit kept confirming, "Yes, my son, it is." I asked God to reveal what was hidden in darkness, and in time, He did. Brother, that gut feeling you've had for a while isn't just a feeling. It's discernment. And yes, it's true.

The sooner you accept reality, the sooner you can prepare your next steps, not in defeat, but in victory. Because

God does not take pleasure in those who quit. He did not create you to be a loser. You have the strength of a lion: "The wicked flee when no one pursues, but the righteous are bold as a lion," and no one has the right to disrespect you. He empowers those who endure and press on with wisdom, dignity, and faith. ***"For God has not given us a spirit of fear, but of power*** *and love and a sound mind to win." 2 Timothy 1:7 "For there is nothing hidden which will not be revealed, nor has anything been kept secret, but that it should come to light." Mark 4:22*

I found undeniable evidence that she had been unfaithful. But it didn't break my heart; it freed my spirit. I had been faithful, and the Holy Spirit had already confirmed what I sensed all along. God had seen my heart, and now the truth was laid bare for her family to see as well. I wasn't surprised, because as a man of prayer, especially one who walks with God, you know. **"But God hath revealed them to you by his Spirit: for the Spirit searched all things, yea, the deep things of God". (1 Corinthians 2:10)**

I planned one last family trip, this time to New York, where her relatives lived. I kept it to myself until the meeting with everyone. Then, under her parents' roof, I revealed everything she had been doing. There was no shouting or insults. Just the facts. Her family looked at her with pain and disbelief. She burst into tears and apologized. But her uncle, a man of integrity and influence, looked her in the eye and said, "Don't you dare to apologize to us. Apologize to your husband, the person you've hurt."

Then I turned to them and said, "I have returned her safe and sound, without conflict, without damage. Now, she can make plans with her affair partner. I am no longer bound to her, and she will soon receive a letter of divorce so she can pursue the happiness and excitement she believes she's found."

I want you to know that over the past twenty years, I have faithfully provided for her and our children. I paid every bill, maintained her cars, cared for her needs, took her on vacation, covered every expense, and remained emotionally and spiritually present. I gave her love and affection to the best of my ability, without negligence. We raised our children together, enjoyed date nights, and took family trips near and far. She lived a life of comfort and protection with me. Now, she is no longer my problem.

So, you might wonder why I arranged this respectful meeting with her family rather than simply walking away, right? To me, respect is paramount. Falling out of love is something I can accept; it's a natural part of life. However, I cannot tolerate deliberate disrespect, especially from someone I once held in high esteem and prioritized above all else in my life. I don't require perfection from others, but I do expect honesty and integrity.

That is why I chose to send her back to her family peacefully and with dignity, because I still believe in acting with honor, even at the end. Am I the only man to have returned an unfaithful woman to her family?

Because everything had already been discussed between us: she would now be divorced and free to join her boyfriends, several of whom, I'm sure, are also married. That evening, I left. I took the car and drove home alone with my sons. She returned by bus a few days later, but I had already closed the door on my heart. *The King said: "Truthful lips endure forever, but a lying tongue lasts only a moment" (Proverbs 12:19)*

Her lies were exposed in that room. Although it hurt many people I care about, I stayed calm. When she got home, whatever she was involved in no longer worried me; she had lost the right to blame me for her choices. My primary concern was protecting our young boys from the harsh reality of growing up too fast in a broken home. Still, I held on to hope, to shield them and keep some sense of normalcy. But deep down, I knew her spirit had no intention of changing.

She kept returning to the same patterns repeatedly. She crossed a line that I couldn't forgive; I checked out, just like 100% of men would. We don't stay after betrayal; we stop trusting and never forget. So, we walk away. As Proverbs 26:11 states, *"As a dog return to its vomit, so fools repeat their folly." Despite this, I chose patience.*

I waited, giving the boys time to mature so they could better understand and not be hurt by her new environment. At the same time, I protected my heart and future. I made sure no more children would come from that relationship, confirming through DNA that my sons were truly mine. This wasn't because I doubted them, but out of wisdom for myself, hard-earned understanding learned through experience and rooted in the lessons of The Book of Men.

I took steps to guard my heart and secure my future. I ensured there would be no more children between us, and I confirmed through DNA testing that my sons are indeed mine. It wasn't about mistrust towards them, but about wisdom for myself, I learning from the best in **The Book of Men**.

Jesus said, "*Behold, I send you forth as sheep among wolves: be ye therefore wise as serpents and harmless as doves.*" *(Matthew 10:16). At this point, protection is reserved only for your children, if you have any. But above all, you must now prioritize yourself. Keep your heart guarded silently and act with discernment.*

Surround yourself with the unbreakable wall of the Holy Spirit; no one should breach the sacred space between you and your faith in God. He has already mapped out your next steps. You only need to remain still and trust Him to guide your path. As it is written in Exodus 14:14, *"****The Lord will fight for you; you need only to be still.****"*

HEAVENLY CITIZEN

CHAPTER FOUR

Real Husband's Laws, Amazing Grace
The Only One Worthy of Our Bow

It was a pivotal moment of true independence. When she went to Florida without informing me, she went on a trip with her "independent" divorced friends and left our children with her father. I arrived home from work and realized clearly: my ultimate door to freedom was opening. Without anger or regret, I packed my belongings, left that house, and never looked back.

Sometimes, walking away isn't a sign of weakness; it's an act of obedience to protect what God has entrusted to you.

Don't forget that this is why He created man in the first place. The Lord will grant you the strength to leave and discover a woman who is more beautiful, younger, and devout

Christian was raised with strong family values by both parents. She is also very fertile and has no children. Just as God did for me. I have now been remarried for five years, and God blessed us with another son. I found my wife in another country.

God created man first to establish a clear hierarchy and order, as part of His design for humanity. The headship is first, which means a man must be fundamentally established, disciplined, grounded in values, guided by vision, rooted in stability, and walking in purpose before a woman can even consider disrupting his life. The Lord has established a model of tender, responsible leadership within the family and society.

According to 1 Corinthians 11:3, 8-9, this **order demonstrates that while men and women are equal in God's eyes, their roles differ: "For man did not come out of a woman, but woman out of a man; man was not created for woman, but woman for man."**

This divine hierarchy emphasizes that the man is to lead with devoted love and stewardship, reflecting God's authority and wisdom in placing the man in charge as the head of the woman and his household. Simultaneously, the woman was created to be a helper and a suitable partner, completing the beautiful harmony of God's creation in marriage.

The Book of Men states, in Deuteronomy 24:1-4, that if a man marries a woman who becomes displeasing to him because he finds something indecent about her, and he writes her a **certificate of divorce**, gives it to her, and sends her away from his house, her life will repeat the same cycle over and over until no man wants her anymore. She has been defiled.

If a woman chooses to leave her husband, deceived into thinking the grass is greener elsewhere, she exposes herself to spiritual corruption and a cycle of deception in God's eyes. Scripture encourages married women to respect and honor their husbands (Ephesians 5:33), not to abandon the covenant lightly. The title "**husband**" should not be taken lightly; it signifies a sacred role.

A husband reflects God's image in his household: he is the head of the home (Ephesians 5:23), a protector, provider, and leader; a man who loves his wife as Christ loved the church, sacrificially and unconditionally (Ephesians 5:25); a faithful steward of his marriage and children; and a servant leader who guides with humility and purpose. To dishonor a husband is to dishonor the divine structure God established for the family when he created the husband in his likeness.

The relationship between the Lord and humanity is to be respected: He entrusted Adam with the responsibility to cultivate (work) and protect the Garden, even before Eve was created, emphasizing humanity's foundational role as stewards and providers. As Genesis 2:15 states: ***"The LORD God took the man and put him in the Garden of Eden to work it and take care of it."***

In *The Book of Men*, this explains what it means to be a man of genuine worth or a high-value Christian man, who is bright and intelligent: we do not need anyone's approval to build and rebuild, to create wealth, and to pursue our vision. We went to the top school, the unique University created and taught by the almighty himself.

Sometimes, after a divorce, a man needs to return to his roots, revisit *The Book of Men*, and rediscover his original purpose. That's why nearly 99% of men succeed within the first five years after divorce: a real man is motivated to work hard and wisely to build wealth and an inheritance. *The Book of Men* also advises men to keep money received as an inheritance or gift in a separate account and never mix it with marital funds. If you can't reach a prenuptial or postnuptial agreement, remember that you are God's first son, you are a man, and wherever there's life, there's always a way. Stay focused.

The leadership of a man in the family reflects the divine plan of fatherhood, establishing a hierarchical order under God: father, mother, then children. Paul's letter to the Ephesians 5:23 states: ***"For the husband is the head of the wife as Christ is the head of the church."*** **From the beginning, God gave Adam a role as leader and steward, entrusting him with the command concerning the tree before Eve was created (Genesis 2:16-17).**

This intentional arrangement clearly shows that man has the primary duty to uphold and teach God's Word within his family.

REAL HUSBANDS

The manner in which one communicates with a husband is distinctly different from the approach taken when addressing a boy. A boy might be corrected with impatience; however, a husband warrants communication imbued with respect and dignity, as he bears responsibilities that children are not yet equipped to handle. Regrettably, numerous men today endure their struggles in silence, particularly Christian men, who frequently feel misunderstood both by society and within their own households.

When I say "***Christian***," I am not referring to a specific denomination, such as Protestant or Catholic, because religious boundaries did not limit Christ Himself. He did not act as an imam, priest, or pastor affiliated with any institution. Instead, He came to announce the Kingdom of God and to fulfill the Law and the Prophets, as He explicitly stated: Matthew 5:17: ***"Do not think that I have come to abolish the Law or the Prophets; I have not come to abolish them but to fulfill them"***.

A faithful husband is a man who understands that his life is not his own but a stewardship entrusted to him by God. He rises each day not only to work for bread but also to cover his family with prayer, protection, and presence. To disregard such a man, to strip him of the fruit of his labor, and to cast him aside as though his efforts mean nothing is not simply an injustice; it is a sin against the God who called him. Scripture reminds us that the cry of the oppressed reaches the ears of the Lord of Hosts. Those who dishonor a faithful husband will answer to his Maker.

At the heart of a genuine husband's character is the reliability of a great father. His promises carry weight, and he strives to keep them. When he speaks, his family can trust in his integrity. His actions reflect his core values, and his character remains uncompromised.

Although he may not always be flawless, his steadfast integrity shines a light on a world often marked by compromise. He establishes his home on honesty rather than deceit, teaching his family to live with integrity through his own example.

Yet a husband's responsibility goes beyond providing bread. A faithful husband understands that man does not live by bread alone, but by every word that proceeds from the mouth of God. His role is not just to earn an income but also to nurture souls. He offers emotional support, listens, and guides with compassion.

He provides spiritually, guiding his family toward righteousness, teaching his children the ways of God, and reminding his household that they belong to a higher Kingdom. In this way, his leadership is holistic, nourishing both body and spirit. Faithfulness characterizes a husband's bond with his wife. Regarding his children, every Christian husband shows sacrificial commitment to their safety and welfare. While the mother's happiness takes precedence, most would accept their roles as the Lord's representatives for their children.

His love is not just superficial affection or fleeting passion but instead a binding commitment. He honors his spouse with words that uplift rather than demean, through attitudes that display respect, and through actions that protect her dignity. A faithful husband doesn't just say he loves his wife; he shows it through consistency, patience, and sacrifice. For his children, love isn't measured by gifts or possessions but by presence: listening to their stories, correcting them kindly, and encouraging them to follow their calling in God.

A real husband is also a protector. His strength lies not only in his muscles but also in his vigilance and discernment. He protects his family physically by shielding them from harm. He protects emotionally by being attentive and refusing to neglect their needs. He protects spiritually by keeping his home free from false values and ungodly influences.

Beyond protection, his voice roared like a lion, providing direction. He offers vision for the household, guiding them toward a future marked not by fear, but by faith. Under his covering, his wife and children find a sense of security, knowing that their home is anchored in both love and wisdom. A husband who looks beyond himself recognizes that his true legacy isn't material possessions, such as cars or wealth, but the character and faith he imparts to his children. He lives with a sense of eternity, laying a foundation meant to last beyond his lifetime. His dedication ensures that his descendants will inherit more than just possessions; they'll inherit values, stability, and faith. A genuine husband is someone who not only lives for today but also plants seeds for the future, creating a legacy that resonates forever.

Why Did God Place a Man as the Head of the House?

From the very beginning, God's design for the family was established in Genesis. Adam was created first, and then Eve was formed as a *"**helper suitable for him" (Genesis 2:18)***. This divine arrangement was never about superiority or inferiority; it was about order. Just as the universe operates with structure, so does the family. God gave the man the role of headship, not as a dictator, but as a servant-leader who reflects God's own leadership over His people. This order ensures harmony and direction because where there is no leadership, confusion reigns.

Headship, therefore, is a position of responsibility, not privilege. The man bears the weight of accountability before God for the well-being of his household. When challenges arise, the family often turns to the husband first. His leadership provides stability in times of uncertainty, direction in moments of confusion, and courage in the face of fear. This is not about domination, but about taking on the responsibility of stewardship.

God holds the man accountable, just as He called out to Adam first in the Garden: "Where are you?" (Genesis 3:9). The Bible makes it clear that husband and wife are equal before God. **"Husbands, live with your wives in an understanding way, showing honor to the woman as the weaker vessel, since they are heirs with you of the grace of life"** (1 Peter 3:7).

The wife is not beneath the man; she stands beside him as a co-heir of grace. Yet Scripture acknowledges that she is the "weaker vessel," not in worth, but in her need for protection, care, and honor. The husband's strength is meant to support his wife's vulnerability, not exploit it. His role is to shield, not to dominate.

This order of headship does not diminish the wife's voice or value; instead, it affirms her place of honor. In God's wisdom, authority and equality coexist within the home. A husband leads with sacrificial love, and a wife supports with respect and wisdom. Together, they reflect the image of Christ and His Church: the bride who is cherished, and the bridegroom who lays down His life in love (Ephesians 5:2527).

When this divine order is disrupted, the home suffers. For example, when a wife raises her voice at her husband in anger, it often communicates dishonor rather than constructive disagreement. The Bible calls wives to respect their husbands, just as husbands are commanded to love their wives (Ephesians 5:33). Raised voices tear down respect, create distance, and wound the bond of trust. ***Proverbs warns, "Better to live on a corner of the roof than share a house with a quarrelsome wife" (Proverbs 21:9).***

Strife erodes peace, but respect strengthens unity. The atmosphere of a household is primarily shaped by the words exchanged between a husband and a wife. Harsh, loud speech stirs anger, while gentle, respectful communication fosters peace. Scripture teaches, "A gentle answer turns away wrath, but a harsh word stirs up anger" (Proverbs 15:1). A wife who chooses calmness, even in moments of frustration, shows spiritual maturity and helps her home thrive. Her voice becomes a source of healing instead of harm.

Ultimately, God appointed the man as the head of the household not to elevate him above his wife and children, but to ensure the family has guidance, protection, and a reflection of Christ's sacrificial leadership. The wife's role of respect and the husband's role of love are not opposing forces but complementary callings. When both partners embrace their God-given roles, the family becomes a strong unit, a testimony to the world of the order, peace, and love that characterize the Kingdom of God.

The Power of Words in Marriage

Raising your voice does more than produce sound; it conveys disrespect, frustration, and even rejection. To a husband, especially one trying to lead his family faithfully, a raised voice can feel like an attack on his authority and dignity. What a wife might see as simply anger can easily be perceived as dishonor.

Over time, these moments accumulate, creating a distance between husband and wife. What should be a partnership begins to break down into defensiveness, silence, or conflict. If left unaddressed, the home, intended by God to be a place of peace, can become a battlefield of pride and hurt. But God has shown us a better way: the way of self-control and gentle words.

"A gentle answer turns away wrath, but a harsh word stirs up anger" (Proverbs 15:1).

Gentleness in speech is not weakness; it is strength guided by wisdom. It requires more courage to remain calm and composed than to unleash anger. A godly woman learns to speak firmly yet with respect, expressing her concerns without undermining her husband's spirit. By doing so, she upholds her husband's dignity while still making her voice heard. Scripture reminds us that a woman's words can shape the atmosphere of her home. *"The wise woman builds her house, but with her own hands the foolish one tears hers down" (Proverbs 14:1).*

Every sentence, every tone, every response can either build the foundation of unity or weaken the walls of trust. Though small, the tongue guides the course of relationships, and within marriage, its influence is vast. A gentle word, spoken patiently, can heal wounds and rebuild closeness. Respectful communication strengthens a husband's heart, encourages his leadership, and maintains peace in the home. Conversely, constant arguing drains joy and weakens the very foundation of marriage. By choosing gentleness, a wife not only honors her husband but also honors God, whose Spirit empowers her to act with patience and grace.

Content English:

The Husband and the Covenant of Marriage

The husband is defined as an individual who has entered into a marital covenant, characterized by mutual rights and responsibilities with his wife. The first husband was Adam, to whom God provided a wife, **Eve**, as a **"helper suitable for him"** (Genesis 2:18).

They remained united until death, exemplifying the permanence of divine design for marriage. A husband is substantially more than a married man; he is a covenantal leader, protector, and servant of his household.

Eve was the first woman, created by God's own hands in a world untouched by sin. Her beauty was pure and flawless, reflecting the perfection of creation itself. She was not only physically radiant but also endowed with a sharp and inquisitive mind. Gifted with intelligence, sensitivity, and reasoning ability, she was designed as an equal partner to Adam, differing in role yet equal in worth. Her beauty was captivating, and her intellect complemented her appearance, symbolizing the divine intention behind womanhood.

Her intelligence and curiosity led her into deception, and from that moment on, she paid a heavy price for her disobedience. Yet even in her failure, she stayed by her husband's side, walking the path of consequences together. Her story became a solemn reminder of the unchanging law of God, testifying that His word cannot be ignored without consequence.

Unlike many modern women of the 21st century who easily leave their husbands and venture alone down unfamiliar paths, wives need to recognize a fundamental truth: men pay attention. If you leave your home once and make yourself accessible to someone else, trust is broken, and they will believe you might do it again. **No wise man wishes to become the next target of instability**. Instead, women should learn from Eve's example; although she faltered, she stayed by her husband's side until the end. True wisdom isn't in walking away but in standing firm, honoring the covenant, and protecting the home God has entrusted to you.

The Bible describes the husband not just as the leader of a social arrangement, but as the caretaker of a divine covenant. ***"For the husband is*** *the head of the wife as Christ is the head of the church, His body, of which He is the Savior" (Ephesians 5:23).*

This leadership is based on responsibility rather than control, reflecting Christ's sacrificial love for His Church. A husband is called to lead with humility, protect with courage, and serve with faithfulness.

Even the word husband itself indicates this role of stewardship. It originates from the Old Norse husband, literally meaning "house-dweller" or "householder." It referred to someone who managed the home responsibly. In the biblical sense, the husband is not just a resident of the household, but its caretaker, entrusted by God to govern with wisdom and love.

The Book of Christian Men gives this counsel: if a man can provide for his household without requiring his wife to labor outside the home, he should do so. "**Why**"?

The reason is not to diminish the wife, but to preserve her primary calling as the nurturer of the children and the heart of the home. Scripture reminds us that the wife is "the weaker vessel" (1 Peter 3:7), not in terms of value or worth, but in her need for protection and covering.

When financial pressure forces her to divide her strength between her children and the demands of outside work, the family may be exposed to tension and temptation. If not guided by the Holy Spirit, the lure of financial independence can distort her priorities and strain her relationship with her husband.

Indeed, I acknowledge that many men may disagree with statement number one; However, if one examines other countries where divorce rates are nearly zero, a common factor observed is that the wives primarily assume the role of homemakers. The value and respect attributed to their work, as well as their respectful care for the children and contributions through their labor, are fundamental to the household. The maintenance of the home and the appearance of the well-dressed husband and children consistently reflect the efforts of the wife. This is the work of the wife.

This does not diminish her dignity nor reduce her equality as a co-heir of grace. A wife is a woman who has entered into a legal and spiritual covenant of marriage, sharing mutual responsibilities, rights, and companionship with her husband. She is a helper, not in the sense of servitude, but as a partner, one who completes what is lacking in the man, just as Eve was given to Adam.

The apostle Paul acknowledged that marriage is a significant calling and that staying unmarried can sometimes allow for greater focus on the Lord (1 Corinthians 7).

However, for those who marry, the responsibilities are substantial, and the vocation is sacred. A wife embodies love, respect, and partnership within marriage. She is entrusted with nurturing the heart of the home, supporting her husband with wisdom, and shaping the family's atmosphere. Together, husband and wife form a single partnership, one flesh and one home, though each may bring different resources to the table.

In marriage, individuality is not erased, but unity takes priority. Finances, responsibilities, and decisions should never be used as tools of division, but rather as instruments of unity. As I often reminded my own wife, money should never be a problem in our home because finances are not meant to divide us but to serve us as one body under God's order.

The Only One Worthy of Our Bow

Furthermore, let it be made clear: certain men will disagree with this conviction, yet the truth stands firm. No matter how powerful another man may be, whether a president, a king, a dignitary clothed in authority, or a figure crowned with great wealth and success, we will not and must never bow in worship to their presence. We will never show reverence by bowing to anyone, whether it is a president, king, or high dignitary. We do not kiss their hands nor shout as if they are saviors. Earthly power, no matter how great, is temporary and doomed to fade away. King David said Psalm 146:3: *"Do not put your trust in princes, in human beings, who cannot save"*

There is only One before whom we fall face down, laying our guards and crowns at His feet. The only power worthy of our worship is the Lord Jesus Christ, who holds the keys of life and the Kingdom of Heaven. *"Therefore, God exalted Him to the highest place and gave Him the name that is above every name, that at the name of Jesus every knee should bow, in heaven and on earth and under the earth" (Philippians 2:9-10).*

All prophets, kings, and celestial beings throughout history have never dared to claim what Christ Himself declared.

The Messiah did not say He had found a way.

He proclaimed, "*I am the Way.*" He did not claim to have read or discovered the truth. He revealed, "*I am the Truth.*" He did not offer a philosophy of life. He declared, "*I am the Life." No one comes to the Father except through Me" (John 14:6).* His words distinguish Him from every prophet, leader, or ruler who has ever lived. As men, as husbands, and as fathers, we acknowledge that no man surpasses the One who holds the keys to our salvation. Our loyalty is not to worldly thrones, but to God's eternal throne. Our praise is not for temporary crowns, but for the everlasting King of Kings and Lord of Lords (Revelation 19:16).

Therefore, a true man of God lives with conviction: He respects authority, but he worships only Christ. He honors leadership, but he kneels only to the Savior, Jesus Christ. He may serve his nation, but he belongs to the Kingdom. We will never kiss anyone's hands as a sign of higher majesty except our Lord Jesus.

This is the mark of a real man, a husband and father who understands that strength, integrity, and legacy come not from earthly titles, but from the eternal Lord who reigns forever. *Psalm 95:6: "O come, let us worship and bow down: let us kneel before the Lord our maker."*

As husbands, we have the responsibility to speak into every matter that affects the family's safety, direction, and well-being. This isn't about control, but about accountability before God. Headship means being trusted with oversight, making decisions with wisdom, prayer, and love, always considering what is best for the household.

When a husband and wife walk together in unity under God's Word, the home is filled with peace, order, and stability. Such a marriage becomes not only a personal blessing but also a testament to God's Kingdom on earth. Psalm 150:1-2: *Alleluia: Praise the Lord. Praise God in his sanctuary; praise him in his mighty heavens. Praise with trumpet for his greatness.*

A Prayer for Peaceful Speech

Heavenly Father, teach me to guard my tongue and temper. Give me the wisdom to speak with love, patience, and respect, even in the most challenging moments. Where I have wounded with my words, bring healing. Where my home has been shaken by anger, restore it with Your peace. Let my voice be an instrument of encouragement, not destruction. Shape my words so that my marriage reflects the love of Christ and His Church. May the atmosphere of my home be filled with gentleness, wisdom, and grace. In Jesus' name, Amen.

HEAVENLY CITIZEN

CHAPTER FIVE

Men: Leaders and Stewards of the Christian
Home Real Husbands Walk by Faith and Stay Sharp

For the husband is the head of the wife, Ephesians 5:23

Christian men are leaders and stewards of the Christian home. God has entrusted husbands with the sacred duty to lead, protect, and provide for their families with integrity and love. "For the husband is the head of the wife even as Christ is the head of the church, his body, and is himself its Savior" (Ephesians 5:23). Genuine husbands live by faith and keep their minds clear, guarding their hearts and households with wisdom and prayer. They do not lead harshly but with the sacrificial love Christ demonstrated to his people.

A wise husband stays alert and purposeful, never lazy about his calling. He leads, provides, and protects without fear or compromise. Meanwhile, his wife embraces her God-given role to build and nurture the home alongside him, under God's supervision and grace. "The wise woman builds her house, but with her own hands the foolish one tears hers down" (Proverbs 14:1). Together, they form a strong household that honors the Lord and leaves a legacy of faith for future generations.

Fleeting emotions, cultural trends, or social quests do not govern faith-driven men. They remain anchored in Scripture and are guided by godly counsel and advice from **The Book of Men**. They understand that marriage is a sacred covenant, not a casual contract; they recognize that God is watching over them. *"Therefore, what God has joined together, let no one separate" (Mark 10:9).*

They also know when to stand firm for their families or, when necessary, to walk away from betrayal or manipulation, not out of pride, but out of righteous discernment to protect what God has entrusted to them. Godly men remember they are called to be as bold as lions.

"The wicked flee when no one pursues, but the righteous are bold as a lion" (Proverbs 28:1). Just as Christ, the Lion of

Judah, reigns with strength and righteousness (Revelation 5:5). Gabriel said in **The Book of Men** that "all real husbands must guard their homes fiercely. No woman should attempt to deceive or use a man's hard work and devotion for selfish gain". Men who read The Book of Men know that manipulation has no place in a household built on God, truth, and honor.

In today's world, if a wife chooses to abandon her role as a helper to pursue self-focused independence, a faithful man does not need to beg her to stay. He understands that peace and purpose come from God alone. Adam worked faithfully and named all creation before Eve was brought to him in marriage. He was whole and purposeful before he had a wife.

"It is not good that the man should be alone; I will make him a helper fit for him" (Genesis 2:18).

Any wife whose judgment is no longer fitting for the husband should be dismissed. If a wife decides to reject that role, let her answer to the Lord for breaking the covenant and depriving her children of a father's daily blessing. A virtuous person understands that living in peace is preferable to living in conflict. *"Better is a piece of dry bread, with peace, than a house full of meat, with strife." (Proverbs 17:1).*

He trusts in God's faithfulness: many godly women honor covenant love and respect men's authentic biblical leadership. That is why men stay steadfast, bold as lions, vigilant stewards of what God has entrusted to them, leading, loving, and protecting with wisdom, courage, and faith. Yes, true love exists, and we honor these biblical laws by respecting and valuing the many women of God who remain committed to their part of the covenant.

There's no shortage of godly women who honor covenant love and respect men's authentic biblical leadership. That's why men remain steadfast, bold as lions, vigilant stewards of what God has given them, leading, loving, and protecting with wisdom, courage, and faith. As men of God, we must stand firm against all forms of abuse. No man should ever raise his hand, his voice, or his mind to be harsh with the woman he has sworn to love and protect.

Abuse violates God's purpose and corrupts the sanctuary of the home. Yet, in a culture where marriage remains sacred and honored by families and communities, the freedom to abandon one's vows on a whim would no longer be so casually considered. If wives knew that running away for no good reason meant living alone for the rest of their lives, without the possibility of remarriage or easy reinvention, they would likely make excuses like "love is no longer there," which would be enough to break up a home. **Would longing for someone wealthier, more thrilling, or more**

indulgent justify breaking what God has joined? Let her explain this to God?

Today, modern mindsets have led many wives to believe they can have it all: the freedom to leave, a fresh start with another man, and the lifestyle they see online, including the wealth and resources they've built with the husband they now despise. This way of thinking has turned many women into dreamers, older and more demanding, but with less to offer in return. They envision a perfect man built from endless checklists, but forget that time changes everyone. The young bachelors they desire are often no match for them, as these men have countless options.

The book of men says "*that the top earners and younger men have options among vibrant women whose hearts are still eager to build, not destroy; whose beauty is still blooming, not fading; whose attitudes bring peace, not rivalry. They are more fertile and ready to follow men's plans. There is no place or chance for old cars with useless engines*".

The book of men teaches that, in the real marketplace of love and commitment, high-earning men and younger men with rising prospects naturally gravitate toward vibrant women whose hearts are ready to build with them, not tear down what they hope to create. Women who are willing to learn from them and listen, cherishing every opportunity to grow alongside their husbands.

These women's beauty is fresh and still unfolding; their spirits are cooperative rather than combative, and their youth makes them capable of bearing many healthy children, helping the family legacy stay strong. Like a brand-new luxury car straight from the showroom, flawless in design and full of promise, such women bring vitality and freshness to a man's life. By contrast, many men avoid older single mothers or women burdened with heavy pasts and weary bodies, the home and heart breakers, regardless of an outwardly polished appearance.

To these men, such women are like a high-mileage used car, once desirable and maybe still shiny, but showing signs of wear like the sole of worn shoes, carrying a lot of baggage, and having little to offer beyond a record of fake stories and body count. They contrast with the bright, fertile, hopeful companionship that a youthful, childless bride can provide to a man.

Christian men often find that life's options grow with time, experience, and earned resources. The older a faithful man becomes, the more he refines his worth, expands his influence, and attracts genuine affection. He becomes a tree offering shelter and fruit, while the woman running away finds herself like a used car on a crowded lot, too many miles, too many past owners, and too few willing buyers.

However, the Bitterness Queens and career divas are out there claiming they are "independent." *"I don't need a man for anything! My job is my husband, I'm married to my career! I live for myself and do whatever I want! Men are good for nothing; I do for myself, and my dog is enough!"*

Recent studies in sociology and behavioral economics have shown that high-earning women are more likely to exhibit hyper-independence, often referred to as **"individualistic detachment"** in the research literature. A 2022 study published in the Journal of Marriage and Family indicates that financially successful women are increasingly delaying or rejecting traditional relationships, often influenced by modern feminist ideas that view submission as weakness and dependence as failure.

Many women enter what can be described as a metaphorical **"island of independence, Lala Island,** a space where self-sufficiency is valued more than connection. However, the emotional, spiritual, and relational costs are quietly accumulating.

Sadly, as time passes, many people don't realize the long-term effects of their self-imposed isolation until it's too late, when beauty fades, options shrink, and genuine companionship becomes increasingly challenging to find. Meanwhile, what the world calls "freedom" starts to feel more like exile to the "independent island forever".

As men awaken through pain, prayer, and discernment, they begin to make more informed choices. **The Book of Men** is not a myth; it's a modern reflection of timeless truths that call men to avoid relationships based on control, pride, or rebellion against divine order. Proverbs 21:9 warns, ***"It is better to dwell in a corner of a housetop than with a brawling woman in a wide house."***

In other words, peace is more valuable to a man than presence. Men are learning to walk away from old patterns and "old bosses," partners who misuse independence as a weapon, and instead seek godly peace, spiritual harmony, and mutual respect. As Jesus said in John 14:27, "***Peace I leave with you; my peace I give to you. I do not give to you as the world gives. Do not let your hearts be troubled and do not be afraid.***"

They discourage each other from embracing marriage and often promote disrespect toward husbands. In their youth, they refused to build families, too busy chasing status and wealth instead; however, now their so-called independence has left them isolated as the applause for their careers fades. Even in their forties or fifties, they can be found alone in clubs or at parties, desperately trying to keep up with young women half their age.

These self-proclaimed "Miss Independents" neglect the deeper purpose for which the Lord created them, believing they are wiser than God's design. They reject the legacy of obedience and submission, mock commitment, and resist engaging with many husbands around them, using "independence" as an excuse to avoid maturity and responsibility.

This harsh reality does not mock women, but instead calls for a return to reverence for marriage. A bond that requires maturity, sacrifice, and a shared sense of loyalty. Only when both husbands and wives remember that marriage is not disposable but a sacred covenant under God will families stay strong and future generations thrive.

The System That Profits from Broken Homes:

Broken Vows, Feminism, Lawyers, and a Government That Wins. **The Book of Men said,** "A greedy woman brings trouble to her home and harm to her children, but she who hates dishonesty will live in peace."

In the early 1900s, women gained the right to vote in the

U.S., marking a significant step toward social equality. By the 1960s and 1970s, the second wave of feminism arose, strongly pushing for workplace equality, birth control rights, legal abortion to free women from traditional roles, and greater freedom from the housewife stereotype. Around that time, no-fault divorce laws were introduced in the U.S. and Canada, making it much easier to end a marriage without proving abuse or adultery. She can leave because her boyfriend's love is newer, and she might also take your life with her.

Welfare systems and well-known courts were not primarily designed to protect women and children, but rather to remove fathers from the home. They often made it easier for women to divorce while still receiving child support or public assistance. In this way, the government created a business model based on naive men who care to stay with the wrong wives. This encouraged single motherhood, leaving many homes without fathers, and resulted in men losing 50% of their wealth, with 35% allocated for child and spousal support after separation.

Sadly, even within the church, many Christian women started to adopt an attitude that views men as replaceable, while neglecting the authority of God's Word. Yet the scripture clearly says, *"**Therefore, what God has joined together, let no one separate." (Mark 10:9) and "Wives, submit to your husbands as you do to the Lord… Husbands, love your wives just as Christ loved the church." (Ephesians 5:22-25).***

Over time, the "independent woman" movement is increasingly recruiting young, innocent women to waste their youth and wait until their late 40s to find a husband. Gradually, these independent home breakers will break your heart if you ignore **The Book of Men**.

Despite this divine blueprint, humanity fell in the Garden and continued to stray from the Lord for generations. Yet today, we stand at a turning point, an awakening for men everywhere: for those who have been married, are newlyweds, men preparing for marriage, or single men searching for a wife. We thank God for unveiling these truths preserved in The Book of Men by Gabriel, a guide to reclaiming our original calling and walking wisely in a world that often mocks true manhood.

The wisdom found in ***The Book of Men*** teaches every man a hard truth; now you have the opportunity to learn this knowledge. It is your responsibility to ensure that other men are aware of this understanding, so they can protect their hearts from straying away from the Lord. The truth is that love alone does not sustain a marriage, and beauty alone does not guarantee virtue.

King Solomon, the wisest man to ever live, discovered this firsthand through his own mistakes and observations. He warned men to be vigilant and discerning when choosing a wife, confessing in Ecclesiastes ***7:28,***

"While I was still searching but not finding, I found one upright man among a thousand, but not one upright woman among them all."

Such a blunt revelation should not foster bitterness or resentment toward women, but rather ground a man's hope and expectations firmly in God, not in the fragile fantasy of perfect companionship. Men should never feel rushed or desperate to get married, as even in 2025, this remains a confusing time for women, and the truth hasn't changed.

Thanks be to God; **The Book of Men** is here to impart timeless wisdom to men that some might have overlooked. Long ago, the prophet Isaiah foresaw a time ***of judgment and social disorder***, the bitter fruit of what we might today call the reckless "independent woman" movement. Isaiah warned that when women abandon their husbands without cause or genuine abuse, they stray away from their God-given role and invite consequences that no fleeting freedom can prevent.

Unlike many, we men are called to be direct and rooted in the truth of life. When one of us strays or falters, we must stand beside them, speak plainly, and help them return to what is right, especially when it comes to staying faithful in their own home and caring for their wife and children. As James 5:19-20 reminds us:

"My brothers, if one of you should wander from the truth and The Book of Men will send someone to bring him back, remember this: Whoever turns a sinner from the error of his way will save him from death and cover over a multitude of sins."

This is our brotherhood's mission to watch each other's backs, restore those who have fallen, and protect the families God has entrusted to us as leaders, husbands, and fathers. Many women may lose sight of their true purpose by listening to misleading voices rather than their husbands' voices, which encourage them to stay home and support their faithful spouses. Titus 2:4-5 says,

"Then they can urge the younger women to love their husbands and children, to be self-controlled and pure, to be busy at home, to be kind, and to be subject to their husbands, so that no one will malign the word of God."

The misguided perception of the so-called "**Independent woman**," endorsed by governments that benefit from fractured families, exploits the generational wealth of hardworking men to promote the abandonment of marriage and traditional family values, forcing many elderly women to rely on pets as companions. Such policies overlook the fact that even children suffer in this turbulent and lonely environment. The ancient prophecy of Isaiah directly addresses this harmful mentality among contemporary women, foretelling a future in which men will become scarce and... **"On that day, seven women will take hold of one man, saying, 'We will eat our food and wear our clothes; only let us bear your name. Take away our shame!' (Isaiah 4:1).**

This is why many proud and visionary North American men are taking their passports and looking for wives abroad, such as the Philippines, Thailand, Vietnam,

Colombia, Brazil, the Dominican Republic, Ukraine, Russia, Mexico, Kenya, Ethiopia, Ghana, Rwanda, Tanzania, Uganda, and the Caribbean all place a high value on family and marriage, often more than radical independence.

Many women grow up respecting traditional gender roles and come from cultures with deep-rooted faith and strong moral values that emphasize loyalty, modesty, and a commitment to caring for a home. Their family names still hold significant importance.

Let every man remember the wisdom found in **The Book of Men:** A virtuous wife is a rare and priceless gift from the Lord, whether she lives across the ocean or just down the street. As Scripture says, *"A wife of noble character who can find? She is worth far more than rubies"* (Proverbs 31:10).

A close friend, married for over fifteen years as of 2025, once shared something that stayed with me: the only speeding ticket he ever received was for driving too fast to get home to his wife. After all those years, she had cultivated a peaceful and joyful home, a sanctuary for his spirit. He found in her a Christian woman who not only honored God but also understood the power of love, peace, and loyalty. Because of that, he gave her the same in return. I asked him, "What's your secret for keeping your marriage strong in these modern times?" His answer was straightforward yet meaningful:

"Our life is not virtual; it's real. If you're not my friend in life, you'll never know how I live. No one outside our union should have a voice in our marriage. Only the two of us stood before God to make this covenant, not three. We don't display our joy or struggles online. Marriage is a sacred space, private, not public. It's a secret place for two hearts to share, grow, and protect. "As Proverbs 11:13 reminds us: ***"Whoever goes about slandering reveals secrets, but he who is trustworthy in spirit keeps a thing covered."***

In a world of oversharing, guard what is sacred. What is built in private often lasts the longest. The solution isn't just about changing your location; it involves walking in wisdom, with respect, in prayer, and with discernment. A man must first become deserving of a good wife and then trust God to guide him to her.

When wives trust and respect their husbands, all men will find peace. We are no longer accepting disrespectful single women, especially those in their thirties to mid-forties, who are already in the red zone. The Book of Men now teaches men to ask the right questions: ***"You will keep in perfect peace those whose minds are steadfast, because they trust in you." Isaiah 26:3***

The Book of Men encourages you to ask meaningful questions beyond surface traits, focusing on her core values, prayer life, relationship with God, view of covenant, willingness to serve, and her perspective on marriage as a form of ministry rather than merely romance. It helps you determine if she embodies virtue, can walk alongside you in purpose, raise godly children, and create a kingdom home founded on Christ:

- What does marriage mean to you?
- What did you admire most about your parents' relationship?
- What role does faith play in your daily life?
- What are your thoughts on raising children?
- What do submission and partnership mean to you in marriage?
- How do you manage finances and spending?
- What are your life goals and dreams? • What do you expect from a husband?

- What do you believe are a wife's responsibilities?
- How do you handle stress or disappointment?
- What does respect mean to you in a relationship?
- How do you handle disagreements with a partner when you feel strongly about being right?
- What are your thoughts on commitment when things get tough or when you're feeling unhappy?
- How do you see the balance between independence and partnership in marriage?
- What would you do if your husband made a mistake or fell on hard times financially or emotionally?
- What would you do if we had a significant disagreement and I asked for time to calm down and pray first?
- Who do you turn to for advice when you're upset with your partner?
- What do you think about divorce as an option if marriage gets difficult?

Women who honor the Lord will naturally show respect to their husbands; their prayer life is an act of reverence before God. They think, speak, and behave differently within the bounds of marriage. *"Charm is deceitful, and beauty is fleeting, but a woman who fears the Lord is to be praised" (Proverbs 31:30).*

Such a woman understands the true meaning of marriage; even if she works and takes care of her family, she remains faithful to her commitment because marriage is a sacred covenant, not just a contract. She cherishes the godly example she saw in her parents' marriage. Her faith guides her every step, giving her strength and wisdom at all stages of life, for *"acknowledge him in all your ways, and he will make your paths straight" (Proverbs 3:6).* She sees the education of children as a blessing and a duty: *"Train up a child in the way he should go, and when he is old, he will not depart from it" (Proverbs 22:6).*

She believes that submission and partnership reflect divine wisdom, knowing that "wives should submit to their husbands as to the Lord"

(Ephesians 5:22), while her husband lovingly guides her. She manages finances carefully, keeping in mind,

Proverbs 21:5:

"*The plans of the hardworking lead surely to abundance.*" Enduring priorities rather than transient desires influence her goals and aspirations. She understands what is reasonable to expect from a husband and what she is obligated to offer sincerely as a wife: "She does him good and not harm all the days of her life" (Proverbs 31:12).

A woman like this is rare, a true treasure among many. She walks among the worshipers of the seraphim in spirit, marked by a pure heart and a well-disciplined mind, often shaped by the blessing of growing up in a God-fearing, two-parent Christian home. These women stand at the top tier, set apart to guide and teach younger brides how to honor their husbands and uphold the laws found in **The Book of Men**.

They belong to the 99th percentile of spiritually intelligent women, not because of worldly knowledge, but because of their faithful stewardship of the marriage covenant. Through honor, loyalty, and humility, they earn the trust of their husbands and enjoy the fruits of a peaceful, prosperous home. Their presence doesn't diminish the man; it multiplies him. Through their love, respect, and wisdom, they help their husbands rise and produce more, for the good of the entire family and the glory of God. When stress or disappointment arises, she responds with gentleness and prayer, remembering that "*a gentle answer turns away wrath" (Proverbs 15:1).*

She defines respect as mutual honor and love, as commanded: "Let each one of you love his wife as he loves himself, and let the wife see that she respects her husband" (Ephesians 5:33). When disagreements arise, she listens and speaks with wisdom, choosing peace over pride.

She views commitment as a promise to be kept, even when storms come, echoing "What God has united, let no one divide. ***She reconciles her independence with the beauty of teamwork, standing by her husband when he falls, just as "two are better than one, if one falls, the other can help him up" (Ecclesiastes 4:9-10).***

When conflict arises, she takes time to calm down and pray: "Be quick to listen, slow to speak and slow to anger" (James 1:19). She seeks God's counsel, not gossip, for *"Blessed is he who does not walk with the wicked"* **(Psalm 1:1).** *She doesn't see divorce as an easy way out, but as a last resort when all else fails, for her heart clings to the vow: "What God has joined together, let no one separate." (Matthew 19:6).*

The words and life of such a woman demonstrate daily that she respects the Lord and esteems the man God provided her, nurturing her home with wisdom and loyalty. *"A wise woman builds her house, but a foolish woman tears it down with her own hands" (Proverbs 14:1).*

The Book of Men requires all men to design a program of loyalty for their potential wives! Let's determine whether she has the temperament and character to be a faithful wife. What influence have her parents had in shaping her values and expectations of marriage? What about her friends? Will they encourage her to honor her husband, or will they intervene and influence her decisions in your home?

Before choosing a wife, a man should look beyond beauty or charm and seek a woman who truly understands sacrifice and loyalty in marriage. It's wise to ask her directly, "Can you describe what sacrifice and loyalty mean to you if we marry?" This question reveals whether she understands what commitment requires when life gets tough and love is tested. A faithful wife knows that true love isn't proven in comfort, but in perseverance:

"Love bears all things, believes all things, hopes all things, endures all things. " All things, hopes all things, endures all things" (1 Corinthians 13:7).

Humility and a willingness to improve are equally important. A thoughtful man should ask her, "What habits or character traits do you think you still need to improve to be a better wife someday?" An honest answer shows whether she's self-aware and willing to admit her shortcomings. True humility is the foundation of respect and support, which must be reflected in actions, not just words. To the question, "What does it mean to you to honor your husband in everyday life?" a godly woman will speak of serving, respecting, and uplifting her husband, even when no one is watching.

A woman of God is a blessing in a man's life; she is a humble person who will never complicate your life.

A wise woman also prepares her heart to protect her marriage. The question "How do you plan to keep your love and commitment strong in the event of conflict, stress, or disappointment? Similarly, the question:

"***What would you do if you felt attracted to another man while married?***" tests whether the woman guards her heart and sets clear moral boundaries, whether she remembers past mistakes of others, but chooses fidelity in thought and action. Asking her how she plans to handle disagreements over money, family, or career choices reveals her maturity and willingness to communicate with patience and wisdom rather than pride or stubbornness.

Finally, a wise woman finds her greatest happiness not in temporary pleasures, but in a strong connection with God, feeling loved and loving well, and living each day purposefully and with grace. This servant said, ***"The joy of the Lord is my strength" (Nehemiah 8:10).***

When asked, "What are the three things that will make you truly happy and at peace with yourself?" her response will demonstrate a heart grounded in faith, family, and contentment with God.

HEAVENLY CITIZEN

CHAPTER SIX

When It's Time to Walk Away:
*A Man's Inner Strength, Solomon's Wisdom,
and the Courage to Let Go*

How the Fear of the Lord, be wise to protect your heart

Proverbs 4:23:
"Above all else, guard your heart, for everything you do, your life flows from it." Ultimately, it is not a passport that protects a man's heart, but the fear of the Lord and the wise counsel of the wise brothers of **The Book of Men** who follow the same virtuous path. This is not an ancient fairy tale, but a divine warning from the author of **The Book of Men** for our modern generation of men. When a society fails to honor the covenant of marriage and disrespects the balance between masculinity and femininity, the result is loneliness, confusion, and a desperate struggle to restore what has been carefully crafted by God.

Men must take this wisdom to heart: don't become bitter, become stronger. You must know when to cherish her and when to fire her from your program. Don't pursue every attractive face, but instead seek a woman of noble character, born of noble parents, for she is worth more than rubies.

Above all, hold fast to the teachings of **The Book of Men** so you can remain steadfast when your wife strays from her role; don't sink with her ship, but let her go. She should know that many women are more beautiful, younger, and more respectful, waiting for you.

May Isaiah's warning inspire you to prayer, strength, and righteousness. May men rise to lead with wisdom, and may women return to the sacred calling of building a home, alongside a righteous husband, under the Lord's blessing.

Brother, **The Book of Men** urges us to abandon childish dreams of winning life's lottery by unquestioningly believing that a beautiful woman, romance, or passion alone can build a godly home. If even King Solomon, the wealthiest and wisest king who ever lived, with 700 wives and 300 concubines, failed to find lasting satisfaction in loyalty and beauty,

What makes you think we can succeed alone? Solomon's wisdom wasn't wasted; he turned his painful lessons into timeless teachings for future generations of men willing to listen. Now is the time for you to listen and not let any woman's pressure push you. If she isn't an asset, reconsider her role and see if she needs to be let go.

My father often said, "We are men created by God to hunt like lions, build, and survive anywhere and everywhere. Wherever there is water and salt, we will adapt, work hard, and prosper." My daddy's name was **(Elie Marcelin).**

Solomon teaches that a good wife is truly a rare and precious treasure and a blessing. In Proverbs 12:4, he writes,

"A virtuous woman is her husband's crown, but a disgraceful woman is like rot in his bones."

This simple yet powerful proverb shows men that a woman's inner virtue is much more critical than her outward charm and beauty. A woman of godly character brings honor and strength to her home; a woman who lacks it will slowly break a man's peace and vitality, leading him away from his purpose.

That is why Solomon constantly warns young men about immoral and seductive women whose charm only leads to destruction. Proverbs 6:24 warns: ***"Beware of your neighbor's wife, the smooth words of a promiscuous woman. A prostitute can be bought for a piece of bread, but another man's wife threatens your very life.***" He vividly shows how a single reckless relationship can cost a man his reputation, his family, his money, and his soul.

That is why you should surround yourself with brothers who read and live according to the principles of ***The Book of Men***. They will hold you accountable and remind you of Solomon's advice: "They will keep you from the adulterous woman, from the seductive woman with her seductive words" (Proverbs 7:5).

Do not underestimate this danger, for as the king says in Proverbs 7:27, "Her house is a road that leads to the grave, descending to the chambers of death." True strength does not lie in conquering many women but in the fear of God, wise choices, and protecting your heart with the wisdom of those who have gone before you.

You are now part of the brotherhood; you are a man and a member of ***The Book of Men***. It is time to remember this enduring truth from the author, a man who left, divorced after two decades, and started over in another country. A wise man should never beg for peace in his own house. When the walls around you and the respect for you crumble, you must gather your strength, lift yourself, and leave, for God has prepared a better place for those who trust in Him. *"When I am afraid, I put my trust in You. In God, whose word I praise, I trust and am not afraid." Psalm 56:3*

A discerning man does not plead for peace in his household; he establishes it through sound judgment, consistent leadership, and deep respect for God. A stable home is not built on emotion or force but through wisdom that lays the foundation, understanding that secures it, and insight that fills it with purpose and blessing. Even the simplest life, if marked by harmony and quiet strength, is far greater than a life filled with noise, conflict, and abundance that brings no rest.

My brother, when love becomes toxic and loyalty turns into betrayal, remember this: staying too long can cost you your soul or your freedom. Leaving at the right moment can save your life and restore your dignity. Leave when the timing is right and trust God to restore what has been lost or stolen from you. *The Lord will restore to you double everything you've lost and give you twice as much as you had before. Job 42:10*

As Jesus said, "If anyone will not welcome you or listen to your words, leave that house or town and shake the dust off your feet. Sometimes leaving is a sign of God's obedience and strength, not of weakness.

He has already shown you that, as a man, your place is no longer in that house. So be a man, pack your bags, and it's time to say goodbye." Never forget that a man does not find his dignity by holding onto what is broken, but by walking away when the Lord says, **"Enough."** Leave when the time is right and watch as the desert transforms into your promised land. For, as it is written: "*There is a time for everything, and a season for every activity under the heavens; a time to search and a time to give up, a time to keep and a time to throw away, a time to love and a time to hate, a time for war and a time for peace." (Ecclesiastes 3:1, 6-8)*

We were created first; (MAN) we are more intelligent, stronger, and wiser. The Lord will not forsake you; He will wait to walk with you, my brother. Deuteronomy 31:6 *"Be strong and courageous. Do not be afraid or discouraged because of them, for the Lord your God goes with you; He will never leave you nor forsake you."*

Guard your heart with all diligence, as it is quick to fall, while your mind must remain anchored to the Lord. Be wise in love. Love with your emotions, but lead with your mind. Cherish your wife and family deeply, but diligently protect the fruits of your labor, as that's where your heart is invested.

Even God doesn't ask you to squander the wealth He has allowed you to gather through years of patience. Remember that what takes decades to accumulate can be stolen in an instant by careless choices or unfair laws. **The Book of Men** reminds us, as Proverbs 13:11 states: *"Wealth gained by dishonesty will dwindle, but whoever gathers little by little will increase it."*

Build steadily, build honestly, and safeguard what God has entrusted to you. A Christian high-value man works diligently and wisely, creating a legacy that endures through betrayal, trials, or loss. In this age of awakening, let us rise as faithful stewards, strong protectors, and wise kings of what God has placed in our hands.

After years of enduring disrespect, betrayal, and loneliness in my own home, I finally decided to leave, not out of anger, but in peace and with dignity, out of necessity. I filed for divorce, grabbed my passport, and left the country. As Proverbs 17:1 says, *"Better a dry morsel with quietness than a house full of feasting with strife."*

I chose serenity and peace over the independence movement, my wife. She called me to demand I return; otherwise, she threatened to take away my freedom. She begged me with promises of anything to persuade me, only to repeat the cycle and find new ways to break my spirit if I gave her the chance. But my heart was already gone. I had devoted decades of my strength, youth, and hard-earned money to her. Eventually, I returned her to her family peacefully.

She became someone else's problem. And truthfully, it wasn't long before she replaced me with a fairy tale, and many after that. Staying would have been a shame, but now I find myself replaced by a freely wandering cat who is now in her mid-fifties, four years older than me. I didn't just leave; I crossed the border and left the country in search of a new beginning. There, God healed my soul and restored my hope.

This is a testimony to you, my brothers and members of **The Book of Men**; my Lord Jesus doubled my portion. He gave me a new life, a new wife, a peaceful home, and a joy that no one can take away.

The Book of Men Call to Courage

The Faithful Fatherhood

The Book of Men urges faithful fathers to show courage. A man's work and money hold no eternal value if they are not rooted in God. Similarly, the modern ideology of radical independence for women, like extremist strands of feminism, has no lasting worth before the Lord. No one has the right to fall asleep at the wheel when children are in the car; the same applies at home. No one should leave children alone, spiritually, emotionally, or practically. Fathers must stay alert. The stakes are too high.

There are still men who fear God, strong and devoted servants willing to dedicate their strength and their days to loving God, raising their children in instruction, and teaching them how to follow Jesus Christ. I can testify that such a man exists among a thousand, which is significant compared to the near-absence of a woman in the millions.

King Solomon said in Ecclesiastes 7:28: *I found one upright man among a thousand, but not one upright woman among them all.*

The Book of Men is for those who dare to rise despite betrayal or abandonment; those strong enough to endure mistreatment from bitter wives or broken families, and those willing to get up and leave when necessary. It calls for you to take your rightful place, for the sake of your children. Ultimately, the only thing that matters is this: don't lose your faith. Hold the line like apostle Paul, *"I have fought the good fight, I have finished the race, I have kept the faith." 2 Timothy 4:7*

Today, some women are fortunate to be good wives in a happy, blessed home under God's protection. They have the good favor of a righteous husband who treats them well. But suddenly, she decided she preferred a younger man, 6 feet tall, earning a six-figure salary, and her mind kept adding to the list. With a fairy tale spoiled in her mind, she thought that this type of man would fall into her arms.

She still has her old life and many children, even though her rivals are much younger, more beautiful, and free of the baggage of her past. She also overlooks that these men would rather drive a brand-new Bentley with zero miles than the old Nissan from the 1700s, abandoned in the parking lot and once blessed by God with an owner who fit her perfectly.

She now calls herself a "**converted independent feminist**" and is prepared to go to court to stop you from seeing your children. Nevertheless, God will still hold you accountable. Whether you were forced to leave your home or you are in the process of packing, the truth remains: you can leave the house, but you cannot abandon your child. God expects a full report from every single father. **God is calling:**

"So then each of us shall give account of himself to God." Romans 14:12.

In a Christian home, there is no debate about who teaches the children to follow Jesus. There is no question about who secures the household in prayer. There is no confusion about who must rise to break the spirit of divorce and destroy the generational curses passed down through bloodlines.

Every rent or mortgage payment, utility bill, grocery run, pair of shoes, drop of fuel, insurance premium, car repair, medical bill, school fee, household repair, family events, and vacations, all of it is carried on the shoulders of a father and a husband who lifts and shoulders the weight.

Fathers are called to pray diligently for their children to become righteous citizens, culture-shapers, and godly leaders. One day, we will stand before the Lord and be accountable for how we managed our homes.

As husbands, we accept the responsibility and privilege to say, "**Yes**, Lord, we fought the good fight." Even when some wives walk away to chase illusions fed by social media, we stand firm. We declare our homes will be filled with the Holy Spirit. We reject passivity and pray for heaven's power to cover and sustain our children. Ask any truly faithful man, "Will you stand for your family and walk with God to take care of your children?" Without hesitation, every single husband will answer: "**Yes**."

In God's courtroom, your lawyers will not stand beside you. The government won't speak on your behalf. Your friends, your online supporters, and the "independent women's groups" movement will hold no weight. You will stand alone before the Lord, and He will ask: What did you do with the husband I gave you?

God does not cast you aside every time you fail. He shows mercy. He is patient. He waits. Yet, some women walk away from their marriages for trivial reasons, because they no longer see the good in their husbands, or because the world has led them to believe they deserve better. But we will not give up on our children. Men, stand up. Fight the good fight. Refuse to be pushed aside. Lead your homes with love, strength, and God's truth. You were created for this; however, you must walk away rather than go to jail.

Christian husband, kindly take a moment to reflect on the young man you were before you got married! *The Book of Men* encourages you to pause and reflect on when you were a young bachelor full of strength, dreams, and aspirations. You dreamed of building something lasting: a family, a home, a future. These were not unreasonable dreams but the seeds of responsibility waiting to grow. The Bible says, ***"It is good for a man to bear the yoke in his youth" (Lamentations 3:27).***

This yoke is not only the burden of work but also the weight of discipline and preparation. Young men need to learn that manhood is not simply gained with age, but with the maturity required to take on the responsibilities of becoming a husband and, later, a noble father.

Deciding to become a husband and father after marriage is a serious choice. No man who truly understands the significance of this role enters into it lightly. Scripture states, ***"Husbands, love your wives, just as Christ loved the church and gave himself up for her" (Ephesians 5:25).***

This indicates that your commitment is not only to your spouse but also to God. This is not a trivial commandment. A husband is called to be a protector, a provider, and a spiritual leader in his family. Marrying and raising children require embracing a life of sacrifice and leadership. God ordains these roles, and taking on them is a calling, not just an option.

The Book of Men is more than just a book; it is a sacred call for every man of God, an invitation to return to the man you were before life broke you down and before the fairy-tale love of this world confused your identity by signing this governmental contract. It's time to go back into yourself, when your soul was pure, when you still believed, before the disappointments, the betrayals, and when responsibilities grew heavy.

The Book of Men isn't written in ink on this idea, but in fire, God's fire, as Hebrews 12:29 states*: "For our God is a consuming fire."*

The Holy Spirit reminds you that even before you were born, you were already part of God's plan. *"Before I formed you in the womb, I knew you, before you were born, I set you apart" (Jeremiah 1:5).*

You are a man of respect, pride, and dignity; someone people respect and even look up to. The Holy Spirit does not speak to your ears but to your soul. It is time to listen instead of arguing by asking questions. It is time to act, not procrastinate. The moment to leave is not the time to run away, but to remove yourself from a situation you cannot resolve. Move forward in obedience and strength to restore your dignity.

Marriage requires more than just a ceremony, a suit, and wedding rings, because getting married doesn't make you a husband, and saying "yes" doesn't automatically make her a wife in spirit. A wedding is only a public beginning; the actual connection is revealed over time. According to a study published in The Journal of Family Psychology (2012), 47% of women reported having doubts before marriage, and Women with doubts were 90% more likely to divorce than those who felt confident.

Although not all doubts in marriage come from lingering feelings for another man, the reality is that many women enter marriage not solely out of love or a genuine desire to be with you, but because it was the "right time, the right age to have a child," social expectations, or simply convenience. Beneath the surface, some of these women may still harbor strong emotional attachments to someone from their past, a love that was never truly resolved or entirely relinquished.

If you marry a woman in the same country or city where she was born and raised, there's a very high chance, let's say 95% that you're not her first choice. Instead, you're simply the most convenient or practical option available at the time. Maybe you offer more material stability, or you're better suited to care for her child from a previous relationship. In either case, you're not the man of her dreams; you're the man who fits her plan.

Eventually, she may break your home, shatter your heart, and take everything you've worked for. If you're sharp enough to see her true nature early, you might catch her before the damage is done, but by then, the betrayal has already started. She will almost certainly cheat, mainly if she stays connected with an ex or gets involved in certain strands of extreme "independent woman" ideology. In such cases, you'll lose her faster than a rocket heading to the moon.

Meanwhile, most men enter marriage with their eyes wide shut. They rarely ask the tough questions that could reveal a partner's true feelings, intentions, or emotional readiness. It's like signing a business deal that looks incredibly promising on paper, so tempting that you jump in eagerly, only to later find out in the fine print that you've sacrificed far more than you expected. By then, it's often too late to undo the damage without serious personal and financial consequences.

This is exactly why preachers, lawyers, and even government courts often recommend that men read "The Book of Men": to establish a prenuptial agreement, either before or after marriage. A prenup isn't a romantic gesture but a sensible safeguard against these thieves, a modern necessity in a system designed to heavily favor one party during separation.

No country has yet repealed the laws that allow a spouse to walk away with significant financial gains, sometimes even most of what the man has worked his entire life to build. In many cases, the economic incentives are so strong that leaving can become a profitable decision rather than a last resort. Divorce has evolved into a trillion-dollar industry that benefits governments, lawyers, and what some call the "independent woman" movement.

In this view, marriage is more than just an emotional or spiritual bond; it's a legal and financial contract that can sometimes turn into a battleground, often to the disadvantage of the unknowing husband.

Therefore, entering marriage without preparation and protection is like stepping onto a chessboard without knowing the rules of the game or the opponent's strategy. Love and commitment are beautiful ideals; however, they should be accompanied by caution, self-awareness, and legal foresight to prevent a future filled with regret and loss.

Statistically, it is not uncommon for men to marry women who are emotionally unavailable or still connected to their ex-partners. Research and counselling insights indicate that 10–30% of men may have married women with unresolved emotional ties or who were not fully emotionally present at the altar, thinking of someone else. This isn't just about cheating; it's about emotional disconnection that existed before the vows. These women might say "I do" while their hearts are thinking of someone else.

Often, when you marry a woman from her hometown or city where she grew up, she is surrounded by history, including romantic attachments. In such cases, 1 in every three women may still be emotionally or physically involved with an ex, especially in tight-knit communities where social circles stay close, and former lovers remain nearby.

The danger of unresolved emotional attachments is that they are often initially unseen and unacknowledged. According to the Journal of Marital and Family Therapy (2018), ***15–25% of married women admit to having had an affair***, whether emotional, physical, or both. Affairs are common. Emotional affairs are commonplace among women, as they often seek connection, comfort, and affirmation. *Many of these affairs are with men from their past, not strangers.*

A study by psychologist Nancy Kalish from California State University found that 62% of people who reunite with an ex-lover while married end up having a sexual affair. Modern technology, especially social media, has made these reconnections more accessible, frequent, and discreet.

Social media platforms like Facebook, Instagram, and WhatsApp have become silent bridges to the past. A conversation that begins with **"How have you been?"** often leads to **"I miss what we had."** What once required effort and travel can now happen in the palm of your hand. A single private message can rekindle an old flame. A 2020 article in Psychology states that 30% of women in long-term relationships still think about or have feelings for a former lover.

These lingering emotions, even if not always acted upon, weaken intimacy and commitment in their current marriages. The heart may be elsewhere, even when the body remains present. God's Word addresses this.

In Jeremiah 17:9, it says, *"**The heart is deceitful above all things and beyond cure. Who can understand it?**"*

Even someone in love might not fully realize how deeply their emotions are tangled. But God sees what no one can. *"**Nothing in all creation is hidden from God's sight. Everything is uncovered and laid bare before the eyes of Him to whom we must give account**" (Hebrews 4:13).*

A woman may deceive her husband, friends, and even herself, but God sees through the disguise. And He is not fooled by empty vows or fake love. To the man who discovers that his wife still clings to another in her heart, take courage in God's promises. He never wastes suffering. *"**I will repay you for the years the locusts have eaten...**" (Joel 2:25).*

If you loved and faced betrayal, God will restore peace, purpose, and healing. Your worth is not based on her confusion or disloyalty. Even if her heart wandered, your faithfulness remains sacred in God's eyes. He is a Father to the forsaken, a healer to the broken-hearted. *"**Peace, I leave with you; the peace I give to you... do not let your heart be troubled**" (John 14:27).*

Lastly, to men of faith: *stay wise and watchful*. "The wise woman builds her house, but with her own hands the foolish one tears hers down" (Proverbs 14:1). If your wife is still secretly building altars to another man, she is tearing down the house with her own hands. But you make your home on the rock. Be a man of peace, truth, and courage. And remember what God says to you:

*"**I will be a Father to you,** and **you shall be My sons**" (2 Corinthians 6:18).*

Your identity is not in her decision; it is in His calling. Let your healing begin in truth. Let your dignity remain in the Spirit. And let your future be rooted in faith, not fantasy. God will never leave you in the dark for long. It demands sacrifice, leadership, discernment, and a strong spiritual foundation. Too many men wear wedding rings without grasping their significance.

Becoming a husband doesn't start at the altar, but when a man submits to God and dedicates himself to a lifelong mission of protecting, loving, and providing for a woman. Likewise, having children doesn't automatically make you a father. Fatherhood isn't just a biological role; it's a spiritual calling. "*But be a doer of the word, and not merely hearers who deceive* **themselves***" (James 1:22).*

Some fathers never meet their children's emotional needs, and husbands share a bed, but not a covenant. This is not God's plan. We live in an era when many marriages prioritize appearance over purpose. People plan weddings with budgets that could cover student loans, yet they never consider submission, sacrifice, or suffering. For modern women, even minor challenges can cause them to leave.

Many are trapped in a toxic race for social media approval, competing not in virtue but in vanity. They were never taught what true wifehood looks like. A woman raised by a godly mother who honors her husband, prays over her children, and serves her husband joyfully will build her home on a solid foundation. However, the woman who idolizes independence over intimacy, pride over partnership, and pleasure over purpose will ultimately destroy both herself and her home. (Proverbs 14:1). I entered into matrimony at the age of 27, not necessarily because I felt prepared, but because I was instructed that it was the customary obligation within the church community.

I aspired to act righteously, yet, introspectively, I had not fully contemplated the repercussions. I succumbed to a romantic illusion common among many men, believing that love alone would bear the burden of responsibility. However, love is insufficient without sacrifice. Over time, I learned to prioritize my wife and my two sons over my own interests. I engaged in cooking, cleaning, and working extended hours, dedicating all my resources to the task at hand.

I was proud of the man I have become, even if no one has ever acknowledged my efforts. For two decades, I have dedicated myself entirely to my role as a husband, sacrificing my personal needs without hesitation, whether it was buying a new pair of shoes or a simple T-shirt, always prioritizing my family's well-being. I put all my energy into creating a secure and comfortable life for my family.

But in the end, it still wasn't enough for her. She wanted more, more freedom, more independence, after embracing a radical ideology that turned her away from the values we once shared. I gave until there was nothing left to give, and it nearly cost me my life; I could have died from the weight of a broken heart or a sudden heart attack.

Yet, in that dark moment, my prayers were answered. The
Lord saw my heart, my sacrifices, and my unwavering effort. He sent the Holy Spirit to whisper to me, ***"It's time to go."*** And in that quiet guidance, I found the strength to walk away from a situation I could no longer fix, finally reclaiming my peace and dignity.

My brother, if you're reading this, listen carefully: the Holy Spirit is with you now and will always be with you. It speaks to your heart, reminding you that it's okay to step away from your current situation. If you can't control what's happening, and things aren't improving, put your hope in the Lord to guide you and let go. Remember Job, the only servant God trusted as a man of true integrity. Job lost everything, yet because he maintained his faith, God restored him with a double blessing.

Begin by taking things one day at a time. Release yourself from the pressure that is breaking your spirit. Return to the gym, go back to church, and call a close friend you trust to share your struggles in prayer.

Don't worry about anything; instead, pray about everything. Tell God what you need, and thank him for all he has done. (Philippians 4:6).

It is no longer your job to keep giving without end; now is the time to ask for help. Start praying for yourself and your children. Accept that you may need to start over, but remember this: starting over is far better than ending up in prison or becoming entangled in actions that will ruin your soul.

If you need to leave town to save yourself, do it without hesitation. In my case, I had to leave the entire country and start over in my fifties. And guess what? With the Lord by my side, I am doing better than I ever imagined. After darkness, in the middle of your wilderness, there is light waiting for you. The Lord is on the other side, waiting with your angel, ready to heal and restore you with a double portion.

I understand, because I was right where you are now, and I didn't believe it at first either. But I chose to trust Him anyway, and when I stepped forward in faith, Jesus was right there, waiting for me and ready to work on my heart and restore my life. He will do the same for you.

Significant changes have taken place. She who once valued my stability has become increasingly restless. She has grown closer to two women who left their marriages to pursue what they called their 'best lives.' These women were neither wise nor healed; instead, they were lost, resentful, and spread illusions. They enjoyed luxury trips I couldn't afford, often showing off their happiness on social media. As a result, she gradually started to believe that I was incapable.

Imagine a woman in her mid-forties with two kids, walking away from a man who offered her stability, love, protection, and support, to chase fantasies sold by women from broken homes, failed marriages, and unresolved traumas. These influencers promote a version of freedom that disengages from responsibility, celebrating a so-called "dream life" of escapism, superficial validation, and curated independence.

However, they rarely reveal the emotional cost, the quiet loneliness, and the spiritual decline that often accompany it. Leaving a solid foundation for illusions isn't empowerment; it's usually a step away from wisdom and a descent into cycles of confusion masked as self-growth.

At this point, self-worth begins to erode for these women. Many men will tell them precisely what they want to hear, only to use and discard them as quickly as yesterday's news. Behind closed doors, they cry silently, while in public, they hide their pain with perfect makeup and forced smiles. Still, even now, the actual color of the sky remains a mystery from Earth's point of view. Science may guess, but only God sees into the depths where darkness once covered the face of the deep. And once she's gone,

The Book of Men warns: "Shut the door behind you.

Keep moving forward with strength and without bitterness."

I recall the day I experienced an emotional breakdown; not for myself, but for the two young men I was about to leave behind. I leaned on her aunt's shoulder, feeling the quiet weight of a relationship I knew had ended long ago. The love was gone, but the memory of it lingered, not for the bond itself, but for the countless efforts I had invested over the years.

After twenty years of commitment, I watched her make reckless choices, acting like a stranger I had never known. It wasn't heartbreak; it was the sobering realization that the woman I once trusted no longer existed in the way I remembered.

Showing disrespect to the very person who kept the household was unacceptable. She started quoting phrases from those advocating independence: "I don't need a man to provide for me anymore." At that moment, I realized that this was not just an act of rebellion, but also deception. Then came the voice.

During the church service on Sunday morning, sitting beside my boys, I felt the Holy Spirit speak directly into my spirit. "You are a good father. God is pleased with you. But it is time to go. Not tomorrow. Today." It was as clear as someone whispering right next to my face. I recognized it was God, because peace accompanied those words. That same evening, she texted me telling me to find another place to sleep; the house I had just paid for was no longer mine. I didn't argue. I didn't beg. I went home, packed my things, and walked out the front door I helped build.

She made her choice, and her mistake isn't my burden to bear. One month later, she had another man in the house. He lasted twenty-two days. From 2018 to the present, she has gone from one man to another. Now, she finds herself sitting alone, her peace somehow slipping away. Her only companion is a gentle cat. It's her moral reckoning. Life of sin might promise freedom, but its fine print is also full of trouble and loneliness.

If a woman in her fifties believes she can do better than you after you've carried the weight, supported her, and covered her back for over twenty years, let her go. Shut the door firmly behind her, and protect your heart. Start focusing on finding your peace and joy again, because your chances of rebuilding and finding happiness are much greater than hers. Your odds are seven to one, while hers are closer to zero, the eternal stillness or silence.

The master of the universe created man first for a reason. No real man is waiting to step into the life of a woman who leaves her husband and children at fifty, hoping to marry and care for her for the rest of her days. That scenario only exists in fairy tales or online fantasies, not in reality. ***"But one thing I do: Forgetting what is behind and straining toward what is ahead, I press on toward the goal to win the prize for which God has called me heavenward in Christ Jesus. Philippians 3:13–14***

Gentlemen, please listen: demonstrating exemplary character does not require begging for recognition. You may act with integrity and still face rejection. Such experiences do not signify failure; they symbolize liberation. God will never overlook your faithfulness.

The Book of Men aims to affirm that you are not irrational; instead, you are called to see your true self.

You are not broken; you are in the process of being built. Certain seasons call for silence and patience, but obedience always brings renewal. Do not stay in environments where you are not valued. Do not struggle for the approval of those who mock your faithfulness and kindness. Trust in God, even in hardship.

You remain a son of God, irrespective of others' departure, falsehoods, or the absence of farewell or gratitude. The Holy Spirit sustains you as your comforter, guide, and source of strength. Your previous failures do not disqualify you; instead, your obedience is your most outstanding achievement.

The Book of Men serves as a reminder that, before you took on your roles as husband and father, and before experiencing betrayal, you were chosen. God's plan for you is ongoing; His work has merely begun. Allow your past to instruct rather than imprison you. Receptively heed the Holy Spirit's call: the moment is now. Proceed accordingly.

The Book of Men encourages each man to reflect on his life and consider, "Have I genuinely embraced my role?" If the answer is yes, it should inspire a commitment to change, not shame. Every man is called to grow, mature, and lead intentionally by God's will. When respect for you as a husband diminishes, there may come a time when, despite your efforts, your wife no longer sees you as a leader but as a burden or just one of the children. This contradicts God's design for the household. ***"The husband is the head of the wife, even as Christ is the head of the church" (Ephesians 5:23).***

This headship signifies guidance, not control. If a wife loses respect, the family could begin to fall apart, because ***you know that the testing of your faith produces perseverance.***

(James 1:3)

Regaining respect, especially after failure or personal loss, isn't about exerting force but about intentionally rebuilding your character. As a man and a leader, you must understand that leadership begins from within. Respect isn't something you can demand; it's earned through consistent actions, clarity, and conviction.

The Book of Men teaches that the road to reclaiming respect is gradual. It's shaped through individual decisions and acts of integrity, one after another. Start by reestablishing discipline: keep your commitments, no matter how small. Practice silence not as avoidance, but as a display of wisdom's restraint. Speak only when necessary, and when you do, ensure your words are firm, honest, and aligned with your new values.

You must also embrace these foundational pillars: Accountability to own your actions without making excuses. Take full responsibility for your life, both past and future; the integrity to live in a way that your private life could be shared publicly without shame. Your emotional Strength should remain calm in challenging situations. Be slow to anger, quick to listen, Jesus said, *"it is a talent to learn", and be thoughtful in your decisions. "Whoever is patient has a great understanding" (Proverbs 14:29).*

Be humble, not thinking less of yourself, but thinking of yourself rightly with God and others. *"Humble yourselves before the Lord, and he will lift you" (James 4:10).*

A real husband maintains discipline to manage your time, habits, and desires. Without inner order, external influences turn into chaos. The spiritual vision involves writing down your purpose and seeking clarity in your calling, as stated in '*Write the vision and make it plain" (Habakkuk 2:2).*

Release bitterness, not for others, but for your own soul's freedom. As Ephesians 4:31-32 advises, 'Get rid of all bitterness, forgiving each other, just as in Christ God forgave you.' Most importantly, walk with a reverent fear of the Lord, for those who fear God lack nothing. Proverbs 10:9 says, 'Whoever walks in integrity walks securely.' Rebuilding respect means rebuilding the man, not for applause, but for legacy.

Let your actions serve as your apology, and let your transformation speak louder than words. Guide your life by a higher law, not of pride, but of purpose. Carefully consider your children and resources. Every man should consider not just the financial costs, but also the emotional and spiritual ones. Remember, *"A good man leaves an inheritance to his children's children" (Proverbs 13:22).*

If your home feels chaotic, your resources are stretched thin. Your children are caught in the middle of marital struggles; it might be time for a spiritual check-in. Reflect on whether your actions come from love or frustration, responsibility or reactive behavior. It's essential to treat everyone in your home with respect and to be mindful of how your actions — or lack of action, might contribute to chaos. As fathers, we're entrusted with more than just money; we're shaping a meaningful legacy. Ensuring that your children are emotionally and financially protected is a vital part of that journey.

God's laws are absolute and not open to negotiation. God does not bargain because his understanding surpasses ours. The Word of God provides clear guidance on how to live until you return home to his heavenly kingdom. **The Book of Men welcomes this law:** *"But if anyone does not provide for his relatives, and especially for members of his household, he has denied the faith and is worse than an unbeliever" (1 Timothy 5:8).*

This provision includes leadership, love, wisdom, and order for children. When that order is broken, when the man abandons his calling, or when the woman resists God's structure, the house will suffer. Disobedience invites consequences. But obedience restores peace. The Book of Men does not just challenge foolish opinions; it calls every man to return, rebuild, and reclaim what God has entrusted to him. Because when a man walks in his divine role, the whole house begins to heal. But when the wife of that house no longer wants you, you'll need to step away with dignity and walk in respect.

The False "Babes"

No man should ever be called babe as a nickname. It is a false label that diminishes the dignity of manhood and reduces covenant identity to a casual term. My name is Gabriel, and my nickname is Gabe, not Babe. Side note: once you start enjoying the false "babe" nickname as if it were a sign of love and respect, you should pay close attention. Watch how quickly one of the letters will disappear. ("**B**")

When a woman starts to pull back her affection, she often does it subtly, even subconsciously. What began as '**babe**,' a sign of closeness, can turn into '**bae**,' a word that seems innocent, but already signals distance. The missing "**b**" already belongs to someone else. When the affection once directed toward you begins to shift, her heart starts to wander. Soon, she calls you only by your name again, not out of intimacy, but out of a sense of detachment. At that point, you may already be outside her heart, and the relationship weakens.

As men, we should indeed appreciate affectionate nicknames, such as "honey," "love," and "sweetheart," as they reflect warmth, closeness, and intimacy within marriage. These words of endearment can strengthen the bond between husband and wife when they flow from a heart that is faithful and true. Yet we must also be discerning, recognizing that the language of affection can quickly turn into the language of detachment.

Endearment must be guarded, not taken for granted.

I learned this lesson firsthand. The first time it happened to me, I picked up the phone and called my friend Jude. I told him,

"*I am heartbroken.* **I've lost one of the letters from my nickname.**" She no longer called me babe. Overnight, it had been reduced to just "**Bae**". That quickly, I had become "**Mr. Bae.**" What seemed like a slight change in words revealed a much bigger change of heart. No big deal, right?

Affection in marriage is fragile, and nicknames, though light and playful, are windows into the state of the heart. Proverbs reminds us, **"Death and life are in the power of the tongue: and they that love it shall eat the fruit thereof"** (**Proverbs 18:21**).

The way we address each other, whether with respect or dismissal, can build intimacy or tear it down. Words matter. Someone else was using my other letter "**B**". Therefore, a real man must pay attention not only to his wife's words, but also to the feelings behind them. Do not dismiss small changes in affection as insignificant. What begins with a language change often signals a more profound shift in the heart. Protect your marriage, cherish the words spoken in love, and stay faithful to your vows.

In your own life experiences, have you ever lost a letter from your name? I am sure you still remember who took it from you and how it happened. The question is, was someone else already using the letter you lost?

HEAVENLY CITIZEN

CHAPTER SEVEN

Getting Old:
*When Time Slips Away and Love
Becomes a Hard Choice*

Waiting too long in the pursuit of perfection in love, career, and lifestyle can cause us to miss out on incredible opportunities for marriage and a fulfilling family life. Sometimes, our desire to get everything just right can make us hesitate; however, embracing the journey and being open to new possibilities can bring unexpected happiness and fulfilment.

In today's world, countless men and women find themselves waiting too long to get married, trapped in a never-ending cycle of searching for the "perfect" partner who meets every condition. They spend years chasing an ideal love that not only fulfils their emotional needs but also adheres to high standards set by society or social media. The right job, a stable income, the ideal lifestyle, even the correct physical appearance and level of physical beauty.

Christian women and men whom the Lord has ordained to be your future husband and wife will pass you by because of their height, body traits, or salary. In doing so, you forget a simple, sobering truth: time waits for no one. If you find yourself in what this book calls the red zone, meaning you've lived more than thirty years on this earth and you're still delaying marriage and family, The Book of Men warns you not to ignore reality. Postponing marriage and parenthood has serious consequences. Many who delay out of fear of responsibility or a desire to keep their options open are neglecting the most valuable gift they don't have control over, "**Time**".

A Divine Responsibility: Don't Delay What God Designed

Look around you; many of your peers have entered into the covenant of marriage, are raising children, or are laying the foundation for future generations. Life moves forward whether we're ready or not. Time, as ordained by God, does not wait. "To everything there is a season, and a time for every purpose under the heaven" (Ecclesiastes 3:1). When we ignore the seasons God designed, such as the time for building a family, we risk not only loneliness but also the deep sorrow of missed purpose.

For those who procrastinate excessively, the initial impacts are often unseen: regret, loneliness, and an emptiness from not witnessing your legacy grow. Eventually, there may be a day when others are holding their grandchildren, and your arms are still empty, not because God is withholding, but because you chose not to build a family.

Yes, nieces and nephews are family, and they are a blessing. But let's be honest: if God were to pour out a divine inheritance meant for you and your household, could you honestly claim those who belong to someone else's legacy as your own? *"A good man leaves an inheritance to his children's children..." (Proverbs 13:22).* That message implies your children and your grandchildren, not borrowed joy from someone else's obedience.

If you were called before the Court of Heaven, could you honestly and humbly explain to the Lord why you rejected the opportunity to build the family He commanded? *"Be fruitful and multiply; fill the earth and subdue it..." (Genesis 1:28).*

Would you tell the Author of time that He moved too quickly, that His plan for the family wasn't suitable for you, or that you wanted more time to decide?

Think carefully. That would be arguing against the wisdom of God's creation, as if you know better than the One who formed you in the womb (Jeremiah 1:5). It would mean putting your timing and preferences above the divine rhythm established before the foundation of the world. God's laws are not open for negotiation. *"Woe to those who quarrel with their Maker..." (Isaiah 45:9).*

Marriage and family are not optional footnotes; they are divine assignments. When we ignore the call, we are not merely postponing happiness; we are delaying obedience. This is not a rebuke, it's a wake-up call. The window does not stay open forever. Choose now to walk in God's purpose. If you are called to marriage, pursue it with wisdom, prayer, and courage. If you are called to singleness for a season, live it intentionally, but do not mistake delay for a lack of discernment. In the end, you will stand before God alone, not as a nephew, an uncle, or a bystander in someone else's blessing, but as a man either faithful to the assignment or one who let the hour pass.

Given the current global life expectancy, typically 70 to 85 years in developed countries, men and women should aim to marry and start a family between the ages of 25 and 35. For women, biology is straightforward:

fertility peaks between 20 and 35, then declines significantly thereafter. Many delays marriage, which increases the risk of complications, infertility, and health issues for both mother and child. While modern medicine can help, it cannot reverse biological clocks.

Men are not exempt, even if their fertility declines more gradually. Sperm quality usually drops around age 40, raising the risk of genetic diseases and health issues for your children. Additionally, fatherhood demands physical energy and emotional presence, both of which become harder to sustain as you age. The red zone for both men and women is equally critical, as waiting too long to start a family can mean missing out on the invaluable opportunity to raise children. At the same time, you're still strong, healthy, and capable of giving your best to shape the next generation.

Ultimately, keep this wisdom in mind: perfection is unattainable, but a good life partner is within reach if you avoid wasting time chasing illusions while life passes by quietly. **The Book of Men** urges you to prioritize courage over fear, commitment over endless choices, and faith over excuses. Your future family and peace of mind in later years depend on these choices.

"Whoever watches the wind will not plant; whoever looks at the clouds will not reap." Ecclesiastes 11:4 Let me ask you a simple question:

Are we any wiser than King Solomon? How many people do you know, perhaps close friends, who have spent years dreaming of the "perfect life"? They desire a successful career, a lot of money in the bank, and a perfect family, but only when they feel completely ready; by then, it is sometimes too late.

Some people dream of marrying a wealthy, tall, handsome husband with a well-toned physique, a luxurious home, and a collection of fancy cars. He must check off every item on an impossible list. Others desire a beauty queen wife they can showcase on social media like a model. My friend Roy is in this metaphorical situation; He said he is still young, despite being in his early forties, and is chasing after a wife he may never find.

Every one of them has issues, he said,

"I have to wait until I find someone who makes sense to me." A forty-year-old man with the mind of a 12-year-old boy. Everyone around him has a family; when he wakes up to this reality, it will be too late. He might not have the energy or mental capacity to handle a household, which can be tough. It's understandable to feel concerned about this.

But here's the hard truth: most of these dreamers remain locked in their fantasies. Real life never matches their unreal expectations. As they continue to search for the perfect time to start a family or open their hearts to true love, they quietly waste the best years of their youth, years they can never get back. Remember what Apostle Paul told James 4:14 says: ***"You don't even know what tomorrow will be made of. What is your life?"***

Many men of God will be saved, but when it comes to their families, they often fail. They wait too long, lost in dreams and hesitation, taking too much time to step out in faith, pursue a godly partner, or ask for help, until it's too late.

That's why I advised my friend Roy: ask your trusted friends and family to help you find a wife. Time is running out. Your best life is not tomorrow; it's now. Unless you have accepted the decision to stay single, unmarried, and childless, and unless that choice is based on calling rather than fear or comfort, then the outcomes will fall on you. And someday, you will stand alone before the throne of heaven to give an account.

Today, many people tell themselves, "Not yet, there's still time. I'll settle down later." However, the common-sense movement, the wise men of The Book of Men, and even scientific studies agree. There's great value in choosing carefully, but there is also danger in waiting forever for a perfect model that doesn't exist to start a family.

A wise man from the Book of Men says: "If you watch the wind, you'll never sow. If you wait for the clouds to clear, you'll never reap. And if you keep telling yourself that you're "not ready yet," one day you'll wake up and realize that you no longer have any time left in your bank to make the choices that everyone else has dared to make. You must choose someone true, imperfect, and human, just like you."

Go and tell God your plan!

Proverbs 19:21 reminds us, ***"Many are the plans in a person's heart, but it is the Lord's purpose that prevails."*** God has appointed seasons for sowing, building, marrying, raising children, and enjoying family life.

Although we often make numerous plans for our careers or personal goals, we must remember that some blessings only thrive in their designated season. If you miss your season, the fruit may never ripen again. There comes a point in life when you must decide whether to remain single or start a family; ultimately, that choice is yours alone.

Research confirms this fact: according to the Pew Research Center, the number of adults who have never married in middle age has doubled in recent decades. Many admit they waited too long, searching for perfect circumstances or the ideal partner, only to find themselves alone and regretting that their youth has slipped away quietly.

Often, while everyone around them was getting married and starting families, they chose to enjoy the single life without seeking the Holy Spirit's guidance. Yet the Lord declared from the beginning, "It is not good for man to be alone."

The confirmed bachelor and the Bachelorette are familiar figures, aren't they? My friend Roy, for instance, is 40 and happily lives with his brother, saying he might "settle down" at 45 or 50. He enjoys spending on himself, flirts with beauty queens to garner social media likes, and flaunts his good looks. Interestingly, some label him a "closet case," if you catch my meaning. When I mentioned, "At your age, my sons were 10 and 12," he chuckled, believing that men can always start at any age", it's never too late."

I believe that if you're keeping your sexuality private, no one should judge you; if you're open about it, you're simply living authentically. Society often pressures people about relationships and life decisions, but I believe in respecting personal timing. My view is that being in the closet is your personal choice, and others have no right to judge. When you're out, you're being true to yourself and living openly. It is up to you to educate yourself on why the Lord burned what He dislikes.

"They serve as an example of those who suffer the punishment of eternal fire." (Jude 1:7)

Similarly, my friend Margarette, who claims to be intelligent, has spent more than 15 years alone. She says she wants to get married, but convinces herself that all her suitors have bad intentions or are "not good enough." In reality, she fears intimacy and disappointment, a clear sign of what psychologists call Peter Pan syndrome. These adult refuses to grow up emotionally and hide behind excuses to avoid commitment. **The Book of Men** advises men to steer clear of such individuals.

Emotional paralysis. Psychologists agree that "fear of commitment" is more common today than ever before. The modern world encourages us to keep all options open, to switch from one thing to another constantly, and to be wary of making definitive choices. However, a study conducted as part of the Harvard Study of Adult Development, one of the longest-running research projects on human happiness, found that warm, stable relationships, not money or fame, are the key to lasting health and satisfaction. Don't be surprised, children also help you live longer, as they are a gift from heaven.

For these reasons, no one will give you happiness; it's up to you to make choices and create it yourself. In other words, while people like my friends Roy, Margarette, and Den convince themselves that they are "free," their freedom can quietly turn into a form of loneliness. My best friend, Den, decided 12 years ago that he would remain single for the rest of his life. He enjoys his freedom and financial independence while living alone, but sometimes wonders how different his life would be if someone were waiting for him at home to share his burdens and joys.

King Solomon explored the nature of life.

"Remember your Creator in the days of your youth, before the difficult days come, and the years draw near when you will say, 'I find no pleasure in them'" (Ecclesiastes 12:1). God invites us to live wisely and fully while we still have strength and energy. Waiting too long risks entering old age with unfulfilled dreams and no one to share them with.

There is a Time for Everything, the king said. Proverbs 5:18 says: "***May your fountain be blessed, and may you rejoice in the wife of your youth.***"

God's design is not for us to waste our strength on fear and excuses, but to build joyful homes early enough to enjoy the fruit of love and family for decades. Ecclesiastes 3:1 King Solomon said: "***There is a time for everything, and a season for every activity under the heavens.***"

Biology confirms this fact. Men and women who marry later often face increased risks of infertility and more health issues during pregnancy. They also miss valuable years of watching their children grow. Research shows that older parents may experience more stress and fatigue when raising teens, especially as their peers become grandparents.

The Art of Waiting, or the Trap of Never-Being Ready, **time will not forgive you**. Some people think they are being wise by waiting until they have "everything figured out" before getting married; Roy thought so, too. Saving money is wise; choosing carefully is wise, but waiting indefinitely for perfect conditions is not. The fear of imperfection becomes a trap that keeps them single, while the world continues to turn, time passes, and they grow older. Like the farmer who never sows, because he watches the clouds, they reap nothing in their relationships.

Many believe, "I still have plenty of time," but is that truly accurate? Psalm 90:10 states that, if we remain healthy, we may live around 70 or 80 years; yet, half of that time can be lost to turmoil and uncertainty. Considering this, is it wise to spend 35 or 40 years alone when God created us for community and family blessings? This is why many African countries encourage girls to marry in their early twenties, when they are strong, fertile, and capable of caring for lively, noisy children.

The Book of Men says, "Love grows in imperfect seasons." My advice to **Roy**, **Margarette**, and **Den** is simple: perfection is an illusion, but love develops in imperfect soil. Life will never be completely problem-free. You will never have enough money to feel entirely secure. But God's purpose for marriage is not to impoverish you, but to enrich you with love, support, and joy. A spouse multiplies your strength, and children become a crown in your old age; above all, two are better than one.

A man who works for decades without ever starting a family will one day realize that money can buy comfort, but not family. A woman who keeps her heart closed out of fear may discover that this fear has robbed her of her chance to love. She will regret having pursued her career while many potential husbands pass her by, and she did not take the time to stop, thinking she would have time.

Plant today, harvest tomorrow: that is the Bible's wisdom.

Sow your seeds at the right time, young man, and trust God for the harvest. Don't waste your time watching the wind or looking at the clouds, waiting for life to be perfect. Act in faith, honor God in your youth, and He will bless the work of your hands. That is the faith of every single husband before you.

Galatians 6:7-9 "Do not be deceived: God cannot be mocked. A man reaps what he sows. The one who sows to please his flesh will reap destruction from the flesh, but the one who sows to please the Spirit will reap eternal life from the Spirit. Let us not grow tired of doing good, for at the right time we will reap a harvest if we do not give up. Paul warns believers not to deceive themselves: we cannot trick or mock God by pretending to live one way while secretly acting another.

My brothers and sisters, don't waste your prime years. There is no perfect moment, but there is a right moment. And that moment is often now.

Happiness and Married Couples.

Men can indeed find purpose and contentment in solitude, but that was never the whole design. From the very beginning, God made His intention very clear: *"It is not good for the man to be alone. I will make a helper suitable for him." Genesis 2:18* God Himself, the Creator of heaven and earth, ordained companionship for man. He didn't just create woman; He initiated the first wedding ceremony. Imagine that moment: the holy and sovereign God, never alone, always surrounded by angels, heavenly hosts, and worshipers before His throne, descended to earth and walked with Adam. The Good Shepherd presented Eve to Adam, not merely as a companion, but as a wife, a partner in purpose, and a living embodiment of divine law.

This was not just a casual introduction; it was a sacred commissioning. God gave them His laws, His blessing, and His purpose: to live in unity, multiply, and raise a generation that would reflect His image here on the earth. "Has not the one God made you? You belong to Him in body and spirit. And what does the true God seek? Godly offspring. So be on your guard, and do not be unfaithful to the wife of your youth. Malachi 2:15

God encourages marriage in youth for reasons beyond fertility or companionship. It is also about legacy, raising children who know Him, walk in truth, and carry righteousness into future generations. Parents and grandparents can fulfill this important task.

Marriage is not just a cultural invention; it is a divine covenant, created and sanctified by God Himself. No one on earth has the authority to redefine or replace it. He alone establishes the terms, and it all began in Eden, with love, purpose, and holy expectation from each of us. *"Therefore, a man shall leave his father and mother and be joined to his wife, and they shall become one flesh." Genesis 2:24.*

What does a wedding mean to you today?

What comes to mind every time you attend a wedding? Take a moment to reflect; have you ever encountered anything more beautiful, more radiant, or more soul-stirring than that sacred moment? Every wedding feels like a glimpse of heaven. The elegant dresses, the perfectly tailored tuxedos, the glow on every face, suddenly, everyone seems to have stepped out of a dream.

You begin to imagine your wedding day: the joy, the trembling emotion, the tearful speeches, the love poems that resonate in hearts.

It's a rare moment when almost everyone steps into their best character: dignified, joyful, united. It's no surprise that many people meet their future spouse at a wedding. People you've never seen dressed up are now standing confidently, radiating beauty and honor. From the music to the spoken vows, from the sacred words of the ceremony to the tender exchange of rings, every moment imprints itself into your memory. Can you see the goodness of the Lord in all of this? He designed this joy for us to taste.

"Every good and perfect gift is from above, coming down from the Father of lights..." James 1:17

Can you imagine a better day in the life of a mother, father, brother, sister, best friend, or faithful companion? All gathered around, standing with you, just as you once stood with them. The gifts, the fragrance, the music... the water becomes wine, and the decorations echo the beauty of Eden. It feels like paradise on earth, where even the angels of the

Lord celebrates the union of two souls He has brought together. God Himself sends His gifts and blessings to His children. **What about the children who are yet to arrive? Futures are being shaped in that moment. "Children are a gift from the lord, they are a reward from him."(Psalm 127:3)**

And that's not all. From the final "I do" to the celebration that follows, the reception, the laughter, the dancing, and the honeymoon adventures, it all begins. The duty of the bride and groom becomes a source of joy: to smile, to love, to live gratefully before the Lord.

Amazing grace. Could any human wisdom create something better than what God Himself designed? The holy laws of matrimony are not just tradition; they are sacred, written into creation itself as God's perfect way to build life, love, and legacy.

"Therefore, what God has joined together, let no one separate."
Mark 10:9

If you are considering marriage, your concerns are valid; marriage is indeed an honorable institution. However, do not be foolhardy enough to think that your main goal is to ensure a woman's happiness at the cost of your soul. The Book of Men states, "If anyone wishes only to be happy, let him remain single, for then he is free to do as he pleases and to answer to no one."

Still, once you choose to marry, it is crucial to understand: God Himself will hold you accountable and write your name alongside these solemn words.

This will be your Solemn Vow before the Lord.

I promise you, before God's throne, before the stars, before our souls, before these hearts, these eyes that see, I pledge my spirit, my life, to thee. Through every dawn, through darkest nights, In storm or calm, in shade or light, In riches full or humble fare, My love for you will not despair. In laughter bright or tearful days, In winding roads or golden rays, In health or pain, in bloom or drought, My faith in you will never waver. With God as my guide, I'll lead with grace, tender strength, and a warm embrace. I'll honor you, both fierce and true, as Christ, His bride, forever knew. Our godly offspring will obey Holy care, full of joy, and God will breathe His blessing. The angels are witnesses.

This covenant, not made by man, is the law by God's loving hand. So, take my hand, walk close to me, together bound forever. This is my vow, my voice, my breath: to cherish you until death parts us. And even then, where angels sing, I'll love you still before the King.

Marriage is not a guarantee of personal happiness; it is a sacred responsibility, a covenant of sacrifice and stewardship. If your sole desire is to chase happiness, then stay single so you do not enter this holy bond only to abandon it later and leave a trail of bitterness and brokenness behind you. Marriage is not for the selfish or the faint-hearted; it is for those willing to love, to be chosen, to lead, protect, and persevere, guided by the fear of the Lord and the counsel of wise brothers from The Book of Men.

Choose wisely.

My relationship with them is the treasure I carried through the fire. It reminds me of Joel 2:25: ***"So, I will restore to you the years that the swarming locust has eaten…"***

God will restore what betrayal attempted to take from you. Men of faith, followers of the Son of God, you'll witness the strong growth of the fruit. They serve as our living testimony that a father's love, anchored in Christ, can withstand any storm.

The idea that "there is a time for everything, and a season for every activity under the heavens" (Ecclesiastes 3:1) helps us remember that relationships, as well as all parts of life, unfold according to God's plan and timing. The desire for love and connection can lead us to imagine a perfect relationship that might not exist.

These fantasies can distort our expectations and make us impatient about love, especially when we compare ourselves to others who seem to have what we long for. However, understanding that God's plan for us includes specific seasons, each with its purpose, helps us trust His timing and stay content, whether we are single or married.

HEAVENLY CITIZEN

CHAPTER EIGHT

Unrealistic Expectations and the Risk of Fantasy

Many people, especially those who use social media and dating apps, romanticize love. These ideals are often false, shaped by media images of romance or social pressures to find the perfect partner. As a result, we sometimes become fixated on finding someone who matches our ideal of love, only to be let down when genuine relationships fail to live up to those expectations. The Bible warns us against these false ideals and encourages us to pursue authentic relationships, as God intended, rather than chasing impossible fantasies.

Self-control plays a vital role in relationships.

The Bible states that "if one cannot exercise self-control, they should marry. For it is better to marry than to burn with passion" (1 Corinthians 7:9). Many people find that they struggle with lust or temptation that can hinder their health and God-centered relationships. Marriage offers a safer space to share love and intimacy, where self-control is both encouraged and expected. It's not about suppressing desires, but about surrendering them to God's will, enabling relationships to grow and thrive according to His perfect timing.

The Biblical view of lust can lead to emotional pain and spiritual separation. In Romans 13:14, the ***apostle Paul urges believers to "put on the Lord Jesus Christ and make no provision for the flesh to fulfil its lusts."***

This encourages rejecting selfish desires and choosing to live in accordance with God's holiness. Lust goes beyond physical craving to include the heart and mind. To resist temptation, believers are encouraged to pursue purity and righteousness, trusting that God's plan is the best path for their lives.

In today's culture, many people delay pursuing love, often prioritizing other aspects of life, such as careers, financial stability, or personal ambitions, over marriage. While these are not inherently bad, they can become obstacles if they hinder the pursuit of a committed relationship. The Bible emphasizes that marriage is part of God's plan for human fulfillment and happiness. Waiting excessively for love, or choosing to stay single out of fear or selfishness, may cause us to miss opportunities to find a partner and fulfil God's intentions for our lives.

The false security of money and independence

For many, the desire to stay single later in life is often linked to financial independence and professional success. People may convince themselves that having money and a well-established career is enough to feel secure. However, the Bible does not affirm that wealth or independence is the ultimate source of fulfillment. It warns against the dangers of idolizing possessions and achievements at the expense of relationships and community. While financial stability is essential, it must not come at the cost of the relationships God has designed for us.

God's plan for marriage and companionship

From the beginning, God's plan for humanity was that we would not be alone. In Genesis 2:18, God declares, *"It is not good for man to be alone; I will make him a helper like himself."*

Marriage is part of God's original design, reflecting His love and care for His creation. The decision to remain single or wait for the "perfect" partner should always align with God's will, rather than being driven by personal desires or fears. God created marriage as a covenant between a man and a woman, a partnership that mirrors Christ's relationship with the Church. The challenge of waiting and the value of patience are virtues that the Bible emphasizes in all aspects of life, including relationships. Psalm 37:4 encourages us to *"delight in the Lord, and he will give you the desires of your heart."*

It's about trusting God's timing and his perfect plan. When we delight in Him, our desires begin to align with His will, and we can trust that He will bring the right partner at the right time. However, impatience can cause poor decisions, including settling for relationships that aren't part of God's plan for our lives.

The Red Zone: Age and the Desire to Marry. When people reach the age of 35 to 45, many feel the pressure of this "Red Zone," a period when they might feel the urgency to get married, especially when they see others around them starting families. This age group can be challenging because many potential partners already have children or have been married before.

Although some may feel they've missed their chance, there's no need to panic; this is a time to reassess. On the contrary,

it should be a period for reflection, prayer, and

discernment. Waiting too long without seriously considering relationships can lead to frustration, but it also presents an opportunity to focus on spiritual growth and align one's desires with God's plan.

The challenge of rebuilding after divorce.

For those in the **red zone** who have gone through divorce, additional layers of emotional and spiritual healing may be needed before considering remarriage. The Bible acknowledges that divorce is painful and calls for God's healing. For those who have experienced separation and are thinking about remarriage, it is crucial to seek God's wisdom and take time to heal. Rebuilding after a broken relationship requires deliberate effort and a sincere desire to establish a healthy, Christ-centered marriage.

Loneliness and societal pressure to conform can feel heavy, especially in a culture that highly values romantic relationships. Although the desire for companionship is natural, societal expectations sometimes lead people to make unhealthy choices. It's important to remember that God's plan for each individual is unique, and feeling lonely isn't a sign of failure. Being single doesn't mean you're incomplete; it simply means you're free to be your authentic self. The Bible emphasizes the importance of contentment and encourages finding fulfillment in your relationship with God, regardless of your marital status.

The myth of "perfect" relationships

Many people, especially those still waiting for the "right" relationship, are influenced by the illusion that a perfect partner exists for them. This belief often results in dissatisfaction with potential partners and a sense that they'll never find someone truly right for them. The reality is that no one is perfect, and relationships demand commitment, effort, and sacrifice. God's plan for marriage emphasizes unity, support, and shared purpose, not perfection that is unattainable.

A significant relationship isn't about perfection but about two people who choose every day to stay together, united in a spiritual covenant as husband and wife. They accept personal responsibility to honor, support, and remain committed to each other for life.

The importance of being complete before committing to marriage is that it's essential to be complete in Christ. The Bible teaches that we must seek to be complete in Him before looking for a partner. In Colossians 2:10, Paul reminds us that *"you are complete in him, who is the head of all principality and power."*

This means individuals must first pursue a deep and fulfilling relationship with God, allowing Him to shape and transform them into the person He has called them to be. Only then are they truly prepared to enter a relationship with the capacity to love, serve, and build a strong, lasting marriage.

Do you trust God's timing to get married?

Marriage is a gift from God, and it's vital to trust His timing and plan for our lives. Proverbs 19:21 states, *"The plans of a man's heart are many, but the purpose of the Lord prevails."* While we may have our own plans and desires for relationships, God's purpose will always take precedence. Trusting His timing, not rushing into His will, and aligning our desires with His are the best ways to experience the fulfillment He has in store for us. While we wait, God is at work. He is never still, never unaware, never absent. Long before we speak a word, He has already written the answers. *"Before a word is on my tongue, you, Lord, know it completely"* (Psalm 139:4).

He has known us from the first breath to the last; our entire journey is already laid bare before Him. "Before I formed you in the womb of your mother, I knew you, before you were born, I set you apart" (Jeremiah 1:5).

He knows your spouse even before you meet. He knows who belongs to your heart and your future. *"The Lord will guide you continually"* (Isaiah 58:11), and His timing is never rushed or delayed. The men of God, those who walk closely with Him, understand that their lives are not random but part of the Lord's sovereign plan.

Therefore, we trust Him with everything, our time, desires, disappointments, and dreams. Even when the outcome is unclear, *"we walk by faith, not by sight" (2 Corinthians 5:7),* and we will praise Him regardless. Our praise is not dependent on results; it is grounded in who He is. We will not allow our minds to return to sadness, anxiety, or fear. Instead, we anchor our faith in Him. *"You will keep in perfect peace those whose minds are steadfast, because they trust in you" (Isaiah 26:3).*

Only the laws of His Kingdom will determine our destiny, not the opinions of men, statistics, or rejection of bad wives. "Many are the plans in a man's heart, but it is the Lord's purpose that prevails" (Proverbs 19:21). If we've tried and failed, we will adapt, not give up, and trust Him again. And again. And again. For we know He is the God who moves mountains for His children. *"If you have faith as small as a mustard seed… nothing will be impossible for you" (Matthew 17:20).*

To the man who feels alone today, trust the Lord with all your heart and pray about everything. *"Do not be anxious about anything, but in every situation, by prayer and petition, with thanksgiving, present your requests to God" (Philippians 4:6).* Watch how He will show up for you, not on your schedule, but on His, and always on time. Surrender to the God of fire. In your silence, He is shaping you. When your strength ends, His begins. *"My grace is sufficient for you, for my power is made perfect in weakness" (2 Corinthians 12:9).*

If you feel like you've reached your limit, been used up, forgotten, or betrayed by those you love, know this: you are not alone. You stand at the edge of something new. "Behold, *I am doing a new thing; now it springs forth, do you not perceive it?" (Isaiah 43:19).* The Book of Men's Laws reminds you: even in silence and sorrow, the God of fire was working for your good. He was moving behind the scenes all along. "The Lord will fight for you; you need only to be still" (Exodus 14:14). No man can reach the depths of your soul, but God can. And in that sacred place, He has always been with you.

The Book of Men focuses on providing practical biblical reasoning. The truth is, if you're approaching your red zone, the critical period when time and opportunities begin to slip away, you'll need to face some harsh realities. You've spent years concentrating on your career, finances, and personal goals, and there's nothing wrong with that. But now that the window is closing, it's essential to realize that the same person who chose to stay single and focus on material success during their prime was you, and now you're dealing with a different landscape.

Your criteria might have shifted, not because you're less deserving, but because the dating scene and your place in it have changed. You might need to consider moving to another city or even another country to find someone willing to build a life with you, often among those who, like you, are starting over from scratch, possibly after a divorce or raising children.

If you still hold the exact expectations and values you had in your twenties, you're not being realistic. Time has moved forward, and so have the options. Younger, more fertile individuals are entering the scene every day. If you don't change your mindset, life and time won't pause to meet your needs. From the moment you read this, the clock is ticking, and it's not in your favor.

At this point, choosing someone who already has children or has been married before can be a wise and meaningful decision. Ultimately, it's you who has decided to wait. But now it's time to determine whether you're ready to adapt and start a new chapter or remain stuck in an outdated idea.

The Choice to Be Alone

Do you choose to be alone? If so, understand this truth:

The choice is yours and yours alone. From the beginning, the Architect of creation declared, ***"It is not good that the man should be alone" (Genesis 2:18).***

By those words, God revealed that companionship was part of His design for humanity. To reject it means accepting the reality of walking a long road of life in solitude. In such a journey, joys are celebrated alone, sorrows are borne alone, and milestones have no earthly witness. The wilderness of solitude can be both a test and a calling. Yet, for those who walk this path for spiritual reasons, Scripture offers encouragement. The apostle Paul himself said, ***"It is good for a man not to marry" (1 Corinthians 7:1)***. Again, he stated, ***"I wish that all of you were as I am. But each of you has your own gift from God" (1 Corinthians 7:7).***

For the believer who chooses celibacy to remain pure and wholly devoted to God, there is blessing, strength, and eternal purpose. Paul reminds us that singleness can free a man to serve the Lord without distraction (1 Corinthians 7:32-34). The Book of Men affirms such a choice with prayer and support. We pray for those who follow this path to stay strong, keeping their eyes on the cross and their hearts cleansed by the blood of Christ, who paid for all sin.

This path is not one of abandonment but of dedication. Living unmarried for the sake of Christ is not a sign of weakness but a sign of spiritual discipline, as long as it is embraced with faith and sincerity. The man who chooses singleness must walk by faith, daily reminded that he is never truly alone. **"I will never leave thee, nor forsake thee" (Hebrews 13:5).**

The Lord Himself is his constant companion, his closest friend, and his eternal portion. In prayer, he finds communion; in the Word, he finds counsel; and in worship, he finds fellowship with the One who knows him better than any human partner ever could.

Such a Christian becomes a testament to the sufficiency of Christ. His life shows that joy, fulfillment, and identity are not dependent on marriage but are rooted in union with the Savior. *"The Lord is my portion, saith my soul; therefore, will I hope in him" (Lamentations 3:24).*

Even if he walks without a wife or children, he walks with the Spirit, and his life becomes an offering of singlehearted devotion to God. In the household of faith, both marriage and singleness are gifts from the Lord. The married man reflects Christ and the Church through his covenant with his wife, while the unmarried man reflects Christ's own undivided devotion to the Father. Neither path is better than the other; both are sacred callings. What matters most is faithfulness to the assignment God has entrusted to you.

Therefore, if you decide to remain unmarried, do so with conviction rather than compromise. Let your solitude be filled with worship, your quiet moments with prayer, and your days with service to the Kingdom. You are not alone; you walk with the Lord who called you, who strengthens you, and who promises eternal companionship. "Lo, I am with you always, even unto the end of the world" (Matthew 28:20).

Who Chooses to Be Alone

Many women find themselves alone, sometimes by choice and at other times by circumstance. For some, relocating for marriage isn't possible; for others, opportunities to meet a husband never align. Over time, solitude becomes familiar, and independence becomes a way of life. They become accustomed to providing for themselves, making decisions independently, and shaping their lives without the daily influence of a partner. In this, many women discover strength and resilience, learning how to stand firmly on their own feet.

However, when a woman accustomed to independence chooses to pursue marriage, she must understand that this shift requires humility and a willingness to compromise. The role of a wife differs from that of a single woman. In marriage, decisions are made together, responsibilities shared, and burdens borne collectively. This does not diminish her dignity but invites her into a new rhythm of partnership. *"Therefore, shall a man leave his father and his mother, and shall cleave unto his wife: and they shall be one flesh" (Genesis 2:24).*

Achieving oneness requires adjustment, patience, and sacrifice. The woman who enters marriage after years of independence must learn to embrace trust, letting go of some of the control she once tightly held. *"Wives, submit yourselves unto your own husbands, as unto the Lord" (Ephesians 5:22).*

Submission in this context is not a sign of weakness but a voluntary choice to honor God's order in the home. Similarly, her husband is called to love her sacrificially (Ephesians 5:25). Marriage is never one-sided; it is a covenant that requires equal faithfulness from both partners.

The adjustment may feel difficult at first. A woman who once made every decision alone must now seek agreement. She who once guarded her own space must now open her life to another. She who once carried her burdens alone must now learn to share them.

But this is the beauty of a covenant: "Two are better than one, *because they have a good reward for their labor. For if they fall, the one will lift his fellow" (Ecclesiastes 4:9-10).* For women who remain single, whether by calling or circumstance, God remains faithful.

"For thy Maker is thine husband; the Lord of hosts is his name" (Isaiah 54:5). In Him, they find companionship, security, and unfailing love. Singleness is not abandonment but a season, or even a lifetime, of divine intimacy where Christ Himself fulfills the roles of provider and protector.

But for those who choose marriage after independence, prayer and preparation are crucial. The heart must be willing to compromise, to let go of solitary habits, and to welcome the joys and challenges of partnership. Marriage won't be like being single with someone; it is a new creation, a sacred promise, and a daily calling. *"What therefore God hath joined together, let not man put asunder" (Mark 10:9).*

Thus, whether single or married, the Christian woman's identity is never diminished. Her worth isn't determined by her marital status but by her relationship with the Lord. However, suppose she chooses to leave the path of independence to embrace marriage. In that case, she must do so with open eyes, prepared to walk in humility, patience, and faith, trusting that God's plan, though demanding, ultimately leads to blessing.

HEAVENLY CITIZEN

CHAPTER NINE

Jesus said, "I am the Life."
"Can any of you, by worrying, add a single hour to your life?" (Matthew 6:27).
When Jesus declared, "I am the way, the truth, and the life: no man cometh unto the Father, but by me" (John 14:6).

God's Design for Humility and Family

The Owner of all creation has spoken clearly so that we may know who is genuinely in charge. "The earth is the Lord's, and the fullness thereof; the world, and they that dwell therein" (Psalm 24:1). Human pride, intelligence, or achievement can never compare with the wisdom and sovereignty of God. As Scripture reminds us, "What is your life? You are a mist that appears for a little while and then vanishes" (James 4:14). Our strength is limited, but His power endures forever.

Throughout His Word, God sets forth laws and guidance to steer our lives under His care and blessing. Marriage, family, and community are recognized as sacred institutions that support human well-being, not only in the Bible but also across various religious and cultural traditions. *"It is not good that the man should be alone; I will make him a help meet for him" (Genesis 2:18).*

In this divine plan, men are called to be providers and protectors, serving their wives, children, and communities with faithfulness and humility. Pride and arrogance are dangerous because God Himself opposes the proud but shows grace to the humble (James 4:6). Therefore, men are called to accept their roles with humility, not as masters but as servants of God, building their families on the foundation of His Word.

A true man understands his responsibility not only to work and provide, but also to love and instruct his children in the ways of the Lord. *"And these words, which I command thee this day, shall be in thine heart: and thou shalt teach them diligently unto thy children" (Deuteronomy 6:6-7).*

Marriage and family are not burdens but blessings. In many cultures, children and family life are regarded as sources of pride and strength. The Bible confirms this truth: *"Children are a heritage of the Lord: and the fruit of the womb is his reward" (Psalm 127:3).*

To dismiss these gifts lightly is to overlook the joy and responsibility of participating in God's plan for humanity. The challenges of modern society often test these values. When material wealth and independence take precedence over faith and humility, families can suffer. Broken homes and neglected children come at a heavy cost when God's design for marriage and unity is ignored. In contrast, in places where family values and community support remain central, children typically grow up in environments of stability, shared responsibility, and respect.

Even justice systems worldwide reflect the impact of broken family relationships. For example, research from the U.S. Department of Justice (Bureau of Justice Statistics) found that 14.6% of state prisoners incarcerated for violent crimes committed offenses against a family member, with men making up the vast majority. These realities emphasize the importance of strong, healthy families guided by God's principles, where love and respect prevent violence and promote peace.

The message is clear: when men and women embrace humility, honor marriage, and raise their children in the fear of the Lord.

Lord, both their households and communities thrive. "Unless the Lord builds the house, the builders labor in vain" (Psalm 127:1). True wisdom is acknowledging God's authority, submitting to His design, and walking in His ways, because in Him we find blessing, stability, and life.

When the Creator spoke, His message was simple and straightforward to all, regardless of their beliefs or affiliations; He revealed the core of the gospel. He didn't offer multiple options, but declared Himself as the only path to eternal fellowship with the Father. In Christ is the Way, the Truth, and the Life, not just directions or truths, but the very essence of life. Rejecting Christ is rejecting life itself. These laws are not optional; you either be with him or separate from him.

The apostle John opens his gospel with this same truth: "*In the beginning was the Word, and the Word was with God, and the Word was God. The same was in the beginning with God. He made all things; and without Him was not anything made that was made*" (John 1:1-3).

The Word, Christ Himself, was not created; He is the eternal God. Paul echoes this in Colossians 1:16: "*For by him were all things created, that are in heaven, and that are in earth, visible and invisible… all things were created by him, and for him.*"

Christ is not merely a teacher or prophet; He is the Creator, God in the flesh, dwelling among us. Because God Himself walked among us in Christ, He instilled within humanity everything needed for life and godliness until we return to Him (2 Peter 1:3).

In Him we lack nothing. Consider this: if parents enroll their child in the finest private school, paying for the best teachers and resources, the child still has the responsibility to learn. If, instead, the child keeps asking his parents for answers rather than applying the tools already provided, he misses the point of their provision.

So, it is with faith in Christ. Many believers pray only to ask for things, rather than to worship and trust Him. But the Lord has already placed within us wisdom, resources, and community to support one another in daily living. The most important virtue is to know Jesus personally:

Jeremiah 4:22 ***"For my people are foolish, they have not known me.***

This does not diminish prayer; it elevates it. We are commanded to pray, but prayer is primarily about reverence and worship, not a list of desires. Too often, Christians pray for things God has already made possible through diligence, wisdom, or the help of others, such as a spouse, a job, or financial stability. These demands require responsibility, not miracles.

Yet when it comes to the impossible, healing incurable diseases, deliverance from death, and breaking spiritual chains, those are the battles where prayer calls upon the power of heaven. ***"Call upon me in the day of trouble: I will deliver thee, and thou shalt glorify me" (Psalm 50:15).***

Every act of Christ on earth testified to His divinity. Only God could raise Lazarus after four days in the tomb, command the dead to rise as if they were sleeping, or drive out demons with a word of authority. Only God could declare, as David prophesied a thousand years earlier. David foresaw the Messiah's death and resurrection, an eternal King whose body would not decay.

"When he prepared the heavens, I was there: when he set a compass upon the face of the depth" (Proverbs 8:27).

The Christ, the eternal Wisdom of God, entered human history to save the very souls He had created in His image. King David understood that life on earth was not the end, but a waiting place for God's promise to be fulfilled. He expressed confidence that even in death, his soul would not be abandoned and his body would not decay.

"For thou wilt not leave my soul in hell; neither wilt thou suffer thine Holy One to see decay" (Psalm 16:10).

Although these words prophetically pointed to Christ, they also showed David's trust in the Lord's power over life and death. David was not afraid to die because he trusted the Lord with his soul. His hope was not in kingship, wealth, or earthly strength but in the eternal God who redeems and restores. Death, for David, was not a final defeat but a doorway into the presence of the Lord. *"Yea, though I walk through the valley of the shadow of death, I will fear no evil: for thou art with me" (Psalm 23:4).*

His confidence was that the Shepherd who guided him in life would also guide him beyond the grave. This same confidence is fulfilled in Christ Jesus, who declared, *"I am he that liveth,* and *was dead; and, behold, I am alive forevermore, Amen; and have the keys of hell and of death" (Revelation 1:18).*

David's hope rested on the promise that God would one day break open the prison of death and set the captives free. In trusting this promise, he looked forward to the day when his soul would rejoice in the presence of his Redeemer.

"But God will redeem my soul from the power of the grave: for he shall receive me" (Psalm 49:15).

For men today, David's faith serves as a reminder to trust God's process with our souls. Life is fragile, death is inevitable, but hope remains secure in the One who conquered the grave. When we anchor our trust in Christ, death loses its sting, and eternity becomes our guarantee. "O death, where is thy sting? *O grave, where is thy victory? ... thanks be to God, which giveth us the victory through our Lord Jesus Christ" (1 Corinthians 15:55, 57).*

Do I believe in prayer? Absolutely. **However,** prayer must be centered on worship and communion with God, rather than merely making endless requests. It is meant to align us with His will, to draw our hearts near in reverence, and to glorify Him as the source of life. When we misuse prayer as a tool for laziness or avoidance of responsibility, we dishonor the One who has already equipped us with the wisdom and strength we need.

"Faith without works is dead" (James 2:26).

We are called to act diligently in matters of daily life while trusting God for what only He can accomplish. The eternal God, who became man, came not only to forgive but also to restore. He entered our broken world to mend what sin has destroyed and to offer eternal life to all who believe. No situation escapes His notice. Even when we stumble, fall into debt, or are in chaos, He remains present. He is the God who restores order, renews strength, and repairs what is shattered. If you trust Him, He will lift you. He is not only the way to follow and the truth to believe, but also the life that sustains you now and will carry you into eternity.

The Alpha and the Omega

Jesus declares, *"**I am Alpha and Omega, the beginning and the end, the first and the last" (Revelation 22:13).*** These words are not poetry; they are authority. Alpha and Omega are the first and last letters of the Greek alphabet, signifying that Christ encompasses everything from start to finish. Nothing exists outside His power, nothing begins without His will, and nothing ends without His command.

From eternity past to eternity future, He remains unchanging. ***"I am Alpha and Omega, the beginning and the end,"*** says the Lord, who is, and was, and is to come, the Almighty (Revelation 1:8). To the fearful and uncertain, He whispers, ***"Fear not; I am the first and the last" (Revelation 1:17).***

To the suffering church, He reassures, "These things saith the first and the last, which was dead, and is alive" (Revelation 2:8). For men, husbands, and fathers, this truth brings unshakable security. Life may feel uncertain, finances may be unstable, and relationships may be fragile, but Christ holds both the first word and the last word over your story. He was present before you were born, He sustains you today, and He will carry you into eternity. Nothing escapes His sight, and nothing can overrule His final authority.

Therefore, we bow not to earthly power but to the eternal King. Presidents rise and fall, kings live and die, but the Alpha and the Omega remain forever. For the man who trusts Him, there is no need to fear tomorrow, because the One who began all things has already secured the end.

A characteristic that belongs only to the God of Israel is His exclusive claim to glory. "I am the Lord: that is my name: and my glory will I not give to another, neither my praise to graven images" (Isaiah 42:8). Unlike the false gods of nations, He revealed Himself personally, giving us His name and making His presence known among us. His glory is not shared with idols, not transferred to images carved by human hands, and not granted to anyone before Him or after Him. The Lord alone is eternal, self-existent, and sovereign, and to Him alone belongs all worship, honor, and praise.

A characteristic unique to the God of Israel is His exclusive claim to glory. *"I am the Lord: that is my name: and my glory will I not give to another, neither my praise to graven images" (Isaiah 42:8).* Unlike the false gods of other nations, He revealed Himself personally, giving us His name and making His presence known among us. His glory is not shared with idols, not transferred to images carved by human hands, and not granted to anyone before or after Him.

The Lord alone is eternal, self-existent, and sovereign, and all worship, honor, and praise belong to Him alone. Jesus reaffirms this truth in His own voice when He declares in

Revelation 1:18: *"I am he that liveth, and was dead; and, behold, I am alive for evermore, Amen; and have the keys of hell and of death."*

Here Christ identifies Himself not only as the eternal God but as the risen Savior who has conquered the grave. No prophet, king, or angel could ever make such a claim. He alone holds authority over life and death, and His resurrection proves His divinity beyond question.

By possessing the keys to hell and death, Jesus demonstrates that the destiny of every soul lies in His hands. This is why all glory must be given to Him alone, for He is the only One who has overcome death and secured eternal life for His people.

Living by the Law of the Lord Deuteronomy 6:5 9:

"And thou shalt love the Lord thy God with all thine heart, and with all thy soul, and with all thy might. And these words, which I command you this day, shall be in your heart: and you shall teach them diligently to your children, and shall talk of them when you sit in your house, and when you walk by the way, and when you lie down, and when you rise.

And thou shalt bind them for a sign upon thine hand, and they shall be as frontlets between thine eyes. And thou shalt write them upon the posts of thy house, and on thy gates"

Every man who chooses to live by these laws of the Lord will see profound changes in his life, his home, and his environment. The foundation of godly manhood is not pride, status, or wealth; it is humility before God and obedience to His Word. Scripture is clear: ***"God resisteth the proud, but giveth grace unto the humble" (James 4:6).***

A proud man will fall under the weight of his arrogance, but the humble man will be lifted by the Lord and strengthened to lead his household with integrity. The same truth applies to women. In our generation, many voices declare independence with pride, boasting, "I don't need a man." Yet that pride often masks hidden pain. Beyond the noise of parties, birthdays, and holidays, many face the wilderness of loneliness, a painful silence that no temporary distraction can heal.

Seasons of selfishness eventually arrive, leaving behind regret and a sense of emptiness. Pride promises freedom, but ultimately, it leads to sorrow. ***"Pride goeth before destruction, and a haughty spirit before a fall" (Proverbs 16:18).***

But God's design for man is different. Every man is called to marry, build a home, and raise children in the fear of the Lord. From the beginning, God declared, ***"It is not good that the man should be alone" (Genesis 2:18).***

Marriage and fatherhood are not optional extras; they are part of the divine calling of manhood. To reject them casually is to neglect the very purpose for which men were created: to reflect God's image through covenant and to extend His legacy through generations.

The command in Deuteronomy 6 is clear: men must love the Lord with all their heart, soul, and might, and they are to pass that love to their children. Faith isn't meant to be kept hidden in private thoughts or reserved for Sundays; it should be woven into daily life. Fathers are called to teach diligently, to talk about God's commands at home, on the road, in the morning, and at night. The family becomes a living classroom of faith, where children learn by hearing and by seeing.

This responsibility is significant. A man who takes seriously the task of instructing his children in God's Word influences not only their future but also the atmosphere of the entire household. His leadership establishes a home characterized by prayer, obedience, and blessing. When the Word of God is inscribed on the posts of the house, both literally and figuratively, the family is under the protection of divine favor. ***"Blessed is every one that feareth the Lord; that walketh in his ways" (Psalm 128:1).***

Therefore, the man who humbly accepts his role as husband, father, and spiritual leader receives God's blessing on his life. He recognizes that strength comes not from pride, but from submission; not from independence, but from covenant; not from selfishness, but from love. Such a man leaves behind not only material possessions but also a spiritual legacy that endures for generations.

"The just man walketh in his integrity: his children are blessed after him" (Proverbs 20:7).

Trusting God's Process

If something truly comes from God and is suitable for you, then you don't need to beg for it in prayer. Guided by the Holy Spirit, you only need to trust His process and wait for His timing. ***"With the Lord a day is like a thousand years, and a thousand years are like a day" (Psalm 90:4).***

What seems delayed in our view is already complete in His eternal plan. To trust God is to rest in the certainty that what He has ordained will happen without striving or fear.

Marriage is one of those blessings. Scripture says, ***"Her husband has full confidence in her and lacks nothing of value" (Proverbs 31:11).***

When God joins a man and a woman, it is not just for romance or temporary happiness, but for a covenant, stability, and the raising of children. Marriage is not meant as an escape from loneliness but as a calling to responsibility. ***"But those who hope in the Lord will renew their strength. They will soar on wings like eagles; they will run and not grow weary; they will walk and not be faint" (Isaiah 40:31).***

The couple who places their hope in God will find strength to endure every season of marriage The apostle Paul reminds us of God's order in creation: ***"A man ought not to cover his head, since he is the image and glory of God; but woman is the glory of man. For man did not come from woman, but woman from man" (1 Corinthians 11:7-8).***

This divine order is not about superiority, but about purpose. The husband reflects the image and glory of God as he leads his family, and the wife demonstrates the glory of her husband as she supports and nurtures the home. Together they form one covenant body, designed to glorify God in unity.

Yet in our generation, marriage is often viewed as a pursuit of happiness rather than a covenant of faith. Many walk away the moment they feel unfulfilled. But marriage was never meant for fleeting happiness; it was designed for perseverance, faithfulness, and growth in holiness. Happiness comes and goes, but the covenant endures. God trusts married men and women to remain faithful, not because every moment is easy, but because the vow was made before Him.

"What therefore God hath joined together, let not man put asunder" (Mark 10:9).

Imagine a father standing alone, watching his wife's back as she walks away with the children because she is "no longer happy." That image is not simply heartbreaking; it is a violation of the covenant. Marriage is not disposable, nor is it subject to the shifting moods of personal happiness. It is sacred, binding, and a choice designed to endure trials. The man who abandons his family betrays his calling, and the woman who leaves for selfishness turns her back on the order of God.

Therefore, the Book of Men counsels this truth: trust God's process in marriage is to trust Him in all things. Pray not for escape but for endurance, not for easy answers but for strength to remain faithful. *"The just shall live by faith" (Romans 1:17). Faith means believing that the God who joined you will also sustain you.*

A man of God, a husband, and a father must walk in this conviction: marriage is not about chasing happiness, but about reflecting Christ's covenant with His Church. The world says, "Leave when you are tired." Christ says, "Remain, for I am with you." Those who trust in the Lord will find that even in seasons of weariness, He renews their strength, teaching them to soar, to run, and to walk without fainting.

God reveals His character through the images of the eagle and the lion, both symbols of power, authority, and dominion under the sun He created.

"As an eagle stirreth up her nest, fluttereth over her young, spreadeth abroad her wings, taketh them, beareth them on her wings: so, the Lord alone did lead him" (Deuteronomy 32:11-12).

Likewise, *"The lion hath roared, who will not fear?*

The Lord God hath spoken, who can but prophesy?" (Amos 3:8). These comparisons remind us that men, created in the image of God (Genesis 1:27), carry within them traits of strength, authority, and responsibility. When you hear the roar in a man's voice, you are reminded of his God-given power to lead, to protect, and to uphold his family. This is why the burden of governing a home or raising children cannot rest solely on the mother. Men are called to respect covenant and commitment, not to chase fleeting happiness.

If marriage were merely about personal happiness, most men would remain alone. But we bow to the laws of the Lord, who declared, "It is not good that the man should be alone" (Genesis 2:18), and we fulfill His promise by building families rooted in His authority and guided by His Word. *Psalm 91:4 "He shall cover thee with his feathers, and under his wings shalt thou trust: his truth shall be thy shield and buckler."*

HEAVENLY CITIZEN

CHAPTER TEN

When God Says Go:
*Obedience in Darkness, Leaving Without
a Map Like Abraham*

"By faith Abraham, when called to go to a place he would later receive as his inheritance, obeyed and went, even though he did not know where he was going." Hebrews 11:8

Every man of faith knows when it's time to go. God speaks in many ways, through Scripture, strangers, and quiet conviction in the soul. When you are a man of prayer, you must learn to listen not only in times of peace but also in the silence of your suffering. God is not absent from your pain; He is attentive to it. And when your heart is bruised and your strength is exhausted, His Spirit will whisper in your soul that "now is the time." Every Bible-believing man who walks with the Lord knows there is a moment when God asks you to act, and obedience becomes your path to healing. It's not about winning; God will be with you in the life you're heading into, however unknown it may be.

There are men today living in silent torment. Although physically stronger, they have become spiritually weak because of the constant emotional, verbal, or even physical violence from their wives. Society does not always recognize a man's wounds because he is expected to endure silently. Some women, too, are broken and capable of causing serious harm; some can manipulate, even hurt themselves, and shift the blame onto others to make it easier to get you locked up. But God sees everything.

The courts of men may ignore you, but the Judge of Heaven observes all. When God reveals to you, through the Holy Spirit, signs, or His actions: it's time to leave. You must trust Him, drop your bag, and go. Abraham must leave.

The Lord told him, *"Leave your country, your people, and your father's house for the land I will show you" (Genesis 12:1).*

Abraham had no map to the unknown, only a promise. Brother, why should you stay humiliated, unloved, and financially drained in a home that no longer welcomes your peace? Pack your belongings, grab a bag, and leave. You're not abandoning your faith; you're answering God's call to protect it.

God told Moses, "**Now go**." I am sending you to Pharaoh to bring my people out of Egypt" (Exodus 3:10). He wasn't just going; he was being sent.

When you leave abuse behind, you're not just escaping pain; you're moving toward divine freedom.

As Hebrews 11:8 says, "by faith **Abraham**...obeyed and went, though he did not know where he was going." You might not see your future today, but faith isn't about certainty; it's about trusting that God will be waiting for you at the other end of the road. If you need to sleep in a car, travel to the next town, visit a friend's or family member's house, or park and leave, like I did when I left everything to start anew in another country...

Brother, don't wait for disaster to strike and bring in those who will be overwhelmed! When the Holy Spirit gives the signal to move, any hesitation will only increase the darkness. Challenges like police involvement, courtroom disputes with convictions in your name, and false accusations become real threats when emotions are uncontrolled.

A woman who no longer shows respect or love cannot be won back solely through your endurance. "Let her go. You're not her savior; Jesus is. Your obedience to God now could be what secures your future, your children's well-being, and your soul.

Trust in God, and you will live a longer, more fulfilled life.

Some people ask me, *"Why did you stay so long?" Why spend 20 years in a home without peace, with someone who only cared about money, and never about family?*

My answer is simple: my sons and the system. I knew my boys needed time to grow. I knew the Western government rarely favors fathers, especially men of faith, trying to protect their children from emotional harm.

So, I prayed, "Lord, give me the strength to be patient."

While their mother embraced a lifestyle of nightclubs, alcohol, and wild independence with her friends, I stayed at home to raise them and managed to hold two jobs simultaneously. I made all the sacrifices silently. Every Sunday, the three of us attended church service. Rain or shine, we worshiped and prayed together. I enrolled them in the Boston Taekwondo Academy to help them learn self-defense techniques and develop discipline and self-respect. I also took them to the Hyde Park YMCA and personally taught them how to swim.

I was not merely passing time; I was sowing seeds. Seeds of discipline, courage, and godly character in my sons' hearts. Though our home was far from perfect, even in its broken state, I understood something vital: I could not offer them a flawless environment, but I could fight to protect their innocence. I could shield them from certain realities, giving them a better chance at a stable, successful life. I am their father, and it remains my sacred responsibility to safeguard their minds, nurture their bodies, and guide their souls.

What I lacked in material provisions, I made up for with presence. A father who was there in the chaos, praying, leading, walking with God, not perfectly, but faithfully. A man they could watch, listen to, and learn from. This is a greater inheritance than any wealth or worldly comfort can offer. ***"A good man leaves an inheritance to his children's children" (Proverbs 13:22)***, and I knew the most significant inheritance was a spiritual legacy.

During this emotional struggle, I held on to God's promise in Jeremiah 33:3: ***"Call unto me, and I will answer thee, and show thee great and mighty things, which thou knowest not." I replied, "Yes, Lord, I'm ready to move forward." Then, I left, stayed in my vehicle for a while, and finally reunited with my sons to say goodbye before leaving the country forever.***

Brothers, listen to The Book of Men: we were created first, not by mistake, not as an afterthought. We are the foundation. "The first man Adam became a living being" (1 Corinthians 15:45), and from the beginning, God gave man purpose, authority, and responsibility. We stand before Him, with both hands raised high, not because we are perfect, but because we have tried. We have stumbled. We have failed.

But he still calls us on the other side of that surrender. He was waiting to open doors I could never force open myself. He gave me a new purpose, a new marriage, more children, and a home filled with peace, order, and mutual respect. And a wife who walks in the fear of the Lord; a servant of God that He chose for me. ***"He who finds a wife finds a good thing and obtains favor from the Lord" (Proverbs 18:22)***.

You, man of God, are not forgotten. You were chosen before you ever fell. "Even before he made the world, God loved us and chose us in Christ to be holy, and without fault in his eyes" (Ephesians 1:4). The God of fire, the same One who spoke to Moses in the burning bush, is still calling men today. He's calling you back to His house, to His presence, to His purpose.

Let's be honest, if it weren't for the Lord, the chaos of this modern age would have overwhelmed some of us. In a world where many women are misled by culture, driven by selfishness, or seeking control, it's only the Lord who protects His sons from ruin. **"Unless the Lord had been my help, my soul would soon have settled in silence" (Psalm 94:17).**

So, rise. Return. Run to Him. The Father waits with open arms, not with shame, but with redemption. Because He is faithful to those who call on Him, He still rescues His sons. The God of men remains faithful, just as it is written: **"If we are faithless, He remains faithful, for He cannot deny Himself" (2 Timothy 2:13).**

I used to believe that my loyalty could secure their future. But fatherhood isn't just about being there; it's also about listening to God's voice and obeying His call to act. When my boys were 10 and 12, we were at church, and I felt the Holy Spirit speaking to me clearly. It was winter, and snow covered the ground, a cold chill filling the air. A deep silence filled my soul as I watched my boys enjoy their time with me, but I knew I had to follow the message: "It's time to go."

I left only with what I needed, without any dramatic exit or conflict, simply because I was obedient. The world became my sanctuary and eventually a gateway to a new life. The Lord sheltered me beneath His wings; I was safe and loved. Elohim was my strength, and the shadow of His presence helped me climb the mountain. He is Jehovah, who never lets His people go nor forsakes us. He is too holy to fail us. Pray about everything and worship Him with all our being.

Today, I am remarried. It's been five years. I am living in another country, raising a new son in a healed and sacred home. While she remains "independent" and continues to look for a dream-rich man. I have stopped looking back. I do not say this to boast, but with quiet hope: that God will bless her, that her eyes will open, and her heart will find the peace that mine now knows. When God says go, we don't argue; we obey. And when we follow, we don't just escape**... we live.**

I understand the difficulty of enduring prolonged waiting, year after year, in the hope of a change that never seems to materialize. You have prayed, endured, forgiven, and attempted once more. However, deep within your spirit, you are hearing the voice of God talking to you: the Holy Spirit is addressing you. This moment is not merely driven by emotion or fear; rather, it is the Lord Himself affirming what you have long suspected. "It is time for you to go."

As Genesis 31:3 states:

"Then the Lord said to Jacob, 'Go back to the land of your fathers and to your relatives, and I will be with you.'"

God never sends a person without also accompanying them with His presence. The Book of Men gets it right every time: when it's time to leave a difficult home, an abusive marriage, or a toxic environment, God doesn't just release you from your duty as a man. He leads you. The Lord understands the investments you've made, financial, emotional, and spiritual. You've poured your life into your family. But now, your name, your dignity, your peace, and even your identity is under attack. You are no longer respected, not even by those you trusted, such as your wife, children, or neighbors.

You may feel like it's too late to start over. But it's not. With God, it's never too late. Whether she asks you to leave or the government does, it's not the end.

Isaiah 41:10 reminds you: ***"So do not fear, for I am with you; do not be dismayed, for I am your God. I will strengthen you and help you; I will uphold you with my righteous right hand."***

Many men before you have faced this same crossroads. Those who found peace were the ones who dared to step out in faith and leave behind what was destroying them. God made a way for them, and He will do the same for you. Even if the path seems dark now, God promises to light it up in the valley.

As Psalm 23:4 says, ***"Even though I walk through the valley of the shadow of death, I will fear no evil, for you are with me."***

He walks beside you with strength and mercy. Even if your world falls apart, His peace will hold you together. His presence is your peace. Brother in Christ, let me be clear: you are not permitted to end your life. That is not your decision. You were bought with Jesus Christ's blood, and your life belongs to Him. No matter how dark it seems, you have no right to take what belongs to the Lord.

And just as important: you are not allowed to abandon your children. No matter how unfair the system feels, and no matter how broken the family courts appear, your responsibility as a father stays the same. You will answer for them, not the judge, not the lawyers, not the government. You are a father in the court of heaven.

So, take courage, faithful man of God. The road ahead may be difficult, but it is a sacred one. You are not turning away in rebellion; you are moving forward in obedience. Trust that God will be your strength, your shield, and your protector. Move slowly, wisely, and prayerfully. And remember: ***"Do not fear, for I am with you… "I will uphold you with my righteous right hand" (Isaiah 41:10).*** You are not alone. You never were. And you never will be.

When the Holy Spirit Becomes the Only Voice: A Message to Christian Husbands in The Book of Men is the only law to move forward. Marriage is a sacred covenant established by God to reflect His love, order, and unity. When a marriage fades, not physically, but spiritually and emotionally, it leaves the man of God feeling confused, rejected, and silent. Sadly, many Christian men are slow to recognize or admit this truth.

They often remain at the altar of a marriage that their wives have long given up on, holding onto loyalty in the hope of reviving what is no longer alive.

God called Adam to lead and protect. He was given the mandate to cultivate the garden, exercise authority over creation, and follow the commands of the Lord. Adam's life not only marked the beginning of humanity but also initiated the countdown to mortality for every subsequent generation. ***"For dust you are and to dust you will return" (Genesis 3:19).***

Eve was his only companion, helper, confidant, and the one who shared in his stewardship of the Garden of Eden. Together, they were to reason, plan, and care for each other's well-being. But in her heart, a dangerous curiosity stirred, similar to what many older women experience today. She longed to know what God had not given them, to taste what was forbidden.

This desire opened the door to deception. *"When the woman saw that the fruit of the tree was good for food and pleasing to the eye, and also desirable for gaining wisdom, she took some and ate it" (Genesis 3:6).*

In that crucial moment, Adam failed to uphold his God-given responsibility. He did not lead in obedience or resist temptation; instead, he followed Eve's choice, placing her voice above God's command. Yet even then, God did not abandon them. He called out to Adam, not because He didn't know where Adam was, but to confront him with his failure.

But the Lord God called to the man, 'Where are you?" Genesis 3:9 Disobedience and its consequences were put into motion. Eve was told, *"I will make your pains in childbearing very severe; with painful labor, you will give birth to children. Your desire will be for your husband, and he will rule over you. "Genesis 3:16* For Adam, time itself came to symbolize how short life is. *"So, all the days that Adam lived were nine hundred and thirty years, and he died." Genesis 5:5*

Yet the Bible does not specify when or how Eve died, nor does it include her in the genealogies of Genesis 5. Scripture emphasizes the male lineage from Adam to Noah, and this silence serves as a reminder: when we break the Lord's covenant and reject His laws, we risk being erased from the testimony of faith.

Though you may still matter to God personally, His love endures; He might choose not to use you to save, deliver, or carry His message to His people. *"Those who honor me I will honor, but those who despise me will be disdained on the surface" (1 Samuel 2:30).*

You might ask: how could this happen? How did Eve, who walked with Adam and God in paradise, fall so far from grace? Why was the consequence so severe as to start the clock toward death? The answer remains the same today: as men ignore their duty, some wives allow themselves to be influenced by voices that reject God's order, voices whispering independence that goes against His design.

They repeat the world's refrain: "I don't need a man." But independence without God creates only a fragile foundation; when the car breaks down, bills pile up, credit cards are maxed out, or unexpected crises occur, the strength of self-reliance fails. And in those moments, the absence of a godly man is felt deeply in the silence, even if it's never spoken aloud.

So, let us learn from Adam's story. Stand firm. Lead with courage. Guard your heart and your home. And hold fast to God's Word, for ***"He is a shield to those who take refuge in him" (Proverbs 30:5).***

Well, think of it this way: when women say they are curious and independent, looking to discover new things, it is a blessing to explore discoveries with your husband. However, when you leave your home and your curiosity unchecked, it is like eating unripe Ackee, which can lead to seizures, coma, or death within hours. The Manchineel, known as the "Death Apple," causes skin blistering, throat and stomach burning, blindness, and even death, sometimes just by touching it. The Strychnine Fruit is equally dangerous; it can cause violent muscle contractions and rapid death through respiratory failure.

These fruits are deceptive. On the outside, they look harmless and even appealing. However, beneath the surface, they hide destruction. Similarly, outside the home, there are men, "boyfriends with broken spirits and hidden agendas," waiting for moments when a woman is weak, curious, or emotionally vulnerable. They observe what you want to hear and mirror your pain with false promises. But as soon as you leave your covenant home and bring your emotional and physical baggage with you, they start to distance themselves. Suddenly, the words of love and care vanish. What follows is heartbreak and disillusionment:

"I can't believe he did that to me... he promised to love me and take care of me." But now, instead of affection, all you hear is: "You're delusional. You're crazy. You're old. You're not attractive anymore." This is the trap of deception. The enemy is a snake, disguising bondage as independence and freedom, and what begins as a quest for happiness often ends in loneliness and regret. Protect your heart. The safest place for your healing and growth remains under the coverage God provides, not in the arms of a counterfeit comforter.

Similarly, some women, blessed by God with a faithful, hardworking husband and children, suddenly desire something "fresh," younger, or more exciting. They chase an illusion of independence and self-fulfillment, hoping it will bring lasting happiness. However, often what seems sweet from afar turns out to be bitter in reality.

Many faithful women of God don't choose that path.

Instead, they kindly ask their husbands to take care of their health, encourage them to visit the doctor, exercise, and eat healthier. They cook, nurture, and speak life into their homes. They might request a change of scenery or lifestyle adjustments, not out of rebellion, but to build a better future together. They recognize the value of what they have and work to strengthen it, not tear it down.

When temptation whispers, "There's more out there," wisdom reminds us that not everything that looks good is good.

Like forbidden fruit, it may cost more than you can afford to lose.

All men are commanded to leave their fathers and mothers and to join themselves to their wives. But what happens when the woman no longer wants to be held? When she emotionally drifts into another world, leaving only her shadow in the home? That's when the Holy Spirit begins to whisper what no one else dares to say or hear to the Christian husbands: "*You don't belong here anymore. She's left the covenant.*"

Men like Jacob left their homes on God's instruction, fleeing from Esau, but also following a divine call (Genesis 28:10-15). Elijah was commanded to leave and hide for protection (1 Kings 17:2-3). Even Jesus left heaven out of obedience (Philippians 2:6-8).

Throughout Scripture, God called men to leave, especially when remaining meant destruction, disobedience, or betrayal of a higher purpose. The same truth applies in marriage. Sometimes God directs His sons to leave, not because they've stopped loving, but because He has already seen the end. Once the spirit of hope has spoken to your heart, you can't think you'll change the heart of a woman who no longer wants to be with you; you need to recalculate your life and leave.

Christian husbands who have sacrificed everything to build a home often find themselves raising their children alone in a cold, empty marriage. She's there physically, but her soul, spirit, and affection have drifted to other men, other fantasies, or other desires. She's no longer fighting for the marriage. And you, as a man of God, find yourself in a spiritual desert.

HEAVENLY CITIZEN

CHAPTER ELEVEN

How many Christian men silently weep in marriages that were spiritually dead long ago?

The Book of Christian Me

The weight of the world, and sometimes even the Church, tells you to keep fighting. But the Holy Spirit knows when it's over. He won't leave you in the dark. He will confirm it to you through dreams, repeated signs, and a deep knowing within your spirit. That's when you begin to hear him say, 'She's no longer part of this covenant.'

Academic research on emotional detachment in marriages uncovers a troubling reality: women often detach emotionally long before they physically leave the relationship. According to the Gottman Institute, 69% of divorces in heterosexual marriages are initiated by women. Michael Rosenfeld, a professor at Stanford University, confirms this finding using data from the "How Couples Meet and Stay Together" (HCMST) survey, which analyzed responses from a large and diverse sample of couples. The results consistently show that women tend to seek emotional intimacy, closeness, and mutual support more deeply, and when these needs are unmet, dissatisfaction gradually grows.

This emotional detachment doesn't happen overnight. Many women start to detach quietly months or even years before filing for divorce, while their husbands, unaware of this, continue to fight to preserve their marriage. Often, men continue to work hard, provide financially for their families, remain faithful, and believe they're doing everything right. However, their wives, who

Often, they seek to reinvent themselves and gain independence, coming to think that they "deserve better," without fully considering the cost of living on their husband's earnings, sometimes even at age 50 or 60, believing it's not too late to start over.

These psychological divides in marriage are rarely visible in superficial statistics. What the data cannot reveal is the silent pain endured by countless husbands, who remain emotionally, spiritually, and physically committed to their wives, even after they have emotionally turned away. These men continue to pray, provide for their families, and persevere, unaware that the woman's love has already begun to detach her heart from the commitment they swore to honor.

For Christian men, the emotional toll is even more complicated. The Book of Men reveals a surprising pattern: many men lose not only their marriages but also their souls in their attempts to hold onto something already dead. They throw themselves into work, silence their own needs, and suffer in silence, hoping that God will restore the bond. But they often confuse fighting for their marriage with remaining stuck in a lifeless relationship.

This form of silent suffering has real consequences. Many men suffer from serious health problems caused by prolonged emotional trauma, spiritual distress, and psychological isolation. These include: death from heart attacks, high blood pressure, chronic stress-related insomnia, depression and anxiety disorders, stress-related weight gain or loss, alcohol or substance abuse, gastrointestinal issues, autoimmune flare-ups due to stress-induced inflammation, panic attacks and chest pain, suicidal thoughts, or spiritual despair.

The Book of Men warns every Christian man.

Never take the sin of betrayal lightly. If a woman steps out on you, emotionally or physically, it is not just a lapse in judgment; it is a violation of covenant and a clear sign that she no longer respects you. Respect is the foundation of a relationship, and when it's gone, so is the bond.

Ask yourself this: why would the same woman who lies to her husband never dare to lie to her boss? The answer is simple: she respects the hierarchy. She fears the consequences at work, but not at home. The moment she loses reverence for your role as head of the house, her spirit detaches; she becomes mentally and emotionally unbound from you. From that point on, even your kindness will be seen as a weakness.

The Bible provides clear guidance:

"But if she has indeed committed defilement and is found guilty, he may write her a certificate of divorce…

(see Deuteronomy 24:1, Matthew 5:32)." God does not command you to stay in a covenant with someone who has already broken it. Do not let guilt or emotional manipulation convince you otherwise. When she says, "It was just a mistake, I'll never do it again," evaluate her words based on her actions. Repentance is not just confession; it's transformation. Without change, there is only deception.

King Solomon, the wisest man to walk the earth, wrote extensively on this very matter. He warned against falling again into the arms of the adulteress. *"Do not go near the door of her house... lest you give your strength to others and your years to one who is cruel." (Proverbs 5:8-9) "For the lips of a forbidden woman drip honey, but in the end, she is bitter as wormwood..." (Proverbs 5:3–4)*

He made it clear: when you return to her, you won't find healing; you'll discover sickness in your spirit. Even the thought of intimacy will turn bitter. Your body may reach out, but your soul will recoil. Proverbs 13:12 "Hope deferred makes the heart sick..."

A man who prays for reconciliation and longs for mutual love and healing, but finds only distance, silence, and coldness, walks through a dark valley. It is a shadowed pain that few people see, and even fewer understand. But every man of God knows what to do: "just leave."

Brother, you're not alone, and loving deeply doesn't make you a fool. Still, God calls you to lead with truth, not illusion. If she has chosen darkness, don't pull your soul back into it to keep up appearances. The ship will sink one day anyway; remove your soul and let her explain the fallen state to the Lord alone. God delivers those who trust Him and honors the man who walks in integrity, even when it costs him everything.

The covenant is broken when your woman continually dishonors it, whether through disrespect, manipulation, emotional abandonment, or infidelity.

Marriage, according to God's design, is not meant to be a one-sided sacrifice. It is a sacred vow between two souls united under heaven to walk in unity, humility, love, and mutual submission. But today, women submit to no one, for no government would advise mothers to return home or prevent women from claiming 50% of their fortune.

God does not call men to stay buried in a tomb called marriage, primarily when it no longer reflects the covenant He established. There is a divine difference between carrying the cross and being crucified by someone who breaks the covenant. One is godly perseverance. The other signifies spiritual and physical death.

Christian men must depend on the Holy Spirit's guidance to discern when to fight for restoration and when to surrender to God, walking away in peace. Healing begins not by pretending that the marriage is thriving, but by accepting the truth and trusting that God can still transform ashes into beauty (Isaiah 61:3). For those mourning in Zion, He gives a crown of beauty instead of ashes, the oil of joy instead of mourning, and a garment of praise instead of despair. They will be called oaks of righteousness, a planting of the Lord to display His splendor.

The Book of Men says: "It's time for you to go."

The Holy Spirit has never let anyone down. His eyes are always watchful, reaching places no earthly husband can, especially when that husband is busy providing, protecting, and stewarding his home. For every Christian man who walks closely with the Lord, the Spirit becomes his eyes, revealing what is hidden in darkness and exposing what cannot be seen with the natural eye. No secret is safe from Him. What man may miss, God sees, and He will surely alert the innocent, guiding and protecting those who trust in Him with a discerning heart.

"For the eyes of the Lord range throughout the earth to strengthen those whose hearts are fully committed to him." (2 Chronicles 16:9)

Suppose a woman begins to humiliate her husband in public, manipulate the children, or use the police or government institutions against him. In that case, the home is no longer a safe place. It is no longer a marriage; it becomes slavery. And God has never called any man to live enslaved to a broken covenant. A godly home cannot thrive under the yoke of fear, shame, and control. Hello, my brother, "It's time for you to go."

Rosenfeld's research further emphasizes that women are more likely to initiate divorce due to emotional dissatisfaction rather than physical or financial instability. Many women report feeling ignored or emotionally neglected, even when their husbands do their best to provide for them materially and remain faithful. The burden of meeting emotional expectations while being the sole financial provider, especially when dowries or bride prices are still in effect, can leave men feeling trapped and devalued. If she raised her voice at you, brother, "It's time for you to go."

It is essential to recognize these patterns, not to assign blame, but to shed light on the truth. When your wife stops investing emotionally, spiritually, or respectfully, the covenant becomes unbalanced. Christian men must seek wisdom through the Holy Spirit to discern when they are truly faithful in love or when they are buried alive under false perceptions of hope. God's plan for marriage was never meant to be a one-sided sacrifice. Mutual respect, submission, and love are required of both husband and wife (Ephesians 5:21-33).

When these principles are lost and one partner chooses independence over the covenant, the other must seek God for guidance, healing, and clarity. The Book of Men says: "It's time for you to go." ***"You have stayed long enough at this mountain. It is time to go." Inspired by Deuteronomy 1:6–7***

The signs that your wife has emotionally distanced herself from the marriage are not minor. She flirts with other men publicly or privately, justifies her late-night emotional texts, withholds affection to punish you, or talks about divorce to control you. These are more than marital issues; they are violations of the covenant. According to the Bible, these behaviors are not those of a god-fearing woman.

Let the Holy Spirit guide you. When God shows you that she no longer respects you, no longer covers you in prayer, and no longer honors your authority, you must ask yourself: Am I still a husband in this house, or just a provider and babysitter? For many, the answer is tragic. She has become a roommate, and you are the forgotten servant. "It's time for you to go."

When your wife begins frequenting places that violate marital trust, such as clubs without you, trips with male colleagues, or private homes of male friends at night, she is signaling to you and God that she no longer sees the covenant as sacred. Proverbs 14:1 warns: "A wise woman builds her house, but a foolish woman tears it down with her own hands."

A brother said he came home around midnight and found his wife watching a movie with male friends in their house, without permission, explanation, or shame. When he confronted her, she called the police. At that moment, the Holy Spirit showed him: "You are no longer her protector. She has turned away from you." "It's time for you to go." The Bible says: **"Wives, submit yourselves to your husbands as you do to the Lord... and let the wife see that she respects her husband." (Ephesians 5:22, 33).**

A woman who dresses provocatively for the Internet but refuses her body to her husband is not confused; she is lost. A woman who entertains the world while rejecting her home is not bound by her husband; she is rebellious. Brother, "It's time for you to go."

Many Christian men endure this pain for the sake of their children. But understand this: Even Jacob left. Even Abraham left. Even Paul left when the Holy Spirit told him, "It's time for you to go." Your children need to see a father who obeys God, not a father who dies silently under the weight of disrespect. There is no reward in pretending that a dead marriage is alive, while your wife is mentally and physically absent.

The Holy Spirit does not comfort Christian men; He warns them. He sends dreams, signs, and even testimonies from other men to help you understand that she is no longer your wife. You need to listen when the Lord says, "She has strayed from My plan." Your mission now is to rebuild your life in obedience, even if that means leaving a structure that has become your prison. Don't let her ship sink with you; your soul is very important to God.

Matthew 16:26 "For what profit is it to a man if he gains the whole world, and loses his soul? Or what will a man give in exchange for his soul?"

In **The Book of Men**, the Holy Spirit calls all men back to dignity, healing, and restoration after divorce. Wholeness and purpose. Joel 2:25 "***So I will restore to you the years that the swarming locust has eaten…***"

God promises to restore what was lost or broken, even after devastating seasons, such as divorce. According to a recent study by the Pew Research Center, along with academic research on aging and remarriage, men aged 55 to 90 are much more likely than women to remarry after a divorce. A study by the National

The Center for Family & Marriage Research at Bowling Green State University shows that men are twice as likely to remarry later in life, with many citing emotional healing, companionship, and spiritual renewal as their main reasons.

After a divorce, men are like former prisoners released after many years, embracing life again. They often remarry younger, more beautiful, and more energetic women to feel young and live longer, while their ex-wives may have passed away or are now living with a dog.

These data are more than just social science; they confirm a vital spiritual truth. Men who accept healing and restoration often find a renewed purpose, even in old age. Remember that man was created first, not by accident, but by divine design. He was made to receive God's command and vision, to cultivate, keep, and lead. ***Genesis 2:15-17: "The LORD God took the man and put him in the Garden of Eden to work it. And the Lord God commanded the man…"***

This means that man will first answer to the Lord for what has been entrusted to him. And because of this responsibility, we cannot afford to stand before God broken and refusing to be healed.

We cannot stand before a holy God with a broken heart and unhealed wounds. No one can stand before the throne carrying the pieces of a soul they refuse to let go of. Don't let anyone, including your wife, your past, or your pain, break your emotional and spiritual heart in a way that prevents you from being close to God. When the Holy Spirit speaks and says, "Go," and He gently begins to pull you out of the dead space where you have remained too long, pack your bags and leave.

He is not calling you to shame; He is calling you to restoration. God does not call us to hide our brokenness but to surrender it to be healed through prayer, worship, and fasting. We were never meant to enter God's presence in fragments and without faith. You cannot approach the king's throne room with the dignity of someone who refuses to acknowledge their vulnerability.

God offers you healing, but He will not force you to accept it. Healing begins with surrender. A growing number of divorced women over the age of 65 report living alone, often with a pet as their primary companion. While this lifestyle may seem peaceful, studies show that it usually leads to higher rates of depression, social isolation, and even premature death. Being alone can feel like a prison sentence because the Lord God said,

"It is not good that man should be alone."

Independent feminists believe they know more than the Creator. These statistics reveal something more profound than numbers can convey: men who choose healing over bitterness and courage over stagnation often find renewed life and purpose, even in their later years.

Carefully listen to the Holy Spirit. Before starting something new, you must return to God's voice. The Book of Men calls on all Christian men: you need to go back, back to who you were before you said "yes." Return to the man who walked alone with God, who heard His voice clearly before life became filled with responsibilities, compromises, emotional confusion, and a disregard for character. That man still exists, and God is still calling. He is at your door to restore your wholeness.

The Holy Spirit still speaks today. He says as He did to Moses in the desert, to Joseph in a dream, to Peter through restoration, and to Paul in prison and tribulation. And sometimes, just as in those days, He says, "Go," my brother. I know this because I was there for two decades. I was fortunate to still be in my forties and left my whole life behind to start a new one in another country. In the first year, I met my wife, and since then, the Lord has been so good to me; a double portion was not enough for Him. He blessed me with more children and an extraordinary woman of God who cherishes her role as a wife. Listen to your Holy Spirit. If He says to you, "Your spouse no longer walks with Me, nor with you. I have a new place for you."

Ask yourself the difficult question: "What am I still doing here?"

If the answer is money, remember: you spent years earning it, and God is the God of double portions; He is still sitting on the throne (Job 42:10). Whether it's the house, material possessions, or even children, understand this: God cannot fully restore you until you obey. That's why, in the beginning, God created man alone (Genesis 2:7). Before there was a woman, there was responsibility, purpose, and God Himself. This period of solitude was not a punishment but a preparation.

You will get through this trial without her. All men between the ages of 50 and 85 who have obeyed the Holy Spirit's leading, who have left a spiritually dead marriage, have found a healthier, stronger, and more God-centered life on the other side. And you, too, will get there. 3 John 1:2 "Beloved, I pray that you may prosper in all things and be in health, just as your soul prospers."

This isn't an excuse to give up easily. God hates divorce (Malachi 2:16), but He also despises hypocrisy, betrayal, and disrespect for sacred vows. The same God who calls us to forgive also urges us to discern (Matthew 10:16). Do not remain in a home where Christ has left the table.

If she is emotionally connected to another man, sexually distant from you, and openly rebellious against God's Spirit, then she has already broken your covenant. Your prayers cannot restore what her rebellion has destroyed. At this stage, only God can help you escape this situation, and saving her is not your duty, because she is no longer spiritually united with you.

Leaving can be extremely painful, but staying in bondage is even worse. Many Christian men have lost their minds, children, finances, and faith, sometimes even their health and lives, because they stayed when the Spirit urged them to leave. Your true peace is found in God, not in her. Your identity isn't defined by your role as a husband but by your sonship to the King and His heavenly kingdom.

So, my brother, if any of these signs resonate with you, take a moment to consider them. Pray. Fast. Ask the Holy Spirit whether you are still standing on sacred ground or on the grave of a covenant that God Himself has declared invalid. When the Spirit confirms it, don't wait. Your healing can begin the moment you leave; the Lord is waiting for you on the other side.

Remember this: you are not alone. You are not beyond repair. You are no less of a man because she left. You remain God's beloved son. You are still called to lead, protect yourself, and be a father, even if your wife has abandoned her role as a covenant partner. The Holy Spirit will never leave you in your wilderness; He will lift you.

For you know that it was not with perishable things like silver or gold that you were redeemed... but with the precious blood of Christ."

God paid the highest price for your soul, His Son's life. (1 Peter 1:18–19)

HEAVENLY CITIZEN

CHAPTER TWELVE

The Law of the Book of Men

A **Study of Man**: A Spiritual Research from Adam to Every Christian Man Chosen by God. The Most-High (El Elyon) is the source of all existence, the One who transcends creation itself. He is not just a higher being among others, but the eternal foundation of all reality.

"I am the Alpha and the Omega, the First and the Last, the Beginning and the End." (Revelation 22:13). This research reveals a God who exists outside of time, unbound by the limitations of past, present, or future. He is eternal, sovereign, and unchanging. *"God is spirit, and those who worship Him must worship in spirit and truth." John 4:24.*

Every knee will bow, and every tongue will confess that Jesus Christ is Lord, in worship, in awe, and complete obedience. One day, every soul on earth will stand before the throne of heaven in the presence of the righteous Judge.

If you are a Christian man, you will be called first. You will give an account, not only for yourself but also for your household. Your wife and children will be included in your spiritual responsibility. Their well-being, direction, and covering have been entrusted to you. You are called to lead, protect, teach, and walk in integrity before the Lord.

If your wife has strayed from her covenant, the Lord will turn to her and ask why she abandoned the role He assigned her, why she walked away from the man she once stood beside and vowed to honor, obey, and love until death parted them. She will answer for her choices, but you, as the head, will answer for your leadership.

The throne of God is not a place for excuses; it is a place of truth. In that court, God will judge according to His Word, not cultural trends or personal feelings. This reminds us that God is not limited by physical form or material dimensions. He is Spirit, omnipresent, infinite, and deeply involved in human affairs. In understanding the nature of man, The Book of Men revisits the foundation. *"For Adam was formed first…" (1 Timothy 2:13)*

"Therefore, just as sin entered the world through one man…" (Romans 5:12)

Adam was not only the first human but also established as the first leader, responsible for humanity's fall. This was not random; it reflects God's intentional design for humans to lead, take responsibility, and serve as stewards of spirituality. Throughout history and into modern times, whenever leadership, authority, and structure exist, we often see men holding positions of responsibility. This isn't about superiority, but about divine order, a reflection of man being created in the image of God to establish, protect, and build.

Now consider: if we imagine a world governed entirely by women or entirely by men, which would better manage progress, order, and long-term results? This isn't about worth but about function and purpose. Men and women were created with different roles, equal in value, but assigned differently. When either side completely departs from that divine order, imbalance and chaos are the result.

God's design was never accidental. From the beginning, He revealed Himself as the Most-High, and He created man to lead, not through dominance, but through divine responsibility. When that role is honored, families thrive, societies flourish, and the image of God is reflected adequately on earth. Whenever disobedience occurs, the Holy Spirit will leave the table, and then you'll know that you are in trouble.

The self-existent One, the One who is, Yahweh, first created man in His image and gave him the Laws of leadership, protection, and provision. In Ephesians 5:23, the chief said, "For the husband is the head of the wife, even as Christ is the head of the church." This divine order lays the foundation for a household that thrives on love, respect, and righteous authority. A Christian husband is called not just to lead, but to lead in love, wisdom, and unwavering faith.

Respect for husbands is sacred. A husband must be respected as the head of his family; this is the first law of the human family. Every Christian man will one day leave his parents to marry a woman and uphold this law established by the Lord God. This decree, which requires all women to respect their husbands (Ephesians 5:33), does not originate from human laws, the government, the district court, US attorneys, any pastor, or the president. This mandate was established by the Creator Himself, under the decree of His government, and it abides by His kingdom from the palace of the heavenly throne.

The reason we see a man who obeys the law prosper in strength and confidence is that God has placed a man in every home as His representative, as a protector and caretaker of the family. The respect a husband deserves includes listening to his advice: "Wives, submit yourselves to your husbands" Colossians 3:18. Trusting his decisions. "A wise woman trusts her husband's judgment, just as Sarah trusted Abraham and called him lord." 1 Peter 3:5-6. Speak kindly of him in both public and private, encourage him when he is weak, and support him during difficult times. A woman who respects her husband builds her house; she who dishonors him tears it down with her own hands (Proverbs 14:1).

A good wife wears her kindness like a crown from heaven. Women are encouraged to show kindness to their husbands, not because they are weak, but because kindness is a strength granted by the Holy Spirit of God. A wife's gentle words, patience, and compassionate support for her husband's dreams will inspire him to achieve great wealth.

Her care for him when he's sick and her prayers for his leadership are ornaments on his head. She honors his work, celebrates his victories, forgives his faults, and encourages him daily. ***The Lord's mindset when He created the first husband was "LOVE": (1 John 4:8)***

The very essence of God is love. His mindset when He created man was not one of loneliness or need, but rather a desire to share His love and goodness. Such was the principle in **The Book of Men:** "Husband, love your wife and treat her like a queen, as I love my Church." The Book of Men describes God's desire for a relationship in Genesis 3:8.

God walked in the garden and talked with Adam. This demonstrates that Man is God's voice on earth, charged with bringing order, naming creation, and embodying divine wisdom. That is why men will be held accountable before the heavenly courts. We were created to bear responsibility, to reflect God's image, and to lead creation with moral clarity and spiritual integrity. For many reasons, we will never allow any woman to take away our power and dignity.

The law from **The Book of Men** aims to help you understand the rule of law from the kingdom of God so that you can faithfully represent Him on earth and uphold your oath to

He, the Creator of all things, visible and invisible (Genesis 1:28).

God blessed them and said to them, 'Be fruitful and multiply, fill the earth, and subdue it. Have dominion over every living thing.' Can we agree that one of these living beings is a woman, right? The Lord asks us to love and care for them as He loves and cares for His church. God gave humankind dominion and stewardship over the planet, to care for the earth and to rule over all things in His name.

King David asked God:

"What is man that You are mindful of him, and the son of man that You care for him? Yet you have made him a little lower than the heavenly beings and crowned him with glory and honor, Psalm 8:4-5

You have given man dominion over the works of your hands; you have placed everything under his feet. This highlights man's honorable position and the authority God has delegated to him (1 Corinthians 11:3). Still, I want you to understand that the head of every man is Christ, and the head of every woman is her husband. It is an order established in God's kingdom: man is under the authority of Christ, yet he has been given authority within the family. Ephesians 2:6 And God raised us with Christ and seated us with him in the heavenly realms in Christ Jesus.

But you are a chosen people, a royal nation, a holy people, the family God has acquired as His special possession, so that you may proclaim the praises of the one who called you out of darkness into His marvelous light. Remind every believer of their royal and heavenly role in God's kingdom. Our work does not end here on Earth. Although we are God's representatives, His ambassadors, and his predestined heirs, we are called to serve in His divine council, seated in the executive throne room of His eternal celestial kingdom. When you see a responsible husband, you are right to think and understand who God is.

God gave humanity the authority to be stewards of the universe, to care for the planet, and to rule on His behalf. As Psalm 8:4-6 says, ***King David asks, "What is man that You are mindful of him, and the son of man that You care for him? You made him a little lower than the heavenly beings and crowned him with glory and honor. You gave him dominion over the works of Your hands; You put everything under his feet."***

This highlights man's honorable position and the authority God has delegated to him. Law of the Book of Men: When a Christian woman respects her husband, she doesn't lose her voice; she enhances their victory. Together, they reflect God's order and walk in divine power. You made him a little lower than the heavenly beings, and you crowned him with glory and honor. You gave him dominion over the works of your hands; you put everything under his control. This highlights man's noble position and the authority that God has given him.

An intelligent woman should study these laws and take the time to understand why God places her husband first and why the Almighty Himself oversees everything he does!

Academic research in psychology and leadership reveals that a strong, virtuous masculine character encompasses responsibility, courage, sacrificial leadership, and a clear sense of mission, qualities that align with this biblical mandate. A man's strength is not meant for domination or self-glorification but for protection, provision, and building under God's guidance. In 1 Corinthians 11:3, Paul teaches, *"The head of every man is Christ, the head of the woman is her husband."*

This statement defines the divine order in God's kingdom. Husbands are under Christ's authority and are called to lead their families with love and humility. Ephesians 2:6 also teaches that Jesus says, "God raised us with Christ and seated us with him in the heavenly realms," highlighting that our identity is rooted in heavenly authority and grace.

The reason Christian women who marry within a community of believers tend to be happier and more satisfied is deeply rooted in their spiritual beliefs. These women have learned to obey the Lord's law, which requires them to respect and submit to their husbands as an act of worship to God (Ephesians 5:22-24). By accepting this divine mandate, they not only honor their husbands but also strengthen the foundations of their marriage.

Research conducted at Harvard by Tyler Vandervelde of the T.H. Chan School of Public Health found that couples who regularly attend religious services are 47% less likely to divorce than those who do not. This protective effect highlights the influence of spiritual values and commitment, particularly under male leadership, for maintaining marital stability.

Furthermore, a University of Virginia study shows that couples who worship together have the lowest risk of divorce, especially when the husband assumes his role as the spiritual leader of the home. This represents God's law and design described in 1 Corinthians 11:3, where Christ is the head of every man; no one disputes this fact, and the husband is the head of his wife.

In North America, when a husband leads in prayer, spiritual teaching, and sacrificial love, and when a wife respects and supports that leadership, marriage becomes a living testimony of Christ and His Church (Ephesians 5). Spiritually rooted marriages build mutual trust, deepen intimacy, and establish a shared purpose that surpasses individual desires. Christian women who embrace these biblical truths learn to see marriage as a sacred covenant, not just a contract with the government to leave with 50%. It is a divine partnership meant to mirror God's love and order in the world.

Their obedience to God's law of respect turns everyday challenges into chances for grace and growth, laying the groundwork for lasting joy and contentment. Moreover, 1 Peter 2:9 proclaims: ***"But you are a chosen people, a royal priesthood, a holy nation, God's special possession, that you may declare the praises of him, who called you out of darkness into his wonderful light."***

This emphasizes that every believer, including men as heads of households, has a royal and divine calling to represent God's glory. Our ministry does not end on earth; we are called to be God's representatives, his senators, and deputies in the heavenly kingdom. When you see a responsible and faithful husband, you are witnessing a living reflection of God's nature and leadership. In him, you glimpse the strength, wisdom, and goodness of the King of kings.

The Mindset of High-Value Husbands

A Christian husband of great value thinks with eternity in mind. The kingdom of God is not just an idea to him; it is the force that governs his life. He builds his house on the rock, as Jesus taught in Matthew 7:24, anchoring his life in obedience to God's Word. The unshakable principles of truth, integrity, courage, self-control, and sacrificial love govern his mind. The Book of Men's Laws is his virtues; they are the keystone of his manhood and leadership. He chooses peace over pride, discipline over indulgence, and wisdom over impulsiveness, prayer over partying, and silence over noise.

He leads his family in worship, setting an example of reverence for God in both his private devotion and his public behavior. He teaches his children to fear the Lord, Deuteronomy 6:6-7: ***"And these words that I command you today shall be on your heart. You shall teach them diligently to your children, and shall talk of them when you sit in your house, and when you walk by the way, and when you lie down, and when you rise."***

Not out of fear of punishment, but out of respect for God's holiness and love. His leadership is not authoritarian but helpful, reflecting Christ, who washed his disciples' feet. He provides not only for his family's financial needs but also for their emotional, spiritual, and moral well-being. He understands that his children are arrows in a holy legacy (Psalm 127:4-5), and he carefully guides them toward their divine destiny.

Wisdom is one of his defining traits. A godly man seeks understanding rather than emotion or impulse. Proverbs 4:7 states, ***"Wisdom is the principal thing; therefore, get wisdom, and with all thy getting get understanding."***

His decisions are not reactive or prideful, but rooted in discernment from God's Word. Wisdom allows him to lead with foresight, humility, and clarity, especially as he navigates the complexities of modern family life. Faithfulness and discipline define each of his steps. He remains consistent over time, faithful to God, his wife, and his children. Luke 16:10 Jesus ***said, "He who is faithful in little things is also faithful in big things."***

A faithful man honors his commitments, even when it's inconvenient. Even when he's not happy, his job is to make it work, work harder, and seek improvement. While most women might instinctively begin to reconsider their next choice and explore a Plan B as a backup when the future seems uncertain, the husband, as God's appointed head of the family, is called to stay focused on Plan A. Why? Because divine leadership requires unwavering faith, not unexpected changes. Plan A reflects God's original instruction by faith, and the man must remain anchored in that vision unless the Lord Himself changes it.

His role is not to be indecisive, but to set an example of steadfastness, trusting that obedience will open doors even when logic suggests otherwise. His focus on Plan A creates stability, inspires faith within the family, and exemplifies the unwavering character of Christ, who "endured the cross for the joy set before him" (Hebrews 12:2).

The Book of Men has studied a law to awaken.

Christian men to the truth about modern cultural changes and the shift in women's mentalities. There is a clear contrast between many women today, influenced by 21st-century ideals of radical, obsessive independence and self-worship, and women of past generations in the 19th century who upheld divine values. In the past, when cultural noise and worldly influences were much less overwhelming, many women respected God's laws within marriage.

Historical and academic research confirms that, in those generations, marriages were often more harmonious and that most men ruled their homes in fullness and peace. This is not to demean women, but to highlight how far modern culture has strayed from biblical laws and how urgent it is for men to rise and lead with wisdom, or even consider leaving.

No husband should be guided by emotions or circumstances, but by his covenant. Whether in times of abundance or difficulty, we stay grounded and stable, reflecting the unshakeable laws of Christ.

Responsibility shapes a man's attitude. Christian men learn not to blame others. Just as Adam was called to account in the Garden of Eden, every man will one day be asked, "Where are you?" (Genesis 3:9). A godly man embraces leadership with humility and courage. He takes responsibility for his mistakes, quickly repents, and sets a good example. Responsibility is not just a burden; it is the foundation of biblical leadership and the way to blessing for future generations. When was the last time you heard a modern woman confess?

Humility builds his influence, and authentic leadership begins with bowing before the Lord. James 4:6 says, "God opposes the proud, but gives grace to the humble." A real man does not demand respect; he earns it by walking in humility, admitting his faults, and depending daily on God's strength. His humility invites peace into the home and opens the door to God's favor.

Justice is his driving force. A just man stands up for what is right and fair, even when it is unpopular. Micah 6:8 instructs, "Do justice, love mercy, and walk humbly with your God." He treats his family, employees, and neighbors with honor and fairness. His leadership is marked by justice, not favoritism. Even when justice costs him his reputation or a reward, he remains steadfast, knowing that it is more important to please God than to please men. Raising Kingdom Children: Sons and Daughters for

Christ's Fathers are called to discipline children in love and truth.

"Fathers, do not provoke your children to anger, but bring them up in the discipline and instruction of the Lord" (Ephesians 6:4).

A father teaches accountability and responsibility to his children, builds resilience and confidence, and instills fear of the Lord and respect for the laws. He shows his sons how to be men with dignity and shows his daughters what a real man looks like.

Children raised with a father's strong presence tend to be more stable, grow up with greater grace and a more faithful character, and feel more confident. A mother comforts, nurtures, and embodies gentleness, but fathers are meant to discipline, correct, and set boundaries.

When a father is absent from the home, children are much more likely to stray from moral and social guidance, including the Lord's teachings, and are also at a greater risk of involvement in crime and incarceration. In contrast, children raised in the presence of their fathers are statistically more likely to succeed in school, maintain stable mental health, and avoid criminal behavior.

A study by the U.S. Department of Justice shows that about 85% of young people in prison come from fatherless homes.

Additionally, research from Princeton University's Fragile Families Study and the National Fatherhood Initiative, both studies, found that children living in fatherless homes are four times more likely to live in poverty, twice as likely to drop out of school, and more prone to behavioral problems. Children who grow up with both parents, especially when their fathers are involved, tend to achieve better academic results and demonstrate stronger moral development.

A Christian husband deserves respect as a reflection of God's purpose, not as a dictator, but as a shepherd. He listens to and understands his wife and children's feelings, but his authority is an act of service, and his decisions should be made with prayer. His wife's support helps him carry this heavy responsibility. She empowers her husband through her faith and prayers, her loyalty, her willingness to follow his example, and her readiness to speak the truth in love.

The foundations of a godly home: A strong family begins with a husband who obeys God. He gets up early to pray, guards his eyes and heart, works hard, loves his wife as Christ loved the Church, and remains faithful in all things. He protects his home spiritually, teaches his children to honor their mother, and creates an atmosphere of gratitude. He accepts God's corrections, seeks advice when needed, and stays humble. He saves for his family's future, teaches his family about stewardship, and sets an example of generosity. A father teaches his sons to be providers, protectors, and leaders in faith. He models strength balanced with tenderness. He teaches his daughters self-respect, discernment, and how to recognize a godly man. He establishes family traditions that foster unity, celebrates milestones, and guides the family in their devotions.

The Christian husband leads by example, admits his mistakes, asks for forgiveness, and quickly makes amends. He shows his children how to love unconditionally, resolve conflicts peacefully, and work hard. He laughs with his family, rejoices in small pleasures, and lives contentedly.

The blessing of a wife's prayers becomes a flowing river of life that nourishes her husband's soul. When a man is respected, he stands taller, speaks more gently, listens more carefully, and loves more deeply. A respected husband becomes more protective, generous, thoughtful, and devoted in prayer.

A man's authority is derived from God's law, which he is entrusted to uphold, not from his jurisdiction. His leadership carries a sacred responsibility, and his respect is earned through sacrifice, maintained with steadfastness, and rewarded with heaven's blessing. Children raised under such guidance see in him a pillar of stability and a source of enduring strength. A wife standing beside such a man exudes joy, dignity, and unwavering resolve.

In this divine design, love and respect aren't separate paths, but two sides of the same coin. A husband sacrifices out of love; a wife uplifts him through her respect. Together, they raise children who become arrows, purposefully aimed at the heart of God's destiny for their lives.

The Laws of Headship and Divine Order from The Book of Men

God did not suggest that man should lead the home. He commanded it. From the beginning of creation, God gave Adam authority, not as a dictator, but as a steward of sacred responsibility. Genesis 2:15 tells us that God placed Adam in the garden "to work it and take care of it." Eve was not yet created, not because she was less valuable, but because the burden of leadership and responsibility was designed to rest first on the man. Eve's creation was an act of grace, forming a helper suitable for him, not a subordinate, but a partner under God's ordained structure.

Every man will one day stand before God's throne, not only for his own choices but also for the condition of his household. This accountability is unique to the male role in God's design. The Book of Men teaches that God does not judge men solely as individuals but also as stewards of their homes. The question will be asked: Did you lead your family in righteousness?

Did you cover them in prayer, provision, and example? Just as God called Adam first after the fall, even though Eve took the fruit, so God still calls the man first.

When storms hit the home, whether it is due to sickness, job loss, business failure, or financial hardship, many modern independent women, instead of standing firm in loyalty and faith, often choose to abandon their husbands. Some not only leave but also drag their husbands into court, demanding more support, even though the husband has faithfully provided for them for years, maintaining their lifestyles and protecting them from every flood. In that vulnerable moment, the very person he trusted becomes an adversary. Jesus warns us about this human nature:

"The heart is deceitful above all things and desperately wicked; who can understand it?" (Jeremiah 17:9).

That is why men must be spiritually, emotionally, and practically prepared to guard their hearts and finances.

HEAVENLY CITIZEN

CHAPTER THIRTEEN

The Laws of The Book of Men.
True Millionaires Are Those Who Obey the Lord.

The Book of Men's Laws teaches that a man must manage his finances independently and discreetly. A husband should never entrust his entire financial life to his wife. He must carefully guard his responsibilities in silence, for God has given him the roles of provider and protector. ***"Be wise as serpents and innocent as doves." (Matthew 10:16).***

When a man wisely guards his resources, he not only secures his family's future but also fulfills the responsibility entrusted to him by the Lord to manage and lead. The government of North America has made it surprisingly simple for women to get a divorce, often citing vague reasons like "growing apart," "lack of fulfillment," "emotional disconnection," or "loss of spark and happiness."

Studies consistently indicate that approximately 70– 80% of divorces are initiated by women. The American

The Sociological Association reported in 2015 that women start about 69% of divorces, while a Stanford study by Rosenfeld (2017) found the figure even higher at 75%.

What happens when the woman leaves, thinking she can "trade up" or find more excitement? Many men, primarily Christian self-made individuals or those referred to in The Book of Men as "Humble Millionaires," do not flaunt their wealth. They live modestly, building quietly in the background, focusing on responsibility and legacy rather than show. These men often hold hidden or undisclosed assets, future business ventures, stocks, or silent investments, as well as unknown bank safe deposit boxes. When a wife leaves, expecting something better, she sometimes later realizes that her husband's actual value, both financially, emotionally, and morally, was far greater than she ever appreciated. This can lead him to resume his business with another, much younger and more beautiful businesswoman.

Regret sinks in deeply when the truth is revealed. A study by Avvo, a legal advice platform, found that 27% of divorced individuals regretted their divorce and wished they had tried harder to save the marriage. This echoes what Jesus has warned us all along:

"A foolish woman tears down her own house with her hands." *(Proverbs 14:1).*

And again: "Charm is deceitful, and beauty is vain, but a woman who fears the Lord is to be praised." (Proverbs 31:30). When a business deal falls apart, society often blames the man involved. However, as men, we must identify where the genuine fault lies by following the laws from the Book of Men. You must protect your wealth as if you're safeguarding your soul, using elite forces like **Navy SEALs, Delta Force**, or **the 75th Ranger Regiment**, so that neither government nor court can easily seize what you have built. Imagine a man sitting confidently in a courtroom, unaffected because the judge cannot find anything to confiscate.

A company owns its luxury car; multiple layers of legal strategies protect its assets in accordance with the country's laws and regulations. This is not greed but wisdom, stewardship, knowledge, and understanding, learning from the Lord of lords.

Nothing on earth should be able to touch your hard-earned wealth, which you have accumulated slowly, with discipline and sacrifice. God Himself has set an example for you: Proverbs 13:11 "Wealth gained prematurely will fade away, but whoever gathers little by little will increase it."

The Lord created you first, spent time with you in His presence, instilled in you His intelligence, knowledge, and understanding before bringing anyone else into the picture. You were designed to lead, to manage everything yourself, and to be accountable only to God, accumulating wealth to ensure the security of your family and the legacy of your lineage.

Now is the time, brother. Let the divine teachings God entrusted to you come alive. Become the man of great value you are called to be, a man who is respected, dignified, and endowed with spiritual authority. Lift your spirit above fleeting emotions, stop mourning a woman who is no longer yours, and let your actions reflect the divine wisdom entrusted to you. Protect your heritage, provide for your children, and stand firm as the pillar of your home, as God intended.

Men often spend more than women on household expenses, not because of luxury, but due to the greater responsibility God places on them. "But if anyone does not provide for his relatives, and especially for members of his household, he has denied the faith and is worse than an unbeliever." (1 Timothy 5:8).

This divine sense of duty calls for careful planning and the courage to make choices that may be unpopular with society but are right in God's eyes. Therefore, every high-value Christian man should consider legal measures such as prenuptial and postnuptial agreements to protect his God-given resources. This is not an act of distrust, but an act of stewardship. ***"The prudent sees danger and hides himself, but the naive who are easily misled go on and suffer for it." (Proverbs 27:12).***

These men's laws are designed to ensure that when a wife chooses to leave the marriage, she does so without unfairly taking what she hasn't contributed. At the same time, the husband remains committed to supporting his children faithfully.

If this principle feels uncomfortable, consider seeking out a trustworthy person, a loyal family member, or a spiritual advisor to help you manage and protect your assets in a way that honors God and preserves your legacy. Remember, God created you to lead and to manage. You are the sole manager, CEO, and director of your hard-earned wealth. ***"The Lord God took the man and placed him in the Garden of Eden to work it and guard it." (Genesis 2:15).***

Your intelligence and wisdom are gifts from God and should not be neglected or handed over unquestioningly. God trusts you to succeed in your exams and to provide for your family. However, if your wife no longer needs your protection, she should find other means of support, not at your expense.

Because biblically, she is no longer bound to you. Finally, consider the heartbreak of a Christian wife who, once devoted in worship and prayer, suddenly discovers she can achieve wealth by leaving her husband, claiming half his estate, lifetime alimony, and child support. What will the government do? They will uphold this secular system to destroy your life.

However, suppose you follow The Book of Men's Laws. In that case, she will leave without taking anything if she decides to go, thereby safeguarding your resources for the children that God has entrusted to you to oversee. ***"Therefore, be careful how you walk, not as unwise men, but as wise,*** *making the most of your time, because the days are evil." (Ephesians 5:15-16).*

The teachings of The Book of Men are divine. You are called to protect, provide, and lead with wisdom and courage, as this is the sacred duty bestowed by the Almighty government. As a Sunday school teacher for many years, I've had numerous Christian men, husbands, bachelors, and young men come to me with serious questions.

They ask why the Bible provides so many warnings to men about the times in which we live, especially regarding relationships and marriage. Why do the Scriptures, from the Lord's own words to the letters of the prophets and apostles, urge men to stay alert? Why are there so many warnings about women with impure intentions and laws that could strip a man of his wealth?

They ask, "Why are we told to be careful, even in marriage?" "How do I manage my finances to protect myself if a woman tries to take everything?" It's a serious concern, especially for older men who can no longer work or accumulate new wealth. What happens when a woman leaves and takes you to court, leaving you with nothing, or even owing her for the rest of your life? Being a Christian man doesn't mean being naive or vulnerable. God calls us to be wise as serpents and innocent as doves (Matthew 10:16). We are to walk in love, but not in ignorance.

This book is a call to wisdom. Please read it and share it with other men. Help them understand how to live by the biblical principles that preserve both their households and their peace.

Adam, our first father, placed too much trust without safeguarding what was given to him. A single moment of unguarded trust led to a tragic outcome. We should learn from his mistake. If a woman emotionally abandons her covenant and connects with another man, either physically or emotionally, she is no longer bound to you. She is no longer your responsibility.

These modern laws and cultural traps might be meant to weaken men, but Scripture provides us with the tools to stand firm. Protect your calling, your family, and your legacy. Don't let the train hit you while you're still waving a welcome flag. Guard what God has entrusted to you. Be generous, but not foolish. Love deeply, but lead wisely.

This divine chain of Laws from The Book of Men flows directly from God, through Christ, to the man, and finally to every household. 1 Corinthians 11:3 Jesus declares, "But I want you to understand that the head of every man is Christ, the head of a wife is her husband." This isn't oppression; it's order. God's authority structure is a shield for the family. The man is called to be the protector, the spiritual warrior, and the gatekeeper who watches over the souls of his wife and children.

Biblical scholars affirm that the role of the wife is just as important, but also different. Her divine responsibility and worth are in nurturing the children, maintaining the home, and respecting her husband's leadership. Titus 2:4-5 encourages older women to teach younger women to "love their husbands and children, to be self-controlled and pure, to be busy at home, to be kind, and to be subject to their husbands." This divine pattern reflects not societal preference but spiritual principle.

In the 20th century, it was the standard in both our communities and our churches. Young men and women had great respect, and even a particular fear, for our parents and leaders. If we weren't ready for marriage, we didn't dare express our romantic love. Was it like this for you when you were growing up? We'd love to hear your story. Please share it with us.

God's laws regarding husbands differ from those concerning wives. The husband must shoulder the heavier burden of spiritual responsibility. He is called to lead through sacrifice, courage, and self-denial. Just as Christ loved the church and gave himself up for her, husbands must give their lives daily for their wives and children (Ephesians 5:25).

Imagine a plane in trouble with only one parachute. Who would be the one to jump? It would be the mother, embodying the father's sacrificial love and serving as an example of love and sacrifice. He would instinctively step forward as a protector, guided by a divine sense of duty, willing to give his life if necessary. Authority laws highlight this kind of sacrifice; he is the first to wake up when danger threatens his family, the first to act as things start to unravel, and the first to pray when darkness descends. His leadership provides both safety and a heartfelt calling.

The Book of Men presents this metaphor: if humanity wants to test the equality of power between men and women, then let us build two new nations, one by men and the other by women, with equal resources and five years to complete their mission. History already provides the answer. While women have made significant contributions to modern progress, the physical demands and deadly risks of nation-building have primarily been borne by men.

Think of the men who built America's skyscrapers: steelworkers called "Skywalkers" who balanced on narrow beams high above the ground, wearing minimal ropes and belts. The Empire State Building and other engineering marvels were constructed under conditions that put their workers' lives at risk. These jobs were never denied to women; they were too dangerous for them. Men walked those beams because someone had to. Someone had to risk everything to build a civilization, both on land and underwater.

The Cu Chi tunnels in Vietnam, the trenches of World War I, the Golden Gate, and the Brooklyn bridges all demanded physical and mental endurance, costing many men their lives. Underground collapses, gas leaks, soaked feet, sniper fire; these were environments for the brave, not the fainthearted. Men went first. Men died first. Men stayed until the job was done.

This isn't about male superiority, but about God's divine design. Offshore oil rigs, nuclear power plants, mountain tunnels, and subway systems have long been constructed by men willing to risk everything. Today, thanks to advances in safety and technology, women are entering these fields. However, the historic burden of danger and responsibility will always be marked by male sacrifice.

Just as Noah built the ark above the waters of judgment (Genesis 6:14-22), men are called to build above the culture. They must rise in faith and prepare their families for what is to come. Noah built without applause, without understanding, without support, but his obedience saved generations. This is the burden of man: to create even when no one sees, to prepare even when no one believes.

Psalm 18:33 says, *"He makes my feet like those of a deer, and he sets me on the heights."*

God equips man to reach the heights of spiritual leadership. The heights are dangerous, but that is also where the view is clearest. Man must learn to live above the noise, see beyond temporary turbulence, and strive for what is eternal.

Men are often called to work in secret. Like Nehemiah rebuilding the wall, with one hand on a brick and the other on a sword (Nehemiah 4:17), modern men must work while staying alert. They need to build walls of emotional security, financial stability, and spiritual defense, all while watching for the enemy nearby. Their work is unseen but vital. Psalm 25:14 David says,

"The secret of the Lord is with those who fear Him."

A man who fears God will not treat his family casually. He will not lead solely by instinct, but by divine wisdom. He will pray in private and act when others remain paralyzed.

A wise woman does not challenge her husband's authority; she honors it. Ephesians 5:33 teaches women to respect their husbands, not because they are perfect, but because God commands it. When a woman respects these laws given to her by God, she does not lose her power; she activates divine protection over her home.

Isaiah 45:2 contains a promise for men who walk in divine order: "I will go before you and level the mountains; I will break down the bronze gates." God makes a way for men who take on the burden of leadership with righteousness. When a man leads in submission to Christ, nothing can prevent his family from walking in blessing.

Luke 12:48 reminds us, "From everyone who has been given much, much will be demanded." The husband has been given a family, his wife's trust, his children's eyes, and God's favor. These are not trophies but trials. Every father and husband must understand that his leadership is not optional but is ordained and established by the celestial law.

Ezekiel 22:30 states, "I looked for someone among them who would build up the wall and stand before me in the gap." God continues to search for gap-fillers, men who will stand between hell and their households. He is not looking for perfect men, but willing men, those who say, "I will take responsibility even when it costs me everything."

Psalm 119:105 declares, "Your word is a lamp to my feet and a light to my path." A true leader does not follow opinion but relies on revelation. The head of the household must lead, with God's Word as the lamp lighting the way. This isn't easy; it demands study, prayer, and spiritual growth.

However, it is the only way the family will reach its destination.

Nehemiah, a key leader in rebuilding Jerusalem's walls and governor of Judah, called on the men of God to rise and fight to protect their families. Nehemiah 4:14 concludes our charge: "Fight for your families, your sons and your daughters, your wives, and your homes." The battle is real. The call is urgent.

Men, rise and lead. The law of God is not a burden, but a blessing. When the man stands in his rightful place, all of heaven stands with him.

The Book of Men's Laws and a study on money and family

True wealth isn't measured by money but by obedience and discipline. A person who obeys the Lord's commands holds a treasure far greater than gold. *"Better is a little with righteousness than great gains without right" (Proverbs 16:8).*

For Christians, money isn't inherently bad; it can be a blessing when used responsibly. Scripture clearly states: "For the love of money is the root of all evil" (1 Timothy 6:10). Money is simply a tool and servant, not the master. The real risk is when money rules the heart, clouds judgment, or leads to sin. It is normal and even admirable to accumulate wealth for yourself, your family, and future generations. *"A good man leaveth an inheritance to his children's children" (Proverbs 13:22).*

Providing and planning are signs of godly stewardship. Still, your primary focus must stay on the Lord's Word regarding wealth. The purpose of money is not to gain status, pride, or comparison, but to provide, be generous, and serve God's Kingdom.

In today's culture, money is often used as a tool for competition. Many pursue wealth not for survival or legacy, but to compare themselves to others, even strangers. This rivalry can lead to bitterness in marriages, as some women and men judge their own worth by income or material possessions. Sometimes, spouses leave marriages simply because one is not "earning enough." This mindset overlooks the true purpose of marriage and goes against its biblical foundation.

God's Word warns us against such distortions. "Keep your lives free from the love of money and be content with what you have, because God has said, I will never leave thee, nor forsake thee" (Hebrews 13:5). Money cannot buy trust, loyalty, or love. A strong marriage rests on faith, respect, and unity, not on the balance of a bank account. When a man builds his home on obedience to the Lord, discipline in his responsibilities, and faithfulness in his marriage, he becomes wealthy, no matter the size of his paycheck.

Psalm 112:1–3:

"Blessed is the man that feareth the Lord, that delighteth greatly in his commandments. His seed shall be mighty upon earth: the generation of the upright shall be blessed. Wealth and riches shall be in his house: and his righteousness endureth forever."

Obedience to God is the inheritance of real millionaires, for they live in the abundance of his favor. The Law of Oneness. In marriage, husband and wife are no longer two separate lives, but one flesh, united in body, spirit, and purpose. *"Therefore, shall a man leave his father and his mother, and shall cleave unto his wife: and they shall be one flesh" (Genesis 2:24).*

Oneness is not only physical intimacy but a covenant that joins hearts, dreams, and callings. Where there is unity, God commands blessing (Psalm 133:1–3). A house divided cannot stand, but a house united will flourish under God's design. Therefore, a man shall leave his father and his mother and be united to his wife, and they shall become one flesh.

The Law of Love is the foundation of marriage. A husband is called to love his wife as Christ loved the Church, sacrificially, faithfully, and unconditionally (Ephesians 5:25). In return, a wife is encouraged to respect her husband, honoring his leadership and partnership. Love in marriage isn't just a passing emotion but a dedicated commitment. It's demonstrated daily through words, attitudes, and actions that build up rather than tear down. The Law of Faithfulness Marriage requires exclusive loyalty, physically, emotionally, and spiritually.

Hebrews 13:4: *"Marriage is honorable in all,* and *the bed undefiled: but whoremongers and adulterers God will judge".*

Faithfulness is more than avoiding betrayal; it is living in truth, speaking with gentleness, and practicing transparency. A faithful marriage guards the heart against secret affections and builds trust through openness and consistency.

The Law of Forgiveness

No marriage can survive without grace. To forgive is not weakness but strength, for it mirrors God's own love toward us. "And be ye kind one to another, tenderhearted, forgiving one another, even as God for Christ's sake hath forgiven you" (Ephesians 4:32). Forgiveness heals wounds, restores intimacy, and breaks the cycle of bitterness. Every husband and wife will fail one another at times, but a covenant thrives when grace is greater than offense.

The Law of Confidentiality

Marriage is a sacred agreement involving three parties:

Husband, wife, and the Lord. It is essential that what is kept within that circle remains protected. The challenges and secrets of a marriage should not be shared online, spread as gossip among friends, or given to family members. Proverbs 11:13: *"A gossip betrays a confidence, but a trustworthy person keeps a secret."*

Respecting privacy is a mark of honor and a valuable skill to cultivate. The foundation of a strong marriage is trust, and this trust is maintained when a couple's private matters are kept safe under God's protection. God created man first for a purpose. He is the Creator, the Master Builder, strong, wise, and sovereign over both the visible and invisible. When God formed man from the dust, He granted him authority, vision, and responsibility to build, protect, and lead. These divine laws are deliberate and not random.

When a woman leaves her marriage, she is not just departing from her husband; she is also abandoning the presence and protection that God intended for her. There is no ethical way for a woman to move from one man to another without experiencing profound spiritual and emotional consequences. Life is not a game of chess; every careless move endangers the soul.

Many men are becoming aware of this. The Book of Men sounds a loud alarm for the Christian community. They read these laws, and now we see the patterns clearly. If you have left your marital home and are knocking on our door, we are not fooled; we recognize the cycle. You are not seeking to rebuild yourself; you are after the next adrenaline rush, the next provider, the next fantasy of control. But religious-minded men, men of actual spiritual value, have learned not to play this game. We do not follow this path.

Too many women today exchange the lasting security of their homes for illusions; they chase after wealth, social status, and the fantasies promoted by social media, seeking men who don't exist. Some individuals become bitter, manipulative, or even self-destructive when reality fails to meet their expectations. Meanwhile, a line of fake suitors waits, men who tell them what they want to hear, play their game, and then disappear as soon as they've achieved their goal. They'll break the bridge of contact.

After a hundred cycles, the soul grows exhausted, the heart becomes numb, and life's engine begins to run low on oil. The vehicle halts, stranded in a desert of loneliness. Remember this: the sons of God do not take this path.

They read **The Book of Men** and gain understanding; they do not pursue broken promises and false hopes. Instead, they rebuild the foundations and stand firm. By wisdom a house is built, and by understanding it is established; by knowledge, the rooms are filled with all precious and pleasant riches. (Proverbs 24:3–4)

Once you leave your marriage, understand this: the door will shut behind you, and it will never reopen for you again. This covenant is no longer valid. We will move forward, building a new life with someone younger, wiser, more faithful, and more beautiful in spirit and truth, faster than the F-15 Eagle, United States Air Force.

Your rebellion will not be rewarded. We won't even wish you good luck because what you've chosen didn't come from God. When you reject the divine order, you cut off the flow of prayer, the voice guiding you, and the protection of the grace of a husband. Heaven does not respond to manipulation or disobedience.

The consequences are clear: without repentance and surrender, a divorced woman can find herself lost in a personal wilderness, wandering, searching, and struggling, yet never finding peace or purpose. Research in relationship psychology and marital restoration shows that a significant percentage of husbands who take back their wives after infidelity or emotional betrayal experience repeated abandonment and deeper emotional pain.

In many cases, the returning spouse continues to exhibit disrespectful or emotionally detached behavior, undermining the husband's dignity and reinforcing a destructive cycle. These results confirm what Scripture and wisdom literature often warn: reconciliation without transformation leads to further brokenness.

The Book of Proverbs, and by extension the "**laws of the Book of Men**," advise men to exercise discernment, not just emotion. Forgiveness is a Christian obligation, but restoration must be based on repentance, truth, and a willingness to rebuild, not on passivity or fear of loss.

When a woman breaks the marriage covenant, the door should be completely and automatically closed. It is not her place to seek reconciliation with remorse for her actions. In such cases, it may be necessary to release her from that role fully; she no longer bears the title or responsibilities of a wife. Otherwise, the husband risks losing his purpose, peace, dignity, and legacy in exchange for an illusion.

HEAVENLY CITIZEN

CHAPTER FOURTEEN

The Book of Men encourages Christian men to practice faithful stewardship of their Christian homes.

The Big Day and Beyond: Embracing the True Weight of Marriage as a husband. The big day has finally arrived. Whether you've already said, "**I do**," you're getting ready to walk down the aisle, or you're dating intentionally with a wedding in mind, that long-awaited moment has come, so what's next? After the excitement, the beautiful photos, and the joyful celebrations, it's time to face reality. A wedding isn't just a festive event, even if we've just celebrated it. It's a sacred covenant and a lifelong commitment. You've just told the world that you're choosing one person to share your life with forever.

As men, we must recognize the serious responsibility that comes with this joyful union. Becoming a husband means making a lifelong commitment not only to your wife but also to caring for your shared home. You, your wife, and "Mr. Bill" are now lifelong partners in handling financial responsibilities. Your wife is like your new home, your new car, and possibly the source of children - each a priceless blessing that brings new opportunities and responsibilities.

That's why, out of obedience to God, we should set aside some of our resources for emergencies and unexpected times. Many couples live as if each year will be smooth, predictable, and abundant. However, as a husband and future father, you're called to think ahead wisely. You must prepare for storms before they arrive, since the Scriptures say, "***The prudent see danger and take cover, but the simple press on and pay the price***" **(Proverbs 22:3).**

As husband and wife, we are no longer two; no more personal decisions. **The Book of Men said**, "*Two is better than one*". Our company has two CEOs, two managers, and the Lord's laws in mind as we plan together.

You are more than just the provider of daily needs. You are the architect of your family's long-term security. Your role extends far beyond making sure your wife has enough today; it involves building a solid foundation that will support her, your children, and even your grandchildren for generations to come. This great responsibility rests on your shoulders, and someday, you will stand before the Lord to give an account of how you protected what He entrusted to you.

"So then, each of us will give an account of ourselves to God" **(Romans 14:12).**

As a man, you must not approach the Word of God casually, as everyone else does. You are called to interpret each word as divine instruction; they are laws coming directly from the throne room of heaven, shaping you into the man, husband, and Father God designed you to be. Nothing God said should be taken lightly. *"Man shall not live by bread alone, but by every word that proceeds from the mouth of God"* **(Matthew 4:4).**

The book of men teaches us that "God's words are not just celestial mandates or occasional advice; they are divine laws and sacred commandments issued from the very counsel of His heavenly throne, approved by angels, and confirmed by the Holy Spirit. Who are you, then, to treat the Lord's Word lightly or to read it as if a casual friend had written it? It's a reminder to approach it with respect and reverence.

God despises ignorance and laziness. "How long will you lie there, you sluggard? When will you get up from your sleep?" (Proverbs 6:9). If you are lazy, irresponsible, and lack discipline, you will first neglect to read and follow God's laws, and then you will fail to work wisely and prepare for your household's safety. A person who refuses to grow in understanding and diligence cannot expect to protect what God has given him.

Therefore, for those of us who are responsible and high-value Christian men, those who obey God's laws and carefully study The Book of Men to protect ourselves and our families, we are walking the right path. The Lord watches over your every move, ready to answer your prayers and strengthen your hands to protect the goods and blessings He has given you. *"The eyes of the Lord are on the righteous, and His ears are attentive to their cry"* **(Psalm 34:15).**

No one should work tirelessly to build and protect their family only to leave the door open for someone to come in and take everything, leaving them empty-handed. If a household member chooses to go, they should take only what they have personally contributed, and nothing more. In the Book of Men's Laws, it is not acceptable for someone to decide to abandon the family and take the life and labor of the husband with them.

Consider Mr. Gabriel's story. Following two decades of marriage and the upbringing of two sons, his wife resolved that she desired greater opportunities, motivated by a network of self-described independent divorcees who persuaded her of her potential. Despite being older than him and facing limited prospects for a fresh start, she compelled Gabriel to vacate the residence, thereby imposing substantial responsibilities on him, including child support, alimony, and her own expenses.

For many years, **Gabriel bore these burdens until he ultimately understood the Word of God correctly**, recognizing it not as mere spiritual narratives but as divine statutes governing human conduct. He understood that God created man initially to serve as a guide and protector for humanity. *"For man did not come from woman, but woman from man; man was not created for woman, but woman for man" (1 Corinthians 11:8-9).*

When a man treats his wife with love, provides for his children, and diligently fulfils his responsibilities, he has no grounds for reproach before God. Upon this revelation, Gabriel realized it was time to act. He took the necessary steps to protect his remaining assets and prepared to leave for a place where his ex-wife, the government, or her lawyers could not seize what God had given him. All of this was possible because, during his marriage, he had already implemented the strategies and safety measures taught by The Book of Men's principles, safeguarding the family's future and making plans to move to a place where his ex-wife could not follow what God had blessed him.

Husbands must remember: your highest duty is to God first. By walking in obedience to His laws, leading with wisdom, and diligently preparing your household, you fulfill your role as a man. Ultimately, you will be rewarded with those treasured words: *"**Well done, good and faithful servant!**" (Matthew 25:23).*

God did not create man to be a passive observer in marriage. Initially, He assigned Adam the responsibility of cultivating and guarding the garden (Genesis 2:15). Similarly, He calls you to lead, protect, and nurture your home environment. You are the steward of every blessing God entrusts to you. A wise man understands that giving unrestricted access to all resources can lead to problems. If your wife mismanages finances and depletes the family's assets, it becomes your responsibility to rebuild and maintain stability. If she continues to mishandle resources or demands more to fulfill her desires, you might find yourself caught in a never-ending effort to meet rising demands.

This is why maintaining divine order and boundaries in financial stewardship is crucial. ***"Moreover, it is required of stewards that they be found faithful" (1 Corinthians 4:2).***

Faithfulness does not imply reckless generosity without accountability; instead, it involves safeguarding what God has entrusted to us, even from those we love, if doing so ensures the safety and well-being of the entire family.

A husband should lead his household wisely by saving for emergencies, investing for the future, and preparing for hard times. It's not just about comfort now but about ensuring survival in the long run. As Proverbs 6:6-8 advises, ***"Go to the ant, O sluggard; consider her ways, and be wise. Without having any chief, officer, or ruler, she prepares her bread in summer and gathers her food in harvest."***

Your primary goal is not to accumulate wealth and knowledge, but to be a faithful provider and protector. By practicing restraint and wise stewardship, you ensure your wife and children are not left vulnerable when hardships arise. Marriage is a joyful gift, but it is also a divine calling. It demands that a man think long-term and act selflessly. When you embrace this calling, God is pleased, and your family thrives.

Remember: you are more than just the man beside your wife. You are the shepherd of your home, the guardian of its resources, and the builder of its legacy. Walk faithfully, lead courageously, and steward diligently, for in the end, you will hear, "Well done, good and faithful servant".

The Book of Men Explains Why Marriage Is Hard

Marriage is not a fantasy. It is not a movie script or a fairy tale ending; it is real, raw, and often challenging. Instead of discussing the "qualities of a trustworthy spouse," we prefer to focus on the qualities needed to be a lifelong partner. The Book of Men states it plainly at times: marriage is a battlefield where love, growth, sacrifice, and sanctification connect. Faithful husbands understand this reality. Men who take the sacred role of husband seriously do not fool themselves into thinking marriage is always easy. They know it demands daily discipline, intentional love, and a heart grounded in the Word of God.

Real husbands understand that marriage isn't easier for their wives, either. They recognize the many sacrifices she makes, both mentally and emotionally, as well as physically and spiritually. She isn't just a helper; she's a warrior watching over the home, gracefully handling pressure. As husbands, we must see the heavy load she bears and support her with strength and compassion.

There is a dangerous and misleading narrative that men have an easy time in marriage. That's all we do: go to work and come home, while our wives suffer in silence, unsatisfied and invisible. But The Book of Men shatters this illusion. Real men are not blind to the burdens their wives carry. We see them. We understand them. We try to lighten them with small gestures: flowers, romantic evenings, unexpected kind words, thoughtful gifts, and our full attention when they need to talk.

It's not just about paying the bills and providing a roof over their heads. A godly husband aims to bring peace of mind, joy, consistency, and spiritual leadership. We want our wives and children to feel safe and loved, not just fed and clothed. We strive to be fully present, not only physically but also emotionally and spiritually.

Being a good wife is no easy task. We recognize that managing a home, raising children, and maintaining emotional availability are incredibly demanding. Protecting the house isn't just about locking the doors; it means maintaining spiritual peace, emotional balance, and a sense of belonging. A wise husband understands this and partners with her, not just to survive the marriage, but to thrive in it.

In marriage, even the tiniest things can spark disagreements, like a sudden summer storm crossing a peaceful sky. My wife and I have had our share of those moments, when a small spark leads to a heated debate. But when tensions rise, I've learned to pause in silence, look at her, and say,

"You're right, I'll do better." Not because I've lost a battle, but because I've chosen to win with love.

Early in our marriage, we silently agreed: never go to bed angry (Ephesians 4:26). This became our guiding rule. Regardless of the argument, we ensure that it is resolved before nightfall, ending each day in unity. At home, if there's a "winner" in an argument, it's usually her, not because she's more assertive or stubborn, but because her heart remains pure, and she never intends to hurt. I stay focused, shifting smoothly from one topic to another, and together, we both come out winners.

As a husband, I have learned that leading doesn't always mean having the last word. Sometimes leading means listening more carefully, responding more gently, or remaining silent, and choosing peace over pride. I find subtle and loving ways to make my point, not to dominate, but to contribute.

All while making sure she feels heard, seen, and valued. Because we are not on opposing sides; we are part of the same team, moving toward the same goal: to love well, grow together, and make our lives work as one. The family will remain peaceful and truly grounded until the cult of modern independence and self-idolatry among women sneaks in like a silent thief, sweeping us away with its tempting and chaotic ideology: "I don't need a man." We are ready to go.

When a husband and wife share the same spiritual, emotional, and aspirational goals, marriage becomes a potent force for good. This doesn't mean everything will always be smooth, but spiritual unity helps couples face challenges without sinking like the Titanic.

When there are no selfish motives and both serve each other in love and honesty, the family becomes unbreakable. *"Love is patient and kind; love does not envy or boast; it is not arrogant or rude. It does not insist on its way; it is not irritable or resentful; it does not rejoice at wrongdoing, but rejoices with the truth. Love bears all things, believes all things, hopes all things, endures all things."* **1 Corinthians 13:4–7**

Communication is the glue that holds a marriage together. It's not just about talking, but also about listening, understanding, and responding with patience and grace. We have learned that planning together, dreaming together, and resolving issues before they get worse make all the difference.

In The Book of Men, we are reminded, "Don't wait until the house is on fire to look for the hose; communicate before the situation gets out of control."

Marriage is not just a contract; it is a covenant. Jesus described it as sacred. He said, "What God has joined together, let no one separate" (Mark 10:9). The truth is, many things will try to divide us. Temptation, offenses, financial stress, health problems, and outside voices will all attempt to break the union. Jesus warned us because he knew that marriage faces constant challenges.

The Book of Men describes marriage as a close and committed bond between two people who choose to love, serve, forgive, and grow together every day. It is not a one-time vow but a daily choice. It is not about three people, family members, or friends, but just two: no parallel relationships, no other intentions. In good times and bad, whether emotionally, financially, or spiritually, we choose each other over and over again.

Illness in marriage is not just physical; it can also be emotional. It can also be emotional and spiritual, often manifesting during times of deep weariness. But these are precisely the moments that test the strength of a marriage, when we support each other. When we don't run away, when we choose to heal instead of hiding, a strong marriage says, "Even here, I will not leave you, and I promise to keep our secrets safe from everyone."

Meanwhile, the world has redefined the concept of marriage. The government has built an industry that tears families apart through divorce courts. It has replaced God's original plan for union with legal terms and paperwork, treating families like companies that can be dissolved at any time. It has even taken fathers out of the home with government checks, breaking down paternal authority, removing responsibility, and causing generations to suffer.

But God's Word remains the unchanging law for those who choose each other for the long journey that is life. The Book of Men encourages every man to understand what marriage truly is before committing himself. It is not about control or convenience. It is about Christ. It is about leading as Jesus did, through love, service, and sacrifice. Ephesians 5:25 makes it clear:

"Husbands, love your wives, just as Christ loved the church and gave himself up for her." This is no easy task. It is a sacred calling.

Marriage is more than a love story; it is a mission. It is a divine partnership created to fulfil God's plan. We are called to build together, raise godly children, and pass on a legacy of faith.

Genesis 1:28 is not just about multiplying, but also about being fruitful, making a spiritual impact, and reigning in your home.

A Christ-centered marriage is a form of discipleship. Two people are shaped together into the image of Christ. You refine each other through trials and forgiveness. You become each other's iron, sharpening, supporting, and strengthening one another.

Ecclesiastes 4:9-10 reminds us, *"**Two are better than one... If one falls, the other lifts his companion."** You are not enemies to each other; you are spiritual allies.*

Ultimately, marriage is challenging, but it is worthwhile. The Book of Men states that godly men must stop pretending it is easy or one-sided. We are called to love deeply, lead humbly, and fight honorably for our homes. With God at the center, prayer as the foundation, and mutual love as the approach, marriage becomes not only bearable but beautiful.

We don't just survive; we glorify. Together. Many men today have forgotten their divine role as leaders and stewards of the home. They enter marriage casually, often driven by emotions and infatuation, without a clear understanding of the sacred responsibility God has entrusted to them.

The Book of Men teaches that the word "LOVE" is Spiritual and emotional. Still, it must also be understood as a serious business exchange, especially in the modern world, where feelings are often confused with loyalty and long-term commitment. The English word "love" comes from the Old English "lufu," which has roots in ancient languages and meant

"To care for," "to desire," or "to cherish."

However, these meanings have been manipulated and distorted over time, particularly as romantic love, women began to dominate how people perceived marriage. Historically, marriage was not based on passion or emotions but on duty, responsibility, mutual interest, and a free choice of commitment. It was an alliance of accountability from one family to another; a social and economic arrangement protected by families and communities. This is why, in the past, many men did not simply "fall in love," but prepared themselves for love by preparing to lead, provide, and protect.

The Book of Men establishes that every man must approach love with wisdom, strategy, and boundaries. Love is not a fairy tale; it is a mental and emotional investment that involves real risks and genuine rewards. In a world where emotional manipulation is common and romantic ideals often overshadow divine wisdom, a man must learn to protect his heart without becoming heartless. This means recognizing different kinds of love: agape love, the divine and sacrificial love that seeks no reward; and philia love, the loyal love of friendship that fosters brotherhood among Christian men with strong values.

Eros love, the physical desire that must be governed by purity and purpose, includes passionate, romantic, or sexual love, as well as Storge love, the nurturing love of family, a bond between parents and children, or siblings. A godly man must never rely on love alone to sustain a home. Instead, he must discern the difference and build his house on the enduring, contractual love described in 1 Corinthians 13: a love that is patient, kind, and does not seek its own interests.

To protect himself from suffering, a man must see love as a covenant with clear roles, a business deal, a spiritual duty, and proven worthiness. He must move away from treating relationships as impulsive emotional adventures and instead view them as a God-ordained mission. This involves setting standards, seeking the fruits of the Spirit in a woman's life, and consulting wise people before making a lifelong commitment.

The modern world has turned love into a gamble, but The Book of Men declares it a divine law where discipline, management, and honor build a home. If love is a business, then man is its manager, not to exploit it, but to safeguard its sacred value. When a man adopts this mindset, he minimizes emotional damage, avoids foolish relationships, and becomes a fortress of strength, capable of loving deeply without losing himself.

Love is not enough to sustain a household on its own. It is only the foundation, but without the structural pillars of leadership, accountability, and spiritual guidance, the home cannot stand firm. A man must not only love his wife but also lead her with wisdom, protect her with strength, and guide the family in truth and righteousness. This is not about pride or dominance, but about divine laws and purpose.

In earlier generations, especially in the 19th century, marriage was treated with respect and careful planning. It was based on community, tradition, and family honor, not on fleeting feelings or digital swipes. A young man couldn't just pursue a woman on his own. He had to first communicate his intention to marry to his parents and, through them, formally approach the woman's family. This process fostered respect, seriousness, and a sense of responsibility. The two families would meet, not only to arrange a marriage but to build a strong foundation of mutual commitment and support for the new couple. Back then, people often married within familiar circles, having grown up together or maintained long-standing family ties.

Divorce was uncommon, not because people didn't face problems, but because the community, friends, relatives, neighbors, and elders were deeply committed to preserving the sacred bond of marriage. A family was not left to handle its own difficulties. All members of the village, neighborhood, or church felt a sense of responsibility for the well-being of the couple and their children. Corrections were not left solely to parents. Elders could step in to discipline, guide, or support children who went astray. Teachers enforced strict moral standards, and community discipline was regarded as an expression of love. It was a collective effort to maintain justice, order, and stability.

Today, this divine system has been dismantled. Governments and modern ideologies have intervened to redefine the family, discipline, and authority. Now, what used to be considered loving correction is treated as abuse. What used to be godly laws is now labelled as oppression. The government profits from broken homes through court systems, child services, and the growing dependence on state programs.

In contrast, the sacred laws of heaven for the family structure are dismissed. Children are raised without correction, marriages collapse under pressure, and men abandon their posts as spiritual leaders. Unless we return to God's original blueprint for manhood and family, society will continue to drift deeper into disorder, and the light of strong, godly homes will grow dimmer.

Ephesians 5:23 Paul said, "For the husband is the head of the wife as Christ is the head of the church, his body, of which he is the Savior." It is a call to sacrificial leadership and humble service. When a man neglects his role, chaos follows. The home turns into a battleground instead of a sanctuary. Many men wrongly think that providing money is enough. But leadership is not just about financial support; it includes spiritual protection, emotional support, and setting a moral example.

As a divorced Christian man, I learned this lesson the hard way. I once believed that giving everything materially would guarantee love forever. I thought loyalty could be bought with comfort. But comfort without a spiritual foundation is like a house built on sand. Proverbs 4:23 King Solomon told all men: *"Above all else, guard your heart, for everything you do flows from it."* Men, if we do not guard our hearts, we leave our homes vulnerable to the enemy. We cannot lead others if we are lost and broken.

In marriage, a man's leadership must be firm yet tender, wise yet accessible, protective yet nurturing. This is not something the world teaches, but it is what the laws of God require. Many modern men fall into the trap of passivity. They let their wives make all the decisions, from financial matters to spiritual guidance. Over time, this passive spirit causes the man to lose his importance in his wife's eyes.

A woman may initially appreciate control, but deep down she longs for a man who stands firm in his convictions, who says "no" when necessary, and who leads her closer to God. When she no longer sees you as her leader, disrespect begins to emerge. Once disrespect starts, intimacy decreases. As intimacy declines, her heart begins to wander, seeking someone else. Brother, understand that love and respect go hand in hand.

Ephesians 5:33 says, *"Each one of you must love his wife as he loves himself, and the wife must respect her husband."*

If she starts to see you as a weak man, she will begin testing your limits. She may question every gift, decision, and expense. Suddenly, you find yourself defending every small action, and you wonder what happened to the sweet woman you married.

That is why The Book of Men teaches that you must always stay in control of your direction and your mind. You are the captain of the ship; she can advise you and make suggestions, but the final decision rests with you under God's authority.

A wise man, like Solomon, knows when to listen and when to act decisively. "The simple believe everything, but the prudent consider their steps." Proverbs 14:15.

If you lead as God commands, you are not oppressive but strong, not tyrannical but protective. There is a difference between leading through fear and leading through love and conviction. You must also protect your financial situation.

Gabriel's father taught these laws to his boys in this way: Just as you pay your taxes without question, you must also set aside resources for your future security, out of sight and out of reach of any temporary storm.

This is the law of men; it's not greed, but wisdom. It's about ensuring that when trials come, and they will come, you will remain standing. Your mission as a man is not to become a slave to your circumstances but to stay steadfast in all seasons. As a Christian, your strength is your testimony.

When others fail, you stand firm. When others panic, you pray. When others give up, you keep going. Stand firm, my brother. "Be on your guard; stand firm in the faith; be courageous; be strong." 1 Corinthians 16:13. This is the first law of the Book of Men: lead as God leads you. Be on your guard; stand firm in the faith; be courageous; be strong.

HEAVENLY CITIZEN

CHAPTER FIFTEEN

The Cost of Blind Love, before you said "I do"

The Law of Strength and Leadership for Christian Men

I once believed I had found my forever partner. I genuinely thought love was enough. I assumed that love, with all its emotion and beauty, could overcome any trial or betrayal. But I learned the hard way that love without wisdom is vulnerable; it can be manipulated, misunderstood, and ultimately lost.

I was lazy and didn't study the principles of the Lord's laws. I failed and took responsibility, but it was too late. I was convinced that giving everything I had, my time, comfort, protection, and money, would guarantee loyalty. I believed that sacrifice alone was enough to preserve the covenant. However, the truth is that I wasn't properly educated about love, and when it became a commercial transaction, I remained blind to it. When love becomes one-sided, it leaves a person broken, questioning everything they once stood for.

The prophet Jeremiah knew what men today often ignore: "The heart is deceitful above all things and beyond cure. Who can understand it?" (Jeremiah 17:9).

Even as men made in the image of God, our hearts can deceive us. My own heart fooled me into thinking that because I was good to her, she would stay.

That was because I worked, served, and sacrificed; she would be grateful. However, I missed something critical: women are wired to seek emotional security first. Her instinct is not evil; it's her design. She needs a clear destination. She wanted the assurance that you are winning, not just trying. If you can't prove to her that you are the man who can take her to a better future, she will walk emotionally first, then physically.

Brother, understand this law: no woman is meant to suffer unthinkingly in the name of love. She may admire your strength, but if she sees no victory ahead, no plan, no leadership, she will start to disconnect, just like your cable bill, if you don't pay on time. And in today's world, she will be overwhelmed with advice from broken women, a fallen culture, and social media telling her to "do what makes her happy."

She will look for reasons to leave, whether justified or not. You may wake up one day and realize that she has already left emotionally, even if she's still sleeping next to you. You will wonder how someone you loved could have become so distant, so cold, so confident in her right to everything you've built, and yet so quick to walk away. Now, the lawyers are coming for you.

That's why I'm urging you: don't wait until your heart is broken to pieces before waking up. You must share The Book of

Men with other men; it was not meant to entertain or impress you. Real life is at stake. Gabriel speaks from the heart and experience, as a man of God, honestly and without emotion. These laws are the most vital teachings heaven can reveal to you, designed to open your eyes and motivate you to take care of yourself now. When a woman takes all your time, energy, compassion, and money, then demands more while your soul is empty, what will you do? Many men give until they are hollow.

Then she abandons him, acts like he never existed, and walks away without remorse. Don't say this won't happen to you.

The facts are clear: 50% of men face social isolation after divorce, 67% never seek help, and 15.3% become homeless. These aren't strangers; they're your brothers, your friends, maybe even your future.

These Laws of Men are more than just ideas; they are spiritual safeguards for your heart, mind, and future. They exist to prepare you, not to frighten you. They are God's way of whispering to you, "Son, pay attention. I am here. I see what's coming your way. Stay close to my laws. Guard your heart." Because once you lose everything, you may never get a second chance.

If your wife becomes unfaithful, it's essential to know the steps to take. What advice would you give another man who asks for your help? Would you tell him to trust her again while she's still emotionally connected to the person who betrayed your marriage? If she refuses to cut ties with him, or if she has crossed that line before, there is a **very high 99.99%** chance she will do it again. This isn't said out of bitterness but from a position of realism. It's not just something that happened to some random brother; it could happen to any of us. Are you married? Do you have a wife at home to care for?

Then understand this: none of us is immune. No man is safe from betrayal. We are all vulnerable to heartbreak if we ignore the warnings, overlook the patterns, or think we're too virtuous to fall into them. This isn't just their story; it could just as easily become yours.

So, I ask you, brother: if God, sitting on His throne in glory, tells you to guard your heart, why do you keep believing, "It could never happen to me"? Why do we ignore the warnings of the Holy Spirit until our hearts are bleeding out? The devil doesn't just attack with bullets to make you cry; he breaks men down with seduction, betrayal, and confusion. That's why this book exists: to warn you, to awaken you, to remind you that you are not above heartbreak. You are not above being broken. But you can be prepared. You can build with wisdom. You can walk with clarity.

And you can protect your soul before it's too late.

Mr. Gabriel's father's wisdom echoes: If you meet a woman with nothing and give her a bicycle, she will ask for a motorcycle. Give her a car, and soon she will demand a specific brand. Give her the brand, and she will want the latest model next. You cannot fill a bottomless cup with worldly gifts. Her steadfast loyalty must be built on your unwavering leadership and her fear of the Lord. Proverbs 31:30 reminds us, "Charm is deceptive, and beauty is fleeting; but a woman who fears the Lord is to be praised."

Solomon teaches men this: "Outward charm can mislead, and physical beauty does not last; but a woman who honors and reveres the Lord deserves true praise." This idea emphasizes the timeless importance of reverence for God over outside appearances. Still, today, it's becoming rarer to find women who genuinely show a deep spiritual fear of the Lord, even within church communities. Many young women who attend church often imitate secular fashion and trends, dressing more like they're heading to a nightclub than to worship. Makeup, flashy clothes, and a focus on outward beauty have replaced the emphasis on inner purity and humility. This cultural shift reflects a broader move away from spiritual priorities toward superficial approval.

A significant factor behind this trend is the widespread influence of social media platforms like Instagram and TikTok, which promote self-promotion and comparison, fostering a culture rooted in vanity and immediate gratification. I once asked a friend to help me find my name or that of my children online to see if any information or pictures could be found, but they were unsuccessful.

This shows that, unless you are a close family member or a real acquaintance, there is no basis for judging or assuming anything about us. If you genuinely want to connect with us, we would be delighted to invite you to our home so we can meet in person. We value our privacy highly, and we keep it protected. Only the Holy Spirit has the proper authority to observe and oversee every part of our family's life without doubt.

According to a 2021 Pew Research Center study, 84% of women aged 18–29 in the U.S. report using at least one social media platform daily. The constant need for likes, followers, and attention has replaced quiet devotion and personal reflection. Instead of seeking God's approval, many women now seek the approval of an ever-watching digital audience.

They no longer have much time to pray. This environment makes it difficult for women to cultivate the fear of the Lord, a virtue that requires solitude, humility, and introspection.

This spiritual erosion aligns with broader demographic and economic trends. A 2019 Morgan Stanley report predicted that 45% of "prime working age" women (ages 25–44) in the U.S. would be single and childless by 2030, creating what it called the "singleton economy." In countries like Germany and Japan, 30– 40% of women born in the 1970s and 1980s are expected to remain childless.

North American projections suggest that 35–45% of women aged 25–45 may remain unmarried and childless by 2030. The root causes include economic independence, higher education, and shifting societal values. Women now prioritize their careers, personal growth, and financial gains over marriage and motherhood, viewing these traditional roles as limiting rather than fulfilling.

Regret often sets in when it's already too late. Many women today focus so heavily on earning degrees and advancing their careers, but by the time they want to get married, it may be too late to start a family. Time doesn't wait for anyone. In contrast, many African families place a strong cultural emphasis on marriage between the ages of 20 and 30.

Whether the young woman is studying or not, parents are actively involved in helping her find a suitable husband and encouraging her to settle down and start a family. Out of respect for their parents, these women often choose to marry with the guidance and blessing of both families. This thoughtful, community-focused approach helps create strong, lasting marriages and dramatically lowers the risk of divorce, sometimes leading to almost zero divorce rates within these communities.

University studies also show that many women cite a desire for peace and freedom as a primary reason for staying single. Research from Harvard University's Institute for Quantitative Social Science indicates that modern women often fear being controlled or losing their independence in marriage. This mistrust, along with stories of emotional manipulation and control in some marriages, pushes them toward independence. The modern focus on self-care and self-sufficiency has reinforced this mindset. As a result, fewer women are willing to submit to their husband's leadership, a biblical principle that is often misunderstood and rejected in today's society.

On the other hand, many men have become increasingly cautious about marriage. Studies consistently show that 70–80% of divorces are initiated by women (American Sociological Association, 2015). In Western societies, especially in America, divorce laws can place heavy financial burdens on men, including alimony, child support, and loss of assets. Not to mention that all the men's hard work and years of labor are at risk.

The University of Michigan's Institute for Social Research found that many men now see marriage as a high-risk venture. Stories of men losing homes, retirement savings, and even relationships with their children fuel this fear. As a result, men are less likely to pursue marriage, particularly with partners perceived as highly independent or career-focused.

Many men today are opting to leave their home countries in search of more traditional wives with fewer problematic backgrounds. Some 12-20% of marriages in the U.S. now involve a foreign-born woman, a trend that is growing. In 2023 alone, about 1.5 million Americans married someone they met through a "mail-order bride" or similar international service.

About 85% of these international marriages involve American men and women from Asia or Latin America. The most common countries for these brides are the Philippines, Russia, Thailand, and Ukraine, where traditional family roles are still highly valued.

An increasing number of these men identify as "Passport brothers," meaning men who deliberately travel or even settle abroad to find wives who embrace a more family-oriented, feminine, and cooperative approach to marriage. For these men, the appeal lies not just in cultural differences but also in lower living costs and a desire for a more peaceful and supportive relationship.

In Europe and East Asia, similar trends are even more noticeable. In Japan and South Korea, for instance, extremely low birth rates indicate a wider societal move away from traditional family structures. Over 40–50% of women in some age groups may stay unmarried and childless. Many of these women have adopted a "lifestyle as a business" approach, investing in travel, wellness, personal branding, and entrepreneurship rather than prioritizing family life. In many urban and wealthy communities, being single and child-free is no longer stigmatized but celebrated. This societal shift profoundly challenges traditional biblical notions of marriage, family, and community responsibility.

From a biblical perspective, masculinity and marriage are not merely social constructs in God's view, but divine callings. Ephesians 5:25 instructs husbands to "love their wives, just as Christ loved the church and gave himself up for her." This sacrificial love calls men to be strong spiritual leaders and protectors, roles that become harder to fulfill as traditional family structures decline.

Likewise, women are called to respect and submit to their husbands (Ephesians 5:22), a concept often misunderstood and misjudged today. As society moves farther from these biblical principles, men and women find themselves isolated and spiritually lost. While the modern emphasis on independence over interdependence may seem freeing, it also risks disconnecting people from the blessings and growth that come from a God-centered family life.

Many men say, "*My wife is different. She is loyal. She would never leave me.*" But trusting without proof and loving without discernment can lead to heartbreak. When sickness comes, will she see you as a burden or as someone to show sacrificial love? When money runs out, will she hold your hand or look for another's promise? The Book of Men teaches that security must be established not only in the wallet, but in the spirit. You must be a fortress: kind, loving, but impossible to conquer by manipulation or deceit.

You must also prepare for the unexpected. Like

Gabriel's father said, "If the government raises taxes, you pay them. So must you tax yourself to secure your future." This means setting aside your reserves before sharing the rest. Not to deprive her, but to ensure your survival. Because a man who is financially broken is easily crushed spiritually, is this selfish? No. It is wisdom. It is stewardship. It is protecting what God entrusted to you. It's a rainy day for you and your family; it's started to rain now. If you have a job, please call HR immediately.

If you own a business, please contact your lawyer or bank immediately.

The Law of Leadership for Christian Men

As a Christian man, you are called to be a pillar of strength and leadership in your relationship. The one who should be stronger is not you. God has designed you to stand firm in faith, carrying the weight of responsibility with courage and humility. You are not meant to be insecure, needy, or constantly seeking emotional validation from your partner. A man grounded in Christ knows that his worth and identity come from the Lord alone, not from a woman's approval.

In moments of doubt or discouragement, remember Psalm 1:3, which describes a righteous man as a tree planted by streams of water, yielding fruit in its season, with leaves that never wither, and who prospers in all they do. Your roots must be deep in God's laws so you can withstand the storms of life without becoming fragile or dependent. Isaiah 40:31 says, "***But those who hope in the Lord will renew their strength. They will soar on wings like eagles; they will run and not grow weary; they will walk and not be faint."***

As a Christian man, you are called to be an eagle, not a caged bird. An eagle soars high above the noise and distractions of the world and the storms, guided by the unseen currents of the Spirit. You must rise above petty arguments, manipulations, and emotional games of women. You are to be steadfast, wise, and discerning, never allowing yourself to be reduced to a passive, defeated spirit. Your strength is not brute force alone but is founded on a quiet, unwavering confidence in God's promises and direction for your life.

The law of The Book of Men, taught by Gabriel, states that a man must guard his heart above all else, as Proverbs 4:23 commands: ***"Above all else, guard your heart, for everything you do flows from it."*** When a man becomes emotionally dependent on his partner, he risks losing his spiritual vision and leadership.

A Christian man must be secure enough to lead with love and authority, yet tender enough to serve and care for others. Your emotional stability reflects your spiritual maturity. If you seek constant reassurance from your partner, you give away the leadership mantle God has entrusted to you. Instead, let your confidence be anchored in Christ, so that your love becomes a source of strength for your family, rather than a burden.

Finally, ***The Book of Men teaches*** that all men must embody Christ-like love, which is firm, sacrificial, and steadfast. "Husbands, love your wives, just as Christ loved the church." This does not mean becoming weak or subservient, but loving from a place of authority and strength. Christ was never needy or insecure; He was the ultimate example of unwavering purpose and identity. As a man, you must model this same confidence and selflessness, ensuring you remain the protector and guide God has called you to be. When you stand firm in your faith, you allow your partner to embrace her God-given femininity, creating a relationship where both partners can thrive in their divine roles.

A man's strength isn't shown by loudness or control, but by the quiet, steady spirit that won't bow to insecurity and fear. Remember Joshua 1:9: "Have I not commanded you? Be strong and courageous. Do not be afraid; do not be discouraged, for the Lord your God will be with you wherever you go." God's presence gives you the power to lead boldly, to protect gently, and to love faithfully. You're not meant to be controlled by emotion or circumstances, but to rise above, soar like the eagle God designed you to be. In this way, you fulfil your divine purpose and set a godly example for your children.

When she starts controlling all spending, questioning every gift, and undermining your decisions, it's a sign: Your leadership has been compromised. You must never apologize for exercising your God-given authority, not with arrogance, but with quiet confidence.

Throughout Scripture, God often uses specific laws and legislative texts to communicate profound spiritual truths to His people, more specifically to men. These Laws are not just figures of speech; they reveal the mind and heart of the

Creator in ways that simple instructions cannot. Prophet Isaiah 64:8, God says, "**But you, Lord, are our Father. We are the clay; you are the potter; we are all the work of your hands.** "Women today may think that they want independence, freedom, and happiness; however, because men were created first and we have received our instruction directly from the Lord Himself, you may travel all over the world asking men the same question: 'Are you depending on anyone? Would you want to be independent"?

God is the potter who shapes, Molds, and refines our lives according to His divine purpose. Just as clay cannot shape itself, we cannot guide ourselves without God's guiding hand. Every single man will answer: apart from God, we are nothing, nothing (John 15:5).

This principle shows that God's Spirit operates with a clear purpose; every part of our lives, whether trials or blessings, is part of His careful shaping of our character. Another powerful law is the vine and branches in:

John 15:5, where Jesus says, "*I am the vine; you are the branches. If you remain in me and I in you, you will bear much fruit; apart from me you can do nothing.*"

Here, God reveals His way of thinking as one of perfect unity, and all people depend on Him. The branches can't bear fruit without getting their life from the vine, just as we can't produce real spiritual fruit without staying connected to Christ. Jesus shows us that God's ultimate goal is relationship and connection, not just performance or rituals. God's Spirit focuses on nourishing us with heavenly instructions so that we bear fruit that honors Him and blesses others, demonstrating His relational and life-giving lessons to those who want to learn.

Don't be surprised that many Christians have never truly read the Bible for themselves, not out of disbelief, but because they were never taught to approach it with curiosity, intention, and reverence.

When you fail to read even the simplest commandment, to understand God's laws and how He wants to guide you and your family, you're not ignorant or incapable. Maybe no one ever told you to read Scripture as if your life, your future, and your legacy depended on it.

God's laws are not just stories; they are divine principles, directly from God's throne, meant to guide you to the right doors, bring healing, promote peace, and open the way to blessings through His grace. Now that you are reading The Book of Men, understand this clearly: the Bible is God's law from heaven to you. Nothing is more important than reading it intentionally, seeking daily the message God has prepared, uniquely and personally, for your soul. God, as a Shepherd, offers a deep view into His heart and character.

In Psalm 23:1, David confidently says, *"The Lord is my shepherd; I shall not want."*

This isn't just poetic language; it's a reflection of faithful obedience and faith. The image of a shepherd shows a leader who is kind and protective, always watching over His Flock with His omnipresence. God chose David over Saul because of his sincere heart and deep knowledge of the Lord. After humble beginnings as a shepherd, he conquered Jerusalem and made it the capital of Israel. Jerusalem has remained the capital of Israel to this day. King David, known as a man after God's own heart (Acts 13:22),

David's legacy endures not only through his leadership but also through his lineage, as he became the forefather of Jesus.

Christ (Matthew 1:1; Luke 1:32), the promised Messiah. He said, **"THIS"** **"O Lord, you have searched me and known me! You know when I sit down and when I rise; you discern my thoughts from afar. You search out my path and my lying down and are acquainted with all my ways. "Psalm 139:1–3**

He guides His sheep to lush pastures, beside quiet waters, and remains near, even in the darkest valleys. God's role as a Shepherd means He is never absent. He stays involved in our lives, guiding us, providing for our needs, and protecting us. This reminds us that His leadership is rooted in compassion and care, that He controls all the dark forces, winds, and storms that come our way.

The Holy Spirit is here beside you and your family. The Shepherd's care is not passive; it is vigilant. God watches over us even when we are unaware of it. He sees invisible dangers, feels our silent struggles, and gently guides us away from harm. His Spirit does not just comfort us in our weakness; it strengthens us with holy confidence. God's leadership is different from the world's. His strength includes tenderness, his authority involves sacrifice, and his power is wrapped in patience. He knows each person by name, and when you cry out in confusion or pain, he listens, not as a distant ruler, but as your Father and Defender.

Jesus assured this same closeness through the Holy Spirit. ***"But the Helper, the Holy Spirit, whom the Father will send in my name, He will teach you all things and bring to your remembrance all that I have said to you." (John 14:26).***

The Spirit of God is both a teacher and a reminder of truth. When no one else understands your pain or you're too ashamed to speak it out loud, the Spirit intercedes with wisdom, comfort, and clarity. Even if your soul is too weary to pray, the Holy Spirit groans on your behalf (Romans 8:26). He speaks to your spirit, leads you through confusion, and tells your heart what to do when your mind can't figure it out.

Revelation 2:7: ***"He who has an ear, let him hear what the*** Spirit ***says to the churches."***

Brother, if you're a Christian man quietly bearing the weight of betrayal, brokenness, or emotional wilderness, God sees you. Maybe you know your wife is stepping outside the covenant of marriage, and you're too ashamed to tell anyone. But it's not your burden to carry alone, and it's not your fault. Your character, dignity, and spiritual calling all hold great significance in God's eyes. You deserve the truth. You deserve healing. And you are not alone. The Spirit is whispering even now, speaking into your pain, calling you to trust in God's justice and mercy.

Brother Gabriel has travelled through the same wilderness. He knows what it feels like to be at your lowest, broken, disappointed, misunderstood. But even in those depths, he never thought of ending his life because he remembered that.

Apostle Paul was also there, crying out in his darkest moment: "Lord, take this thorn from me." Yet, Paul endured. He stayed the course because no matter how deep the pain, God's presence is deeper still. You are not forgotten. If you are breathing, there is still purpose.

The Book of Men was written for such a time as this, to give you the truth, unfiltered, as a man of God. This moment, when you're at a breaking point, is not the end. It's the proving ground of your faith. The Holy Spirit isn't just comforting you; He's calling you to action. He's telling you that what you decide today will have an impact on your future. Find a quiet place, such as your prayer closet, the woods, or your car, and cry out to God.

Scream, weep, worship. Pour out your heart.

Let the spirit minister to you. "He is seated on the throne," watching you with eyes of fire and love. He holds the keys to your breakthrough. Nothing and no one can stand between you and your God unless you permit it. **Jesus said, "You shall love the Lord your God with all your heart, with all your soul, and with all your mind." (Matthew 22:37-38).**

That kind of love is complete; it leaves no part of your life untouched. Even when you're in the fire, remember: "Our God is a consuming fire." (Hebrews 12:29). Fire refines; it does not destroy those who belong to Him. And like Job, you can declare with holy confidence: "For I know that my Redeemer lives, and at the last He will stand upon the earth." (Job 19:25). No servant of God suffers in vain. Your story, wounds, and wilderness, God will redeem them all with twice as much, just as He did for your brother Gabriel.

It might be difficult for a while. The pain feels real. The thoughts are loud in your mind. But you will be fine, because the Lord will never abandon you. "Be strong and courageous. Do not be afraid or dread them, for it is the Lord your God who goes with you. He will neither leave you nor forsake you." (Deuteronomy 31:6). Just as He told Moses: *"I will never leave you nor forsake you." (Hebrews 13:5).*

That promise still belongs to you. So, stand firm, man of God. Embrace the fire, worship in the valley, cry during the storm, and trust that the Shepherd walks with you. And He always brings His children home. ***When***

Jesus calls us "the light of the world" in Matthew 5:14, He commissions us to illuminate a dark world.

This principle reveals God's strategic and redemptive plan for humanity. God created light on the first day (Genesis 1:3), demonstrating that his first act was to make man in His own image, reflecting His knowledge and understanding as He overcame darkness and established order. When He calls us light, He invites us to join Him in His creative and restorative work. This principle from His throne shows that God is not willing to leave the world as it is. He desires transformation and renewal. As lights, we reflect His glory and serve as agents of His redemptive plan.

Finally, when comparing believers to eagles, as in Isaiah 40:31 ("***They will soar on wings like eagles***"), God reveals His desire for His people to experience freedom and spiritual elevation. The eagle soars above storms and perceives everything on earth and beneath the surface from great heights, symbolizing spiritual insight and strength.

When life feels delayed, uncertain, or heavy, we are reminded that our strength doesn't have to come from ourselves alone. True strength is found in God, the limitless source. Instead of rushing ahead or forcing results, we are called to trust in His timing and to find hope and patience in His promises.

Just as an eagle soars above the storm with ease, those who rest in God's guidance will rise above fear, burnout, and disappointment. "They shall renew their strength" applies to all who wait with faith, not only for personal breakthroughs, but also for healing, restoration, and unity within their families. God's timing is always perfect, and when we trust Him, even the toughest seasons can become foundations of peace, wisdom, and purpose.

God does not want His children to live in fear, sin, or the opinions of others. His goal is to lift us above worldly distractions, so we can see His perspective and live in accordance with His purpose. By establishing these laws, God invites us to understand His mind through intentional, relational, compassionate, redemptive, and empowering critical thinking.

When you lead in this way, your heart stays guarded, your home remains peaceful, and your soul stays connected to God's purpose. Remember, brother:

"He who walks with the wise grows wise, but a companion of fools suffers harm." Proverbs 13:20. Choose wisdom in love.

HEAVENLY CITIZEN

CHAPTER SIXTEEN

The Silent Thief
How Time Steals Manhood in Plain Sight, and What You Must Do Before It's Too Late.

Time is the only resource the richest person cannot buy back. You think you have plenty of it, so you wait. You wait for the perfect woman, the perfect career, the perfect moment, and a big bank account. You assume you will have time to sort things out later, to mature, to get serious, to settle down finally. But one day, you wake up and realize that four decades have slipped away. Like steam, your youth has vanished, and you barely noticed the passage of time.

Proverbs 27:1 warns us: *"Do not boast about tomorrow, for you do not know what a day may bring." And yet, many men live as if the future were guaranteed.*

This message isn't just about love or missed opportunities; it's about reality. You kept believing that your moment would come sooner or later. Perhaps you were afraid, perhaps you were too demanding, or maybe you were too focused on finding something better. But while you waited, life moved forward. Your friends got married. They had children. They built their lives. And you? You told yourself that you were "just taking your time." You were "*being wise*." But wisdom, my brother, isn't proven only by waiting; it's proven by discernment and decision-making.

In many cultures, especially outside North America, family pressure grows when a man remains single after a certain age. Your parents start questioning what's wrong. Your aunts, uncles, and siblings ask you awkward questions.

"Is everything okay?" "**What are you waiting for?**" Don't you want to start a family?" And while you nod and smile politely, you feel a sense of inner tension. You know what they mean. Deep down, you realize you've been avoiding something, whether it's commitment, vulnerability, or simply growing up.

Maybe you have high standards. That's fine, but standards are no excuse for emotional isolation. You didn't want to date someone whose values didn't match yours. You wanted someone pure, beautiful, feminine, respectful, and grounded in faith. And that's legitimate. But in avoiding the wrong people, did you also ignore the right ones? You protected yourself so well that no one could enter your life, even those who sincerely loved you.

And now, your most fertile period has passed, and the possibilities for meeting someone have changed without you even realizing it.

Let's be honest: sometimes we have to face the reality that opportunities have slipped away. If you've missed your chance before, now is the time to seize it and take the necessary steps forward. Stop waiting endlessly for the "perfect" person or the ideal situation. If someone suitable is already around you, open your eyes and heart to recognize them. If it means traveling or making sacrifices to meet someone, do it. Not just for yourself, but to fulfill the Lord's commandment to be fruitful and multiply (Genesis 1:28).

You will multiply your happiness by sharing love with someone, by traveling, by walking in the park, or by simply having companionship. The Lord has created approximately 8.24 billion people on this planet. With such a large number, it's unrealistic to think that no one is suitable to live with you, marry you, or share life with you. The issue isn't that God has failed to provide; it's often that our own hearts, our pride, unrealistic expectations, or reluctance to act are the real obstacles.

Proverbs 18:22: *Scripture reminds us: "He who finds a wife finds what is good and receives favor from the Lord."*

Finding a spouse is not about waiting passively but about actively seeking with wisdom, prayer, and humility. If you desire marriage, you must act in faith and take steps toward it. Stop saying, "There is no one for me," and instead believe that among God's children, there is someone with whom you can become one flesh (Genesis 2:24), living together in love, respect, and covenant.

Marriage is not centered solely on perfection, but on obedience. It involves two imperfect individuals coming together under God's divine plan to exemplify His love, establish a family, and create a legacy. You are capable of accomplishing this. Proceed with faith, trust in God's provision, and take decisive action. Reach out, select one of the Lord's children, and commence the journey of covenant love. In doing so, you will not only experience companionship but also honor the Lord, who ordained marriage as a blessing for His people.

Typically, the best time to find a compatible life partner, who is young and with whom you can grow together, is between the ages of 20 and 35. At this stage, you grow together, build together, and learn patience together. But if you're now in your forties and still searching for this ideal wife with the same mindset, you have a problem. Your circle of acquaintances has changed.

The women available in your dating market no longer expect the same things. Many are divorced, single mothers, or emotionally wounded. While some are sincere, others carry heavy pasts they haven't yet overcome and might expect you to help them do so. Today, you want someone young, kind, beautiful, and without children. But how is that fair?

Especially if you have a past, a child, or missed opportunities, it's not about blame, but about telling the truth. For 20 years, you lived your life as you saw fit. You may have had romantic relationships, but you avoided marriage. You cooked, cleaned, travelled, and slept alone. You only know how to function solo, but do you know how to function as a couple? Or do you make yourself believe you do? Do you even have the skills to live with another person in love, patience, and peace under your care?

You ask, "**Is it too late**?" It depends. It's never too late to love, change, grow, and learn. But it might be too late to keep pretending you're still 20. It could also be too late to find the perfect woman, with no past and no expectations. That market no longer exists. You're past that age, and that's not an insult; it's a wake-up call. The world keeps turning, as does your body, your mind, and your value in others' eyes. So, what do you do now?

The Book of Men is here to remind you of reality. **Life isn't a video game with a** *"restart button"*. **Everyone agrees, right?** You only live once, "**YES**." So why haven't you chosen someone?

What are you waiting for? Do you still think you have time?

Try talking to a 22-year-old woman today and see how she describes you. "**Old. Outdated. Scary**." You might be in good shape and have money, but to her, you're not interesting. And she's not entirely wrong. That pain you feel is called the truth. You missed your chance, not because it didn't exist, but because you didn't seize it. And now fear is holding you back again; fear of making the wrong choice, fear of getting hurt. Look around at everyone you know in your age group.

How many are single or have never tried?

So, here's the real question: Are you a Christian? Because if you are, God never intended for you to go through life alone. In Genesis 2:18, God says, **"It is not good for man to be alone."**

As a believer, you are part of a community of faith. And in that fellowship, we don't let men drift indefinitely. We help each other rise. If you receive solid teaching, your pastor would have already guided you toward a woman who is right for you. The elders would have intervened through prayer and counsel. Your brothers in Christ would have helped you build a godly home.

In many strong Christian communities, we ensure our men do not fall behind. If you are seriously considering marriage, the church will step in. We will provide financial support for your wedding. We will pray with you. We will even help your wife walk in biblical femininity. That is the benefit of being surrounded by righteous men. We do not abandon one another. Whether you are broke, wounded, or indecisive, we will help.

If you are an introverted man, we are committed to walking beside you. Our leaders will help connect you with a suitable bride within the family of Christ and support you as you prepare for your wedding. No man will be left behind. We will stand with you, offering guidance, encouragement, job support, and the resources every man needs to fulfill his responsibilities with dignity.

When others see you standing with your wife, they will no longer call you by your first name alone but will honor you as Mr. and Mrs., a testament to God's laws, order, grace, and faithfulness in your life. If you don't have a wife yet, don't fall into silence; seek a solution and ask for help. You must be willing to take that step. In the Kingdom of God, no man is meant to stay a child forever, and no one is called to walk through life alone. Marriage is not just a desire; it's a responsibility and a blessing. If you're ready, the right help and guidance will come to you, but it starts with a willing heart.

The bad news, however, is that life doesn't wait for you to get organized. Whether you're not **"ready,"** **"healed,"** or **"rich,"** the train has already left the station. You missed your first chance. Now what? The worst thing you can do is keep procrastinating. If you're still in limbo, waiting for someone who fits your ideal criteria to appear magically, it's time to wake up. Accept the situation you're currently in on the dating market. You may still be attractive, yes. But in today's world, that's not enough.

You'll need either significant wealth or radical humility.

If you don't have a fortune, you'll need to change your approach. You may need to expand your search, consider international options, and consider traveling. Yes, join the "passport bros" to the Philippines, Thailand, Colombia, Brazil, the Dominican Republic, Mexico, and South Africa, if necessary.

Look for a personality. Search for a woman who values commitment, sacrifice, and faith. Seek a woman who still believes in God, family, and respect. But before you do that, look in the mirror and ask yourself: Have I matured? Am I ready to lead, love, and protect with wisdom, not just feelings? What about the girl down the street, at the local church, or the supermarket? Your wife may pass you by every day.

Before asking God to send you a wife, test yourself as a soldier prepares for war. Marriage is not a vacation; it is a lifelong mission that requires emotional endurance, daily sacrifice, and sacrificial leadership. Want to know if you're ready? Invite a trusted fellow believer to live with you for a week. Share your space. Prepare meals together. Make decisions together. Pray together. When tensions rise, pay attention to how you respond.

Do you shut down? Do you lash out? Or do you show grace? These are exercises in discipline.

If you can't handle having a trusted friend in your home for seven days, you're not ready for a wife, whose heart and future you are called to protect. These small moments will reveal whether you are truly prepared for marriage or still bound by self-centered independence. Emotional maturity is not measured by age, but by the ability to consistently serve others without resentment.

The worst kind of man is the one who waits too long and then blames the entire world. Don't be that man. Don't become bitter, cynical, or delusional. Be honest. If you made a mistake, admit it. If you wasted time, repent. If you have delayed for selfish reasons, change. This is what The Book of Men invites you to do: face the truth, accept it, and move forward like a man. Not with excuses, but with vision. Not with shame, but with courage. Your life is not over, but the longer you delay, the higher the price you will pay.

Now that you're in your forties, you don't have the same energy you once had. You can no longer afford to play games or wake up every hour during the night to chase after young children. The truth is, waiting for a woman without children at this stage is a risky and unrealistic gamble. Your season has changed. You need to be honest with yourself about what you can handle and what is still truly available.

God has not abandoned you. You are still alive for a reason. But do not tempt the mercy of time any longer. Do not gamble with your future, your inheritance, or you're calling. Start over if necessary. Make different choices. Seek advice. Submit yourself to the community. Let your brothers help you get back on your feet, for no Christian is called to live alone. And if you have spent the first half of your life drifting, let the second half be defined by purpose. Let it be guided by faith, not fantasy. Let it be marked by boldness, not procrastination. And above all, let it be lived with someone who walks beside you in God's will.

The fear of the Lord is the highest law for all Christian men.

"The fear of the Lord is the beginning of wisdom." (Proverbs 9:10) The power of a man begins with the one who rules him. The value of a person is not measured by their bank account, title, or public image, but by the one who rules them. A man of great value does not rule himself. He understands authority, not only in the worldly realm of men, but also in the Kingdom of God.

True greatness is rooted in divine laws and order. He is not a lone wolf but a submissive son. He understands that to reign in life, he must bow before the throne of grace. The man who rules his life without God builds his house on sand. But the man who submits to God's rule and builds on the Rock of Ages will be saved.

Christian wealthy men understand the divine hierarchy. A man of great worth possesses a spiritual understanding of how authority operates; he knows he must be ruled before he can rule. Although it is often said, "Behind every successful man is a strong, wise, and hardworking woman," the man of God recognizes that both the man and the woman are ultimately under God's hand. The proper order is spiritual: Christ is the head of man, man is the head of his household, and the law of Jesus governs everything. It is this alignment with heaven that enables the household to prosper, not just through human effort, but through divine instruction. The law of obedience governs our hearts:

"If you love me, keep my commandments." John 14:15.

This is not optional for a Christian; it is a commandment from the King Himself. Before a man can value himself, he must first recognize the sufficiency of God. God is sovereign, directing all things freely according to His royal counsel. It is the highest form of love and power. It shows that our allegiance is not to culture, ego, or even emotion, but to the voice of the Almighty. A person of great value lives in obedience, even if it costs them popularity, comfort, or relationships. Their identity is grounded in faithfulness. The law of responsibility guides his actions:

"From everyone who has been given much, much will be required. From the one who has been entrusted with much, much more will be asked." Luke 12:48.

A man of genuine worth not only accepts his responsibilities; he embraces them with respect. He recognizes that leadership is a burden, not a crown. He understands that God has entrusted him with gifts, people, and influence, and that he will one day be held accountable for them. Whether in business, family, or community, he acts thoughtfully. He builds with eternity in mind, knowing that in an instant, everything could be lost if he loses sight of the One who gave him everything. The law of integrity protects his legacy:

"The righteous man walks in his integrity; his children are blessed after him." Proverbs 20:7.

Integrity is the core of masculinity. A Christian man of high value doesn't say one thing and do another. He doesn't follow the crowd; he follows his convictions. He chooses the narrow path, not because it is easy, but because it is right. His reputation isn't just for his benefit; it also protects his children and acts as a fortress for future generations. The man of integrity builds a spiritual legacy that no amount of money can match.

The law of self-control elevates his soul: "Better a patient person than a warrior, one with self-control than one who takes a city. « Proverbs 16:32. Power means nothing if a man cannot control his mind. Gabriel prays that this law will benefit his three sons: Isaiah, Gabriel Jr., and Gershom, because a man who does not control his mind will be a slave to his appetites. Anger, lust, pride, and fear will dominate him; he must learn to control them.

The fear of the Lord is the most important law that high-value men are to live by. The man of great worth wins the inner war before he even enters the outer battle. He is the man who will stand even in the face of loss, rejection, or betrayal. The Law of God's Sufficiency humbles a Christian man's confidence.

"No matter how much money, power, or status a man achieves, without the laws of God, he is nothing." The Apostle Paul says in 2 Corinthians 3:5:

"Not that we are sufficient in ourselves to claim anything as coming from us, but our sufficiency is from God." A high-value Christian man lives with this truth engraved into his soul: Without Christ, I am nothing, you are nothing, and no one is. The strength of the righteous man flows from a daily dependence on the Heavenly Father: Lord Jesus, you are:

- Our Father, and Our Shepherd (Isaiah 64:8)
- Our Healer, and Our Fortress (Psalm 18:2)
- Our Provider, and Our Peace (Genesis 22:14)
- Our Righteousness and Redeemer (Genesis 22:8)
- Our Shield and Everlasting Light (Isaiah 60:20)

The law of reverence guides your every step.

You live under God's supreme authority. Every decision, ambition, and relationship is filtered through the fear of the Lord. But this fear is not terrifying; it is sacred reverence. It is trembling before the glory of a God who is both loving and just. The fear of the Lord is the beginning of wisdom (Proverbs 9:10), and a person of great value begins and ends each day recognizing that he is dust, but redeemed. He walks with caution, not carelessness, knowing that eternity weighs on every choice. When love fails, faith remains.

"I thought I was committing myself forever." Like many men of God, Gabriel once entered into marriage with hope, faith, and purity. Mr. Right and Mrs. Right, united in the sacred bonds of marriage. Mark 10:9 still rings true: "What God has joined together, let no man separate." Yet the world is broken, and sometimes our vows are broken too. Gabriel is a divorced Christian man, not because he stopped loving, but because faithfulness sometimes must continue alone. A man of significant worth stays loyal to God regardless of circumstances, even when personal relationships fail. The law of vision protects its goal:

"Without vision, the people perish." Proverbs 29:18.

A man without vision is someone who drifts through life. But a man of great value sees beyond his current struggles; he stays focused. He finds a goal within pain, a direction amid delays, and a calling even in his desert. He walks by faith and not by sight. He builds where others scatter. His chest is covered with the shield of vision; he perceives what God sees with eagle eyes, free from distractions.

This vision keeps him from compromising, giving up, or sinking into despair or suicidal thoughts when things don't go well. Vision is not ambition; it is a prophetic alignment with the laws passed by the Congress of the Heavenly Angel, signed by the blood of Jesus Christ, our Lord and Savior. The law of brotherhood reinforces his circle. *"Iron sharpens iron, and one man sharpens another." Proverbs 27:17.*

A man of great value surrounds himself with men of truth, character, and courage. He rejects the company of fools because he knows that bad company corrupts good character. Brotherhood is not just friendship; it is spiritual warfare. Together, we support each other when marriage becomes difficult, when loneliness sets in, and when temptation whispers.

A circle of men of faith is a fortress against the enemy's attacks. We are not alone; we pray, worship, and fight together. The Law of Divine Purpose Clarifies His Identity. *"Before I formed you in the womb, I knew you, before you were born, I set you apart; I appointed you as a prophet to the nations." Jeremiah 1:5.*

A high-value man doesn't wander; he lives with purpose.

He understands that God intentionally created him. His pain, calling, experiences, and failures are all part of a divine story being woven. He wakes up each day asking, "Why did God create me?" and he dedicates himself to fulfilling that purpose with all his might. A strong man isn't perfect, but he is committed to discovering, protecting, and completing the purpose God set for him before the foundation of the world.

Leadership begins with submission. Before I can lead a woman, I must be guided by Christ. Before I raise children, I must be disciplined by the laws of heaven. Before I speak as a father, I must listen as the Son of God, because the head of every man is Christ.

A man who heaven does not guide cannot rule on earth. The Book of Men begins here: Under God's authority. Every kingdom has laws, and every high-value Christian man must uphold the divine laws that define his calling. In the beginning, God created man and entrusted him with the responsibility to lead, protect, and provide (Genesis 2:15). These duties are not cultural; they are eternal. The kingdom of heaven affirms this principle: "For the husband is the head of the wife, even as Christ is the head of the church."

The laws of The Book of Men are not just motivational quotes. They serve as spiritual architecture for shaping masculinity. Think of these as your commands and instructions:

- **The Law of Divine Primacy:** God is first in everything.
- **The Law of First Accountability:** You are responsible for all that is under your charge.
- **The Law of Purpose Over Pleasure:** Pleasure is a servant, not a master.
- **The Law of Emotional Mastery:** Emotions are tools, not gods.
- **The Law of Reasoned Action:** Don't just react; respond wisely.
- **The Law of Measured Investment:** Never sow where there's no fruit.
- **The Law of Legacy Thinking:** Think three generations ahead.
- **The Law of Sacrificial Prioritization:** Die to self for what truly matters.
- **The Law of Consistency and Integrity:** Let your life reflect your faith.

These laws are tested in the fire of marriage, tested in the pain of divorce, tested in the long nights of waiting and rebuilding. These are not laws of comfort. These are laws of kings. To be God's man, follow the teachings of the Book of Men. You must build your life on these principles. Not your feelings, not trends, not popularity. These laws stand eternal.

The Gospel of The Book of Men

Today, women make up approximately four billion of the global population. These are the beautiful and diverse creations of God, placed on this earth not to confuse you, but to give you a meaningful choice rooted in wisdom, not impulse. Walking by faith, not by sight, is a principle that applies to every area of life, especially in choosing a wife.

If you rely solely on what your eyes see, such as outer appearance, trends, or feelings, you risk becoming a man lost in confusion, chasing illusions. True Christian men don't choose based on sight alone. They walk by faith, guided by purpose, values, and spiritual discernment. When looking for a wife, it's wise to choose a woman who grew up in a stable, two-parent household. Why? Because she probably had the chance to see what marriage looks like through both good times and bad. She's observed her mother respect and support her father, and she understands the rhythm of partnership, sacrifice, and commitment.

That kind of foundation matters. It doesn't guarantee perfection, but it indicates she has already learned some essential principles, lessons many people still lack today.

Choosing a wife is one of the most important decisions a man will ever make. Please don't leave it to chance or charm. Walk by faith, think clearly, and build with legacy in mind.

Silence, at times, speaks louder than words. As Christian men, we have come to understand these more profound truths not by chance, but through intentional and prayerful study of the Word. With open hearts and curious minds, we have uncovered timeless instructions that were written for us all along. Now, we must pass these truths to the next generation, to young men and unmarried brothers around the world. Building and securing your future isn't an act of greed; it's an act of stewardship. You are safeguarding the legacy and purpose God has entrusted to you. *"A good man leaves an inheritance to his children's children" (Proverbs 13:22).*

Let us walk boldly in this calling.

Marriage taught men many things:

- Love is not enough.
- Good intentions are not enough.
- Desire alone won't sustain a relationship.
- Promises aren't enough.
- Attraction by itself isn't enough.
- Feelings alone can't hold a marriage.
- Chemistry isn't enough.
- Words aren't enough.
- Money and hope alone fall short.
- Faithfulness, patience, and wisdom are the actual weapons. Genuine husbands live by faith, not by emotion or opinion, but by faith.

Headship is not dictatorship; it is sacrificial leadership.

Christ didn't rule over others; He knelt and washed the feet of those who were his followers. He carried His cross and bled for His bride. That exemplifies true manhood at its highest. Many Christian men wake early and work late. They bear the weight of their homes on tired shoulders, doing everything they can to keep everything intact. Yet sometimes, she walks away. Not bound by covenant, but tied only to a bank account, she used the marriage as a means to leverage her next move, ***not for love. Not for legacy. Not for you.***

The Book of Men says:

"Even in intimacy, keep your eyes open and your words measured." **Why?** Because discernment doesn't stop at the bedroom door; it protects you even there. What you say during those vulnerable moments will be remembered, replayed, and potentially used to define your character. Many men have been caught off guard because they let their guard down at the wrong time, believing that love means abandoning wisdom and judgment. But love without discernment isn't truly loved; it's risk without a plan. It's like riding your motorcycle without wearing a helmet.

Understand this: in relationships, every move counts. Life, like chess, demands foresight. You don't just make moves; you play to win. That doesn't mean controlling or manipulating her, but leading with purpose and vision. Some might call it selfish. In reality, it is wise stewardship that protects your peace, your reputation, and your future.

If you genuinely love her, observe her closely. Understand her emotional patterns. Recognize her strengths and wounds. Just as you study Scripture to understand God's will, study your wife to lead with clarity and compassion. Leadership in the home should develop into true headship, spirit-led, rooted in respect, and decisive in direction.

And yes, if there ever comes a time when love diminishes and alignment is broken, Scripture does not overlook that reality. **"If a man marries a woman who becomes displeasing to him because he finds something indecent about her, and he writes her a certificate of divorce, gives it to her, and sends her from his house." (Deuteronomy 24:1).**

She will be fired from her position and evicted from the residence. This isn't an excuse to walk away but a reminder that every choice carries responsibility and consequences. Marriage is serious, not a game, but it requires strategic thinking. Lead with intention. Love thoughtfully. Continue to seek discernment, even during your most personal moments.

Sometimes, choosing to walk away is an act of wisdom, not a sign of weakness. When betrayal wounds deeply and reconciliation seems out of reach, a man must remain faithful to God. Solomon didn't pursue every woman who left his court. Samson's downfall wasn't because he loved a woman, but because he entrusted his strength to someone who did not fear God. As Proverbs 4:23 warns, *'Above all else, guard your heart, for everything you do flows from it.'*

A high-value Christian man guards his emotions like a soldier protects a castle. Not every woman deserves access to your vulnerability. Not every relationship deserves your effort. Not every wife should be granted access to your wealth. Protect your heart and safeguard your net worth legally.

"By faith Abraham, when called to go… obeyed and went, even though he did not know where he was going." Hebrews 11:8

Obey when it's dark. Leave when He says go. Move when there is no map. That's called Manhood University. The Lord is the superintendent, and all you need is a little faith. For truly, I say to you, if you have faith like a grain of mustard seed, you will say to this mountain, *"Move from here to there," and it will move, and nothing will be impossible for you.' Matthew 17:20*

Understanding a husband's mind can give us valuable insights into how he thinks, feels, and relates to others. It helps us appreciate his perspective and build stronger, more connected relationships. By exploring these traits, we can foster empathy and deepen our mutual understanding, creating a more harmonious bond.

HEAVENLY CITIZEN

CHAPTER SEVENTEEN

The Book of Men:
A Husband's Sacred Responsibility

Covenant to Legacy: Building Homes of Faith, Integrity and Kingdom Vision. **The Book of Men** guides Christian men to take full responsibility for their homes. Being a husband isn't a reward; it's a primary duty that's blessed. Marriage isn't just about the Big Day; it's about every day after. The responsibility of a family rests on your spiritual shoulders. Love isn't blind. You can see how love costs, yet you still move forward and say "yes." Before you say "I do," ask yourself, "Can I carry her pain, her future, her flaws, and her fears with the strength of Christ?"

Before entering marriage, a man must cultivate the mindset of a husband, a clear, purpose-driven mental framework rooted in intention rather than impulse. This involves not only understanding a husband's thought process in theory but also practicing daily leadership, decision-making, and spiritual discipline in real-life situations. He should reflect on the inner workings of his mind, guided by a vision that goes beyond emotions.

Essentially, he needs to develop the mental habits of a godly husband, where his thoughts are grounded in truth, integrity, and obedience. Holding the title alone isn't enough; he must consistently demonstrate these qualities with clarity and conviction. These are the reasons why a wife should, and must, show respect to her husband.

The Lord recognizes the heavy responsibility a man carries before he becomes a husband. Therefore, God provided clear guidelines and qualities for him to develop so he can walk with dignity, lead honorably, and earn respect. Respect is not something to be demanded; it is something to be gained through obedience, character, and fulfilling divine responsibilities.

This begins with taking full responsibility, owning his past, leading in the present, and shaping the future without excuses. He must protect what's sacred: his mind, his money, his purity, and his God-given vision, treating them as holy ground. He must lead with vision, not emotion, because feelings are fleeting, but purpose is eternal. A faithful husband honors women without idolizing them, knowing they are his partners, not his gods. He must speak less and act more, letting his life and actions speak louder than words.

He builds legacy, not just wealth, investing in generations, not just numbers. He surrounds himself with a brotherhood of accountability because iron sharpens iron, and no man thrives alone. And above all, he refuses to live in half-obedience, because anything less than complete obedience is quiet rebellion.

Christian men persevere to the end. They don't abandon their wives emotionally or leave their children spiritually lost.

They don't mourn losses and then repeat the same mistakes.

Mastery, Legacy, and Kingdom Vision ***"No One serving as a soldier gets entangled in civilian affairs, but instead tries to please his commanding officer; in that case, "God." 2 Timothy 2:4***

A high-value Christian man does not chase thrills. He pursues purpose. He asks, "Does this woman, this job, this opportunity serve my mission?" Your emotions are servants, not masters. Fear, lust, or pride will not rule you if Christ reigns within you. You must train your spirit to respond with wisdom, not impulse. Don't believe you can change a woman; her actions and happiness are not your responsibility.

The bigger loser is never you, because, according to The Book of Men's Laws, if one leaves now, there will always be more opportunities for men. ***"And in that day seven women shall take hold of one man, saying, we will eat our bread, and wear our apparel: only let us be called by thy name, to take away our reproach." (Isaiah 4:1)***

Your decisions should be guided by both faith and logic. A man who is all passion and no principle is an unstable measure before you invest. Your time and energy are sacred. Don't waste them in fruitless relationships, toxic environments, or fantasy-driven goals.

Every decision has repercussions that extend beyond your own life. You are laying the foundation for your grandchildren.

Think legacy. Think eternity. Proverbs 13:22 King Solomon said, ***"A good man leaves an inheritance to his children's children."*** Live a life that is consistent, holy, and disciplined, so that your sons inherit your character and your daughters inherit your standards. This is the legacy of a high-value Christian man. Not fame. Not power. But unshakable faith. Let your inner beliefs and outer actions align. This is integrity. This is manhood. Is this book only meant for believers in Jesus Christ?

That's a fair and important question!

If you're reading this and you don't see yourself as a Christian, or perhaps you identify as an atheist or skeptic, I'm not asking you to believe everything immediately. What I am asking is for you to be curious enough to explore. Consider the possibility that if there is truth beyond what we can see, it is worth searching for.

I believe you have enough education, reason, and life experience to understand simple truths. If you've ever believed in anything, whether it's a poet, a philosopher, a public figure, or a personal experience, then I invite you to ask yourself the most important question of all:

Who is Jesus to you?

Was he just a prophet? A moral teacher? Or is He truly the Messiah, the Lord, and the Savior of the world? "But what about you?" He asked. *"Who do you say I am?" Simon Peter answered, "You are the Messiah, the Son of the living God."*
(Matthew 16:15-16)

Have you ever seriously considered the things He said?

Do His words spark any curiosity in you? He claimed to be more than a teacher or a healer. He claimed to be the Son of God. He claimed to forgive sins, to raise the dead, and to be the only way to eternal life. *"I am the way and the truth and the life. No one comes to the Father except through me." (John 14:6)*

Did he die and rise again? Are His miracles authentic? Did He walk on water, feed thousands, and restore blind eyes? *"He was delivered over to death for our sins and was raised to life for our justification." (Romans 4:25). "Jesus performed many other signs in the presence of his disciples, but these are written that you may believe that Jesus is the Messiah, the Son of God…" (John 20:30–31).* Why did he make it so simple for us to be saved?

The Book of Men describes the laws of Christ like this:

Imagine if the Bible were the only book on Earth and cost $1 million. Think about that. Almost no one could afford it. Only the wealthiest among us could even see its pages. Now ask yourself the most significant question you've ever gotten to answer: How valuable would Jesus's words suddenly be to the world? Wouldn't people be more curious, eager to read just one page, one paragraph, or even a single quote?

If the truth of Jesus were concealed behind wealth, the world would regard it as sacred and rare. However, the paradox remains: through His mercy and the gracious gift of His blood, Jesus ensured that every soul, regardless of wealth, would have free access to His truth in a book. This is exemplified by a simple book, yet, unlike others, it is a sacred text held in reverence by all souls on the planet, guiding them towards the Kingdom of Heaven.

His words now appear in paperback and hardcover books, are broadcast on TV, read on phones, heard in music, and shared across the internet, freely and in every language.

He did not restrict access to a select few; instead, he shared it with the entire world.

And yet, we often ignore this divine wisdom. We scroll past it, leave it on the shelf, and tune it out, forgetting that these are the powerful, eternal laws of the Creator Himself, spoken from the throne of heaven to guide us through life and into eternity.

What many overlook is this:

What is free to us costs Him everything.

So, the question remains: Why wouldn't you be curious to hear what He said?

Among the countless books ever written, none have had a greater impact on the world than His words. Could it be worth your time, even just once, to read them for yourself? Not out of religious obligation, but with a heart that asks: "**What if it's true?**"

If you're intellectually honest and spiritually curious, you'll discover that His truths are both eternal and straightforward. He didn't come to confuse but to save. And he said something extraordinary: ***"Anyone who has seen me has seen the Father." (John 14:9) "The Father and I are one." (John 10:30)***

This promise still holds today: "***If you declare with your mouth, 'Jesus is Lord,' and believe in your heart that God raised Him from the dead,*** *you will be saved." (Romans 10:9)* He is not just a man from history. He is the Resurrection and the Life. *"I am the resurrection and the life. The one who believes in me will live, even though they die." (John 11:25).*

Suppose you can read this book and reach this part during your lecture. In that case, it means you have the capacity and a certain level of intellect to understand the difference between complex and straightforward definitions of experiences, whether they are real or not.

Now, would you agree with this definition of the word "**LIFE**": Life is the experience of existence, the sacred journey between birth and death. It is a divine gift, a condition that distinguishes living things from non-living entities. But true life goes beyond mere biological function; it is found in purpose, in meaning, and ultimately, in connection with God. Physical existence may define our beginning, but it is our relationship with the Creator that gives life its true essence.

What do these words have to do with religion? Let's be honest. Jesus wasn't religious in the way people define it today. He wasn't preaching a set of rituals, rules, or traditions to earn God's favor. He was God in the flesh, coming down in a form we could understand, speaking in ways we could receive, and paying a price we could never afford.

Reading **The Book of Men** makes you a wiser person, not just because you've read it, but because you can now explain its truths to others. However, what's remarkable is that God designed these truths to be so simple and straightforward that even someone without formal education can understand them when they are shared with clarity and conviction.

This book has provided you with insight and understanding. However, remember that its wisdom doesn't solely stem from human intellect; it originates from God's mind. As Scripture explains why Jesus came and died for every unspoken person:

"For my thoughts are not your thoughts, neither are your ways my ways," declares the Lord. As the heavens are higher than the earth, so are my ways higher than your ways and my thoughts than your thoughts." (Isaiah 55:8–9)

The gap between God's wisdom and ours is large, but by His grace, He lowers His truth to our level, so that anyone with a willing heart can accept it, and now, it is your turn to explain this to others. The Lord Jesus had nothing to lose by staying in heaven. He came because you needed saving. He stepped into time, into suffering, into the human experience, so that you could be redeemed.

Let's not pretend you've never experienced a moment when faith suddenly felt real, perhaps when you were 30,000 feet in the air and turbulence shook the plane. In those moments, people who usually claim to be atheists suddenly whisper desperate prayers. Your heart pounds. Your mind races. You don't become "religious," you become aware, aware that you want one more minute of life, one more chance. Why is that?

Because deep down, we all know eternity is genuine, and Jesus made access to eternal life simple and free. He paid with His blood. He died so you wouldn't have to. And He extended this invitation so that anyone, even at their last breath, could call on Him and be saved. ***"Call to me, and I will answer you and tell you great and unsearchable things you do not know." (Jeremiah 33:3)***

You might ask, "But what about those who died before Jesus came?" That's a fair and thoughtful question. Let's go back 1,000 years before Jesus, to King David, the father of Solomon, who reigned around 1010–970 BC. After the death of King Saul, David became king over all Israel. That's about a thousand years before Jesus was born in Bethlehem.

Yet even King David, through the Holy Spirit, prophetically spoke of the coming Savior. He wrote: "Because you will not abandon me to the realm of the dead, nor will you let your faithful one see decay." (Psalm 16:10). These words were also spoken by the Apostle Peter during his sermon on Pentecost after receiving the Holy Spirit

: ***"Because you will not abandon me to the realm of the dead, you will not let your holy one see decay." In Acts 2:27.***

If you read Acts 2:25-26, you'll see how Peter, after Jesus had ascended into heaven, went back to the basics to explain to the people of Israel a profound truth: that no one from the past, present, or future who believed in Jesus will perish. He quoted King David, who prophetically spoke of the Messiah one thousand years before his coming:

Psalm 16

A Miktam of David

- **Keep me safe**, O God, for in You I take refuge. I say to the Lord, "You are my Lord; apart from You I have no good thing."
- As for the saints who are in the land, they are the glorious ones in whom is all my delight. The sorrows of those who run after other gods will multiply; I will not pour out their libations of blood, nor will I take their names on my lips.
- **Lord, you alone are my portion and my cup**; You make my lot secure.
- The boundary lines have fallen for me in pleasant
- places; surely, I have a delightful inheritance. I will praise the Lord, who counsels me; even at night, my heart instructs me.
- I have set the Lord always before me. Because He is at my right hand, I will not be shaken.
- **Therefore, my heart is glad and my tongue rejoices**; my body also will rest secure,
- because You will not abandon me to the grave, nor will You let Your Holy One see decay.
- You have made known to me the path of life; You will fill me with joy in Your presence, with eternal pleasures at Your right hand.

Peter used these words to show that David wasn't just speaking about himself, but foretelling Jesus' death and resurrection, that even death could not hold Him. And through Christ, all who believe will share in that same hope, resting in the promise of eternal life.

Why? Because Jesus had to confront death itself and conquer it from within. He entered the realm of the dead to release every soul that had trusted in God before the cross, and for all who would believe in Him afterward. He overcame death so you wouldn't have to face eternal death. "In him, we find redemption through his blood and forgiveness of sins, all in line with the richness of God's grace."

Even if you have never encountered Him or were not
Present 2,000 years ago, Jesus still extends His call to you today. Because every soul matters to Him, and that includes you. You don't need to become "religious" to have faith in Jesus. Faith isn't blind tradition; it's a pursuit of truth. Since you're someone who can understand both complex and straightforward issues, Gabriel, a brother just like you, encourages you to stay curious. Ask questions. Search deeply. Begin your honest investigation about this man who lived only 33 years, but changed history forever.

Consider this: He lived 33 years, and your body has 33 vertebrae to support your spine. You have 12 ribs on each side of your chest, symbolizing the 12 disciples and the 12 tribes of Israel. This isn't accidental; it's intentional. His covenant isn't just written in the pages of Scripture; it's embedded in your very being.

You are a living tabernacle, fearfully and wonderfully crafted in God's image. The smallest and the most potent part of your existence, the breath, is what links you to Him. When that breath escapes, even for a moment, everything shifts. Without it, you revert to dust. Compared to any dignitary, king, royal figure, or president, most are forgotten within months, sometimes even days, after their tenure ends. Their names fade, and their influence diminishes.

However, one name remains: Jesus. Over 2.9 billion people, nearly a third of the world's population, identify as Christians or followers of other faiths, meaning they consider themselves followers of Jesus.

Think about that. **No president in history has ever needed 2.9 billion votes to win an election**. Yet, Jesus has garnered the loyalty and devotion of billions over the centuries, without relying on political power, military force, or wealth.

That should make you stop and ask: **Why?** Men are inherently endowed with intelligence and curiosity, divine gifts that drive us to seek truth and ask meaningful questions. By studying the teachings of Jesus and the wisdom of Scripture, we start to see why much of what He and the prophets conveyed about women and relationships remains relevant today.

The Bible doesn't call men to distrust women, but it does call them to walk in discernment, wisdom, and self-control, especially with the woman who shares our bed. Not everything should be spoken, and not every emotion should be exposed. Even love must be guided by wisdom.

"Do not give your strength to women, nor your ways to that which destroys kings." (Proverbs 31:3) "A fool vents all his feelings, but a wise man holds them back." (Proverbs 29:11)

These scriptures remind us that a man must be intentional about what he shares, how he leads, and when he speaks. Why? Because trust is earned, not assumed, and wisdom protects a man's legacy.

The Book of Men said:

"Think of being as clever as a serpent and as pure as a dove. It means loving wholeheartedly, guiding wisely, and being attentive to women without losing your sense of judgment. Keep your discernment strong and balanced." What is it about this man, who lived over 2,000 years ago for only 33 years, that continues to move the hearts, minds, and lives of so many?

That's why I urge you, as someone intelligent, educated, possibly a university graduate, with the ability to discern truth and seek meaning, just to be curious. Investigate for yourself. Don't simply dismiss what billions have embraced.

The Book of Men isn't asking you to convert, follow the rules, or join any religious group or anything like that. It simply invites you to take a moment to read the teachings of Jesus, his words and laws, and to ask yourself what they mean. Ask yourself what they mean. No pressure. No cost. No religion required. No sign-up is expected. No one else can decide for you. No better time than now. Just truth, waiting to be received, and a chance to decide for yourself what it's worth.

So, ask yourself: What if it's all true? Could it be that the One who created you is softly calling you back to life, to purpose, to truth? Could it be true, and you've just ignored it all along?

Consider this: anything in your life could have been a glimpse of the miraculous, such as the birth of a child, healing from an illness, a significant victory, a wedding, a close call with an accident, or even an unexpected encounter with a stranger who awakened something spiritual within you.

Maybe it was a subtle reminder. A word. A feeling. Or perhaps it was your instinct, an inner awareness or intelligence you didn't even realize you had, suddenly sparked by a challenge, a moment of beauty, or a new adventure. Has anything in your life ever sparked a thought, a memory that led you back to the teachings of Jesus? To the goodness of God quietly unfolding in your story?

If you're reading this, you are one of the blessed. The Book of Men has opened your eyes, and the Holy Spirit is making these heavenly truths clear to you, not by coincidence, but by divine appointment. These words are not just religious talk. They are life. Truth. Your invitation.

Have you ever had a dream so vivid that it felt like your soul left your body as if you were somewhere else entirely? Now imagine if your soul never returned from that realm. That would mean, quite literally, that your body has died. Your loved ones would bury your physical body, which, as Scripture says, returns to dust:

Genesis 3:19:
"For dust you are and to dust you will return."

Your soul? It wouldn't disappear. It would continue its journey, fully aware, fully conscious, and completely separated from your physical body. The truth is, the soul doesn't perish with the body. It endures forever and ultimately will reside in one of two places: either in the presence of God or eternally apart from Him.

You might not know the day or hour, but your soul's destination is not random. It's determined by how you respond to the truth in this life. So, ask yourself now, while you still have breath in your body: Where is my soul headed? Because eternity doesn't wait. And once the soul leaves the body for good, its course is final.

The answer to that question alters everything, both now and forever. Gabriel is asking, 'Who is Jesus to you?' I invite you to reflect on just two scriptures, not as a demand, but as an open door, one that I pray the Holy Spirit Himself will illuminate for you beyond argument or debate to your answer:

"I am the way, the truth, and the life. No one comes to the Father except through Me." (John 14:6)

Jesus didn't claim to be one of many options. He claimed to be the only way to God, offering salvation, forgiveness, and eternal life to all who place their trust in Him.

According to His own words, there is no other path, no philosophy, religion, or moral effort that can substitute what He alone offers. No room for debate or negotiations.

"Anyone whose name was not found written in the book of life was thrown into the lake of fire." (Revelation 20:15)

That may sound harsh, but it's a warning spoken in love. Scripture makes it clear: all people will stand before God someday, and those who reject His invitation will face eternal separation from Him, not because He hates them, but because they refused what He freely offers. *"The fool says in his heart, 'There is no God.'" (Psalm 14:1)*

This isn't meant to insult your intelligence; it's a reflection of spiritual blindness, not mental capacity. Many brilliant people have once said, "There is no God," until life, death, suffering, or even beauty opened their eyes to something more profound than intellect alone can reach. **But here's the good news: "The Lord is not slow in keeping His promise... He is patient with you, not wanting anyone to perish, but everyone to come to repentance." (2 Peter 3:9)**

God is not against you. He is for you. He is patient. He allows space for questions, doubts, and even rebellion because His goal is not to condemn but to redeem. Many people come to Christ later in life, some after years of denial, pain, or searching. Some even meet Him at their final breath. *"For since the creation of the world God's invisible qualities, His eternal power and divine nature, have been seen... so that people are without excuse." (Romans 1:20)*

God has left His fingerprints everywhere: in creation, in conscience, in love, and even in the longing for meaning that never goes away. He is not hiding from you or anyone. He is revealing Himself. The question is whether we're willing to see. **"Through him, all things were made; without him, nothing was made that has been made." (John 1:3)**

This isn't about God discarding people. It's about individuals rejecting the cure for a shared problem, sin. Jesus is the solution. And belief isn't a jump into the dark; it's a step toward the light. ***"Whoever believes in Him is not condemned, but whoever does not believe stands condemned already" (John 3:18)***

Is this book for you? Yes, it is. Because truth belongs to everyone willing to seek it. You don't have to believe everything today. But if anything in your heart stirs while reading these words, consider this an invitation, not from me, but from the One who made you.

If you're willing, ask this one simple question in your own words: "God, if You're real… show me." He listens to your prayer. He understands that kind of honesty. And if you take one step toward Him, you'll discover He's already been walking toward you all along. Jeremiah 29:12: "Then you will call on me and come and pray to me, and I will listen to you."

The Graduation: Now Go and Lead, you made it to the end.

This is not just a book; it is your gateway to divine masculinity. You have experienced heartbreak, the quest for purpose, patience, obedience, and the pursuit of truth. You have studied the principles of manhood under God's laws. Now, go live them. You are God's anointed. You are His son.

"Touch not my anointed ones; do my prophets no harm."
(Psalm 105:15)

You are no longer a boy driven by impulse, but a man guided by eternal law. You are no longer pursuing love; you are building a legacy. You are no longer asking, "Am I enough?" You now walk in the confidence of Christ, knowing that your worth is based on who rules you and the universe.

This is your graduation from Kingdom University. You were the first. You graduate first. Lead your wife. Lead your children. Lead your community. Lead with wisdom. Lead in prayer. Lead in silence. Lead in sacrifice. The laws of The Book of Men are now yours. Use them. Sharpen them. Teach them. And most of all live them. ***When Jesus declared, "I am the way, the truth, and the life: no man cometh unto the Father, but by me" (John 14:6).***

God's Design for Humility and Family

The Owner of all creation has spoken clearly so that we may know who is genuinely in charge. ***"The earth is the Lord's, and the fullness thereof; the world, and they that dwell therein" (Psalm 24:1).***

Human pride, intelligence, or achievement can never compare with the wisdom and sovereignty of God. As Scripture reminds us, "What is your life? You are a mist that appears for a little while and then vanishes" (James 4:14). Our strength is limited, but His power endures forever. Throughout His Word, God sets forth laws and guidance to steer our lives under His care and blessing. Marriage, family, and community are recognized as sacred institutions that support human well-being, not only in the Bible but also across various religious and cultural traditions.

"It is not good that the man should be alone; I will make him a help meet for him" (Genesis 2:18).

In this divine plan, men are called to be providers and protectors, serving their wives, children, and communities with faithfulness and humility. **Pride and arrogance are dangerous because God Himself opposes the proud but shows grace to the humble (James 4:6).**

Therefore, men are called to accept their roles with humility, not as masters but as servants of God, building their families on the foundation of His Word. A true man understands his responsibility not only to work and provide, but also to love and instruct his children in the ways of the Lord.

Deuteronomy 6:6-7:

"And these words, which I command thee this day, shall be in thine heart: and thou shalt teach them diligently unto thy children"

Marriage and family are not burdens but blessings. In many cultures, children and family life are regarded as sources of pride and strength. The Bible confirms this truth: ***"Children are a heritage of the Lord: and the fruit of the womb is his reward" (Psalm 127:3).***

To dismiss these gifts lightly is to overlook the joy and responsibility of participating in God's plan for humanity. The challenges of modern society often test these values. When material wealth and independence take precedence over faith and humility, families can suffer. Broken homes and neglected children come at a heavy cost when God's design for marriage and unity is ignored. In contrast, in places where family values and community support remain central, children typically grow up in environments of stability, shared responsibility, and respect.

Even justice systems worldwide reflect the impact of broken family relationships. For example, research from the U.S. Department of Justice (Bureau of Justice Statistics) found that 14.6% of state prisoners incarcerated for violent crimes committed offenses against a family member, with men making up the vast majority.

These realities emphasize the importance of strong, healthy families guided by God's principles, where love and respect prevent violence and promote peace. The message is clear: when men and women embrace humility, honor marriage, and raise their children in the fear of the Lord, both their households and communities thrive.

"Unless the Lord builds the house, the builders labor in vain" (Psalm 127:1).

True wisdom is acknowledging God's authority, submitting to His design, and walking in His ways, because in

We find blessing, stability, and life in Him. When the Creator spoke, His message was simple and straightforward to all, regardless of their beliefs or affiliations; He revealed the core of the gospel. He didn't offer multiple options, but declared

He himself is the only path to eternal fellowship with the Father.

In Christ is the Way, the Truth, and the Life, not just directions or truths, but the very essence of life. Rejecting Christ is rejecting life itself. These laws are not optional; you either be with him or separate from him. The apostle John opens his gospel with this same truth:

"In the beginning was the Word, and the Word was with God, and the Word was God. The same was in the beginning with God. He made all things; and without Him was not anything made that was made" **(John 1:1-3).**

The Word, Christ Himself, was not created; He is the eternal God. Paul echoes this in Colossians 1:16: ***"For by him were all things created, that are in heaven, and that are in earth, visible and invisible… all things were created by him, and for him."***

Christ is not merely a teacher or prophet; He is the Creator, God in the flesh, dwelling among us. Because God Himself walked among us in Christ, He instilled within humanity everything needed for life and godliness until we return to Him (2 Peter 1:3). In Him we lack nothing.

Consider this: if parents enroll their child in the finest private school, paying for the best teachers and resources, the child still has the responsibility to learn. If, instead, the child keeps asking his parents for answers rather than applying the tools already provided, he misses the point of their provision.

So, it is with faith in Christ. Many believers pray only to ask for things, rather than to worship and trust Him. But the Lord has already placed within us wisdom, resources, and community to support one another in daily living. The most important virtue is to know Jesus personally: ***Jeremiah 4:22 "For my people are foolish, they have not known me.***

This does not diminish prayer; it elevates it. We are commanded to pray, but prayer is primarily about reverence and worship, not a list of desires. Too often, Christians pray for things God has already made possible through diligence, wisdom, or the help of others, such as a spouse, a job, or financial stability. These demands require responsibility, not miracles. Yet when it comes to the impossible, healing incurable diseases, deliverance from death, and breaking spiritual chains, those are the battles where prayer calls upon the power of heaven.

"Call upon me in the day of trouble: I will deliver thee, and thou shalt glorify me" (Psalm 50:15).

Every act of Christ on earth testified to His divinity. Only God could raise Lazarus after four days in the tomb, command the dead to rise as if they were sleeping, or drive out demons with a word of authority. Only God could declare, as David prophesied a thousand years earlier. David foresaw the Messiah's death and resurrection, an eternal King whose body would not decay. ***"When he prepared the heavens, I was there: when he set a compass upon the face of the depth" (Proverbs 8:27).***

The Christ, the eternal Wisdom of God, entered human history to save the very souls He had created in His image. King David understood that life on earth was not the end, but a waiting place for God's promise to be fulfilled. He expressed confidence that even in death, his soul would not be abandoned and his body would not decay. ***"For thou wilt not leave my soul in hell; neither wilt thou suffer thine Holy One to see decay" (Psalm 16:10).***

Although these words prophetically pointed to Christ, they also showed David's trust in the Lord's power over life and death. David was not afraid to die because he trusted the Lord with his soul. His hope was not in kingship, wealth, or earthly strength but in the eternal God who redeems and restores. Death, for David, was not a final defeat but a doorway into the presence of the Lord.

"Yea, though I walk through the valley of the shadow of death, I will fear no evil: for thou art with me" (Psalm 23:4).

His confidence was that the Shepherd who guided him in life would also guide him beyond the grave. This same confidence is fulfilled in Christ Jesus, who declared, "*I am he that liveth*, and was dead; and, behold, I am alive forevermore, Amen; and have the keys of hell and of death" (Revelation 1:18). David's hope rested on the promise that God would one day break open the prison of death and set the captives free. In trusting this promise, he looked forward to the day when his soul would rejoice in the presence of his Redeemer. ***"But God will redeem my soul from the power of the grave: for he shall receive me" (Psalm 49:15).***

For men today, David's faith serves as a reminder to trust God's process with our souls. Life is fragile, death is inevitable, but hope remains secure in the One who conquered the grave. When we anchor our trust in Christ, death loses its sting, and eternity becomes our guarantee. ***"O death, where is thy sting? O grave, where is thy victory? … thanks be to God, which giveth us the victory through our Lord Jesus Christ" (1 Corinthians 15:55, 57).***

Do I believe in prayer? Absolutely. However, prayer must be centered on worship and communion with God, rather than merely making endless requests. It is meant to align us with His will, to draw our hearts near in reverence, and to glorify Him as the source of life. When we misuse prayer as a tool for laziness or avoidance of responsibility, we dishonor the One who has already equipped us with the wisdom and strength we need.

"Faith without works is dead" (James 2:26).

We are called to act diligently in matters of daily life while trusting God for what only He can accomplish. The eternal God, who became man, came not only to forgive but also to restore. He entered our broken world to mend what sin has destroyed and to offer eternal life to all who believe. No situation escapes His notice. Even when we stumble, fall into debt, or are in chaos, He remains present. He is the God who restores order, renews strength, and repairs what is shattered. If you trust Him, He will lift you. He is not only the way to follow and the truth to believe, but also the life that sustains you now and will carry you into eternity.

The Alpha and the Omega

Jesus declares, **"I am Alpha and Omega, the beginning and the end, the first and the last" (Revelation 22:13).**

These words are not poetry; they are authority. Alpha and Omega are the first and last letters of the Greek alphabet, signifying that Christ encompasses everything from start to finish. Nothing exists outside His power, nothing begins without His will, and nothing ends without His command.

From eternity past to eternity future, He remains unchanging. *"**I am Alpha** and **Omega, the beginning** and **the end**," says the Lord, who is, and was, and is to come, the Almighty (Revelation 1:8).* To the fearful and uncertain, He whispers, **"Fear not; I am the first and the last"** (Revelation 1:17). *To the suffering church, He reassures, "**These things saith the first and the last, which was dead, and is alive**" (Revelation 2:8).*

For men, husbands, and fathers, this truth brings unshakable security. Life may feel uncertain, finances may be unstable, and relationships may be fragile, but Christ holds both the first word and the last word over your story. He was present before you were born, He sustains you today, and He will carry you into eternity. Nothing escapes His sight, and nothing can overrule His final authority.

Therefore, we bow not to earthly power but to the eternal King. Presidents rise and fall, kings live and die, but the Alpha and the Omega remain forever. For the man who trusts Him, there is no need to fear tomorrow, because the One who began all things has already secured the end. A characteristic that belongs only to the God of Israel is His exclusive claim to glory. ***"I am the Lord: that is my name: and my glory will I not give to another, neither my praise to graven images"* (Isaiah 42:8).**

Unlike the false gods of nations, He revealed Himself personally, giving us His name and making His presence known among us. His glory is not shared with idols, not transferred to images carved by human hands, and not granted to anyone before Him or after Him. The Lord alone is eternal, self-existent, and sovereign, and to Him alone belongs all worship, honor, and praise. A characteristic unique to the God of Israel is His exclusive claim to glory. ***"I am the Lord: that is my name: and my glory will I not give to another, neither my praise to graven images"* (Isaiah 42:8).**

Unlike the false gods of other nations, He revealed Himself personally, giving us His name and making His presence known among us. His glory is not shared with idols, not transferred to images carved by human hands, and not granted to anyone before or after Him. The Lord alone is eternal, self-existent, and sovereign, and all worship, honor, and praise belong to Him alone. Jesus reaffirms this truth in His own voice when He declares in Revelation 1:18: "*I am he that liveth, and was dead; and, behold, I am alive for evermore, Amen; and have the keys of hell and of death.*"

Here Christ identifies Himself not only as the eternal God but as the risen Savior who has conquered the grave. No prophet, king, or angel could ever make such a claim. He alone holds authority over life and death, and His resurrection proves His divinity beyond question. By having the keys of hell and death, Jesus shows that the destiny of every soul lies in His hands. This is why all glory must be given to Him alone, for He is the only One who has overcome death and secured eternal life for His people.

Living by the Law of the Lord

"And thou shalt love the Lord thy God with all thine heart, and with all thy soul, and with all thy might. And these words, which I command you this day, shall be in your heart: and you shall teach them diligently to your children, and shall talk of them when you sit in your house, and when you walk by the way, and when you lie down, and when you rise. And thou shalt bind them for a sign upon thine hand, and they shall be as frontlets between thine eyes. And thou shalt write them upon the posts of thy house, and on thy gates" (Deuteronomy 6:5 9).

Every man who chooses to live by these laws of the Lord will see profound changes in his life, his home, and his environment. The foundation of godly manhood is not pride, status, or wealth; it is humility before God and obedience to His Word. Scripture is clear: **"God resisted the proud, but giveth grace unto the humble" (James 4:6).**

A proud man will fall under the weight of his arrogance, but the humble man will be lifted by the Lord and strengthened to lead his household with integrity. The same truth applies to women. In our generation, many voices declare independence with pride, boasting, *"I don't need a man."*

Yet that pride often masks hidden pain. Beyond the noise of parties, birthdays, and holidays, many face the wilderness of loneliness, a painful silence that no temporary distraction can heal. Seasons of selfishness eventually arrive, leaving behind regret and a sense of emptiness. Pride promises freedom, but ultimately, it leads to sorrow. ***"Pride goeth before destruction, and a haughty spirit before a fall" (Proverbs 16:18).***

But God's design for man is different. Every man is called to marry, build a home, and raise children in the fear of the Lord. From the beginning, God declared, ***"It is not good that the man should be alone"* (Genesis 2:18).**

Marriage and fatherhood are not optional extras; they are part of the divine calling of manhood. To reject them casually is to neglect the very purpose for which men were created: to reflect God's image through covenant and to extend His legacy through generations.

The command in Deuteronomy 6 is clear: men must love the Lord with all their heart, soul, and might, and they are to pass that love to their children. Faith isn't meant to be kept hidden in private thoughts or reserved for Sundays; it should be woven into daily life. Fathers are called to teach diligently, to talk about God's commands at home, on the road, in the morning, and at night. The family becomes a living classroom of faith, where children learn by hearing and by seeing.

This responsibility is significant. A man who takes seriously the task of instructing his children in God's Word influences not only their future but also the atmosphere of the entire household. His leadership establishes a home characterized by prayer, obedience, and blessing. When the Word of God is inscribed on the posts of the house, both literally and figuratively, the family is under the protection of divine favor. ***"Blessed is every one that feareth the Lord; that walketh in his ways" (Psalm 128:1).***

Therefore, the man who humbly accepts his role as husband, father, and spiritual leader receives God's blessing on his life. He recognizes that strength comes not from pride, but from submission; not from independence, but from covenant; not from selfishness, but from love. Such a man leaves behind not only material possessions but also a spiritual inheritance that lasts for generations. ***"The just man walketh in his integrity: his children are blessed after him" (Proverbs 20:7).***

Trusting God's Process

If something truly comes from God and is suitable for you, then you don't need to beg for it in prayer. Guided by the Holy

Spirit, you only need to trust His process and wait for His timing. ***"With the Lord a day is like a thousand years, and a thousand years are like a day" (Psalm 90:4).***

What seems delayed in our view is already complete in

His eternal plan. To trust God is to rest in the certainty that what He has ordained will happen without striving or fear. Marriage is one of those blessings. Scripture says, ***"Her husband has full confidence in her and lacks nothing of value" (Proverbs 31:11).***

When God joins a man and a woman, it is not just for romance or temporary happiness, but for a covenant, stability, and the raising of children. Marriage is not meant as an escape from loneliness but as a calling to responsibility. ***"But those who hope in the Lord will renew their strength. They will soar on wings like eagles; they will run and not grow weary; they will walk and not be faint"*** (Isaiah 40:31).

The couple who places their hope in God will find strength to endure every season of marriage. The apostle Paul reminds us of God's order in creation: ***"A man ought not to cover his head, since he is the image and glory of God; but woman is the glory of man. For man did not come from woman, but woman from man"*** (1 Corinthians 11:7-8).

This divine order is not about superiority, but about purpose. The husband reflects the image and glory of God as he leads his family, and the wife demonstrates the glory of her husband as she supports and nurtures the home. Together they form one covenant body, designed to glorify God in unity. Yet in our generation, marriage is often viewed as a pursuit of happiness rather than a covenant of faith.

Many walk away the moment they feel unfulfilled. But marriage was never meant for fleeting happiness; it was designed for perseverance, faithfulness, and growth in holiness. Happiness comes and goes, but the covenant endures. God trusts married men and women to remain faithful, not because every moment is easy, but because the vow was made before Him.

"What therefore God hath joined together, let not man put asunder" **(Mark 10:9).**

Imagine a father standing alone, watching his wife's back as she walks away with the children because she is "***no longer happy.***" That image is not simply heartbreaking; it is a violation of the covenant. Marriage is not disposable, nor is it subject to the shifting moods of personal happiness. It is sacred, binding, and a choice designed to endure trials. The man who abandons his family betrays his calling, and the woman who leaves for selfishness turns her back on the order of God.

Therefore, **The Book of Men** counsels this truth: trust God's process in marriage as you trust Him in all things. Pray not for escape but for endurance, not for easy answers but for strength to remain faithful. ***"The just shall live by faith" (Romans 1:17).***

Faith means believing that the God who joined you will also sustain you. A man of God, a husband, and a father must walk in this conviction: marriage is not about chasing happiness, but about reflecting Christ's covenant with His Church. The world says, ***"Leave when you are tired." Christ says, "Remain, for I am with you."***

Those who trust in the Lord will find that even in seasons of weariness, He renews their strength, teaching them to soar, to run, and to walk without fainting. God reveals His character through the images of the eagle and the lion, both symbols of power, authority, and dominion under the sun He created. *"As an eagle stirreth up her nest, fluttereth over her young, spreadeth abroad her wings, taketh them, beareth them on her wings: so, the Lord alone did lead him"* (Deuteronomy 32:11-12). Likewise, *"The lion hath roared, who will not fear? the Lord God hath spoken, who can but prophesy?"* (Amos 3:8).

These comparisons remind us that men, created in the image of God (Genesis 1:27), carry within them traits of strength, authority, and responsibility. When you hear the roar in a man's voice, you are reminded of his God-given power to lead, to protect, and to uphold his family. This is why the burden of governing a home or raising children cannot rest solely on the mother. Men are called to respect covenant and commitment, not to chase fleeting happiness.

If marriage were merely about personal happiness, most men would remain alone. But we bow to the laws of the Lord, who declared, **"It is not good that the man should be alone"** (Genesis 2:18), and we fulfill His promise by building families rooted in His authority and guided by His Word.

Psalm 91:4 "He shall cover thee with his feathers, and under his wings shalt thou trust: his truth shall be thy shield and buckler."

www.ingramcontent.com/pod-product-compliance
Lightning Source LLC
Chambersburg PA
CBHW061216070526
44584CB00029B/3864